Labour Law and Industrial Relations in Great Britain

Labour Law and Industrial Relations in Great Britain

by
Bob Hepple
Sandra Fredman

This book was originally published as a monograph in the International Encyclopaedia for Labour Law and Industrial Relations

1986

Kluwer Law and Taxation Publishers
Deventer . The Netherlands

Antwerp . London . Frankfurt . Boston . New York

Distribution in Canada and the USA
Kluwer Law and Taxation
101 Philip Drive
Norwell MA 02061
USA

Library of Congress Cataloging-in-Publication Data

Hepple, B. A.
Labour law and industrial relations in Great Britain.

"Originally published as a monograph in the International encyclopaedia for labour law and industrial relations."
Bibliography: p.
Includes index.
1. Labor laws and legislation – Great Britain.
I. Fredman, S. (Sandra) II. Title.
KD3009.H47 1986   344.41'01   86-15202
ISBN 90-6544-262-6   344.1041

ISBN 90 6544 2626

D/1986/2664/53

© 1986, Kluwer Law and Taxation Publishers, Deventer, The Netherlands

Foreword

The aim of this book is to provide an introduction to labour law in the context of British industrial relations. It assumes no prior knowledge of law or of industrial practice, and is aimed at four main classes of reader: (1) students of labour law and industrial relations for whom it provides a general framework to accompany detailed study with any of the standard collections of materials and specialist monographs (a select bibliography of such works will be found at pp 257-59); (2) students of other disciplines studying labour law as an ancillary subject who may use this as a main text; (3) trade unionists, managers and the general reader who want to understand the framework of legal intervention in industrial relations; and (4) practitioners, teachers and students in other countries who want an outline for comparative or practical purposes. This monograph is off-printed from the *International Encyclopaedia for Labour Law and Industrial Relations* (ed. R. Blanpain).

The Introduction places British labour law in its comparative, historical and socio-economic context with emphasis on the restrictions on trade unions and the neo-liberal policies of labour regulation through the market since 1979. The basic concepts and major institutions are explained and there is also a short account of how transnational problems are dealt with. Part I covers the individual employment relationship, including the effect of labour market changes on the legal definition of the relationship, as well as working time, remuneration, incapacity for work, job security and discrimination. There are brief outlines of the law on competition by former employees and employee inventions. Part II discusses collective labour relations and the law, including such topical subjects as trade union freedom, secret ballots, workers' participation, trends in collective bargaining, and the new legal restrictions on industrial action. The appendices include a chronological summary of the main labour legislation since 1813.

The law is stated as at 1 January 1986, although it has been possible in some sections to take account of more recent developments. The Sex Discrimination Bill and the Wages Bill 1986 have already undergone amendments since the text was written and may be further altered before enactment in summer or autumn 1986. Attention is drawn to the Government White Paper *Building Businesses ... Not Barriers,* Cmnd 9794, published on 29 May 1986, which proposes further deregulation including a fee of £ 25 for employees bringing cases in industrial tribunals (p 59); extending from 6 months to 2 years the qualifying period after which employees are required to give a statement of reasons for dismissal (p 157); exempting firms with fewer than 10 employees from the requirement to allow a woman to return to work within 29 weeks after the birth of a child (p 136); exempting firms with fewer than 20 employees from the requirement to provide staff with a written statement on disciplinary and grievance procedures (p 88); restricting the industrial relations duties for which time off with pay must be allowed to union officials (p 109); raising the hours of work thresholds above which employees qualify for the main employment rights from 8 to 12, and 16 to 20 hours per week respectively (p 149); and amending the transfer of undertakings regulations (p 149).

Table of Contents

Table of Contents

Table of Contents

8

Table of Contents

List of Abbreviations

ACAS	Advisory, Conciliation and Arbitration Service
All ER	All England Law Reports
CA	Court of Appeal
CAC	Central Arbitration Committee
CBI	Confederation of British Industry
CIR	Commission on Industrial Relations
CO	Certification Officer
CRE	Commission for Racial Equality
DE	Department of Employment
EA 1980	Employment Act 1980
EA 1982	Employment Act 1982
ECJ	European Court of Justice
ECR	European Court Reports
EEC	European Economic Community
EOC	Equal Opportunities Commission
EPA 1975	Employment Protection Act 1975
EPCA 1978	Employment Protection (Consolidation) Act 1978
HL	House of Lords
ICR	Industrial Cases Reports (formerly Industrial Court Reports)
IRLR	Industrial Relations Law Reports
ITR	Industrial Tribunal Reports
KIR	Knight's Industrial Reports
MLR	Modern Law Review
MSC	Manpower Services Commission
QB	Queen's Bench Division of the High Court
RRA	Race Relations Act 1976
SDA	Sex Discrimination Act 1975

List of Abbreviations

TLR	Times Law Reports
TUA 1984	Trade Union Act 1984
TUC	Trades Union Congress
TULRA 1974	Trade Union and Labour Relations Act 1974
TULRA 1976	Trade Union and Labour Relations (Amendment) Act 1976

Acknowledgments

The authors of this monograph and the publishers gratefully acknowledge the permission of the Comptroller, Her Majesty's Stationery Officer to reproduce the Table in Part II, Ch. V from the *Employment Gazette*, and of Sweet & Maxwell Ltd. to draw on material in *Hepple and O'Higgins Employment Law* 4th ed. (1981). Some of the Introduction, section III, originally appeared in Bob Hepple's contribution to *Industrial Relations in Britain* (ed. G. S. Bain), published by Basil Blackwell, 1983.

The authors wish to thank Andrew Glyn, Fellow and Tutor in Economics at Corpus Christi College, Oxford for contributing the section on the economy, and Philip Trott, solicitor, for his assistance with the section on foreign workers. We were extremely fortunate to have the services of Bernadette Hurd in word processing a tangled manuscript and saving us from a number of errors.

Introduction

I. General Features

§1. A COMPARATIVE PERSPECTIVE

1. A traveller making an organised tour of the world's systems of labour law and industrial relations is likely to begin the journey in Great Britain. This is the country in which industrial relations began, as the product of the first industrial revolution in history. It is here that labour law took shape. Great Britain was for a time not only the 'workshop' of the world, she was also an exporter of labour law. The 21 million British citizens who emigrated during the 19th and early 20th centuries to the United States, the British Colonies and overseas dominions, took with them not only the attitudes and behaviour they had learnt in the industries of the mother country. They also built on to the age-old English common law which, ideologically, epitomises the *laissez-faire* liberal capitalism which became ascendant in Great Britain between 1820 and 1850. So Great Britain is a natural starting point for any study of the labour laws and industrial relations of the United States and the Commonwealth countries, and also for a comparison of the common law with Roman-Germanic (civil law) systems, and of capitalist with socialist systems.

2. Britain was the first country (1824) to legalise trade unions, and the liberal and utilitarian beliefs behind this era of toleration, in which collective bargaining could begin to develop, spread over the next 70 years to other parts of Europe. French and German workers, sponsored by their governments, came to Britain at the time of the Great Exhibition to study how the new reformist British trade unions worked. The 19th century British factories and workmen's compensation legislation served as a model in many parts of the world, as far apart as France and Japan. Stephan Bauer, first secretary of the International Association for Labour Legislation, described the adaptation of this model as being at least as important for humanity as the reception of the Roman law of property and obligations.[1] 'His claim was extravagant, not least because the British Acts cannot be compared with the Romanistic legal techniques which promoted national civil laws. But his analogy serves to emphasise the historical relationship between the labour laws of different countries.'[2] It was the pioneer of British socialism, Robert Owen, who can be regarded as the 'father' of international labour law because as early as 1818 he carried his campaign to end the exploitation of human resources into Europe and presented a petition to the Five Powers then meeting at Aix-la-Chapelle, appealing to them to regulate working hours throughout the Continent. His petition was dismissed, but when at the end of the century the movement was revived Britain played a leading role in the various conferences which culminated in the founding of the ILO in 1919. Successive British governments promoted international standards not infrequently based on British practice.

1. S. Bauer, 'Arbeiterschutzgesetzgebung', *Handwörterbuch der Staatswissenschaften* (ed. L. Elster, A. Weber, F. Wieser) 4th ed., vol. I, Jena 1924, p. 401.
2. B. Hepple, A. Jacobs, T. Ramm. B. Veneziani, E. Vogel-Polsky, *The Making of Labour Law in Europe: a comparative study of 9 countries to 1945*, London 1986.

3. When our traveller moves on to other parts of the capitalist world in which industrialization came later, under different social and political conditions, he or she will be quick to discover the many disadvantages of pioneering. By comparison with those countries British trade union organisation seems archaic, the structure of industrial relations appears to be chaotic, labour law is uncodified, the common law contract of service is still the cornerstone of legal thinking, and there is an absence of positive legal rights to organise, to bargain collectively and to strike. In 1954, Otto Kahn-Freund could write that 'there is, perhaps, no major country in the world in which the law has played a less significant role in the shaping of [labour–management] relations than in Great Britain, and in which today the legal professions have less to do with labour relations',[1] and in 1959 he again remarked on the British 'policy of abstention on the part of the law and the reluctance to apply legal sanctions'.[2] In some senses, this reference to 'abstention' of the law was misleading. For one thing, it was wrong to imply that the state was an essentially neutral party to industrial conflict. For another thing, there *was* a great deal of regulatory legislation on subjects such as health and safety in factories, mines and some other workplaces, minimum wages in 'sweated' trades, workmen's compensation for accidents, and the law of social insurance, the latter inspired by Bismarck's welfare system. However, as William Robson, a leading scholar, commented in 1935 'many foreign countries now lay down much higher legal standards in these and cognate matters than we do; and it is no longer possible to fall back on the complacent belief that whereas English law is enforced, the legislation of foreign countries is ignored in practice'.[3] Moreover, Kahn-Freund's *description* of British voluntarism could be regarded as an accurate one right up to the 1960s and, in some respects, even later. In the field of collective labour relations, British labour law unlike that in most comparable countries, conferred no positive rights to organise and to strike, despite the growing political power which the unions could have used, but did not, to secure these rights. Legal intervention was largely limited to a series of negative immunities from the judge-made common law, which was hostile to collective action, and to some relatively weak supports for collective bargaining.

1. O. Kahn-Freund, Chap. II, 'The Legal Framework' in *The System of Industrial Relations in Great Britain* (eds. A. Flanders and H. A. Clegg), Oxford 1954, p. 44.
2. O. Kahn-Freund, 'Labour Law' in *Law and Opinion in England in the 20th Century* (ed. M. Ginsberg), London 1959, p. 238.
3. W. Robson, 'Industrial Law' *Law Quarterly Review* (1935) vol. 51, p. 195 at p. 201.

4. Between 1963 and 1979 it seemed that Britain was feeling its way towards a more legally-regulated system of industrial relations. In 1963 Britain became the last country in Europe (apart from Ireland) to introduce statutory minimum periods of notice to terminate employment, and this was followed by a whole series of new rights, especially on unfair dismissal, for individual employees. The American model of anti-discrimination legislation was transplanted into the different social and legal climate of Britain, and membership of the EEC (from 1973) brought with it a new range of social legislation on matters such as collective redundancies, acquired rights on the transfer of undertakings and equal pay. For a time, between 1971–1974, it seemed that American Taft-Hartley style laws would serve as the main instrument for the restructuring of collective labour relations in Britain, but the Industrial Relations Act 1971 failed not least because it was based on the mistaken assumption that employers would use the law and that trade union leaders would co-operate with it. It was followed by a 'social contract' between the Labour Government (1974–1979) and the Trades Union Congress (reminiscent of such other famous accords as the Danish September 1899 agreement, the French Matignon Agreement (1936) and Grenelle *constat* (1968) and the German Margaretenhof agreement (1954)). This produced a great volume of new legislation and enhanced the role of the industrial tribunals (established in 1964) which like labour courts in other countries are composed of employer and worker members alongside a legally-qualified chairman.

5. This period was marked by a growing conflict between incomes policies, which interfered with collective bargaining, and reformist legislation, which aimed to support and encourage the development of collective bargaining. Since May 1979 Britain has had a right-wing Conservative Government which has abandoned both direct incomes policies and support for collectivism and has substituted a consistent strategy of legal restrictions on trade unions and the restoration of market regulation. It is the preoccupation of state policies since 1979 with the power of trade unions which distinguishes the response of Britain to the economic crisis from that of other Western European countries. In many countries the inflexibility of labour markets is seen as a major cause of the crisis, and measures have been adopted to reduce labour costs and to deregulate employment protection laws. The British government since 1979 has also resorted to measures of this kind, and this has, so far, involved the denunciation of no less than three ILO conventions (on public contracts, minimum wage-fixing machinery, and the protection of wages), and a British veto over proposed new EEC directives on part-time and temporary work and on parental leave. In developments of this kind Britain has moved earlier and further than other Western European governments. The trend to deregulation is not unique, but in those other countries the systems of labour law have generally retained the values of democratic pluralism. Unions are still seen as the 'social partners' of the employers; collective bargaining remains at the centre of labour relations. In Britain, by contrast, the main thrust of the government's strategy has been built around attempts to weaken trade unions, through measures such as the privatization of heavily-unionised public corporations, the devolution of industrial relations to the workplace where unions

19

are relatively weak in a time of high unemployment, and legislation which severely restricts the freedom to organise, to bargain and to strike. These policies have been put dramatically to the test, notably in a series of conflicts between the unions and the law in the miners' strike (1984–1985) and in the disputes in the printing industry (1983–1986). In this new period the British government has shown a willingness to defy international standards, such as in its refusal to accept the findings of the ILO Committee on Freedom of Association in 1984 that the withdrawal of trade union rights for some civil servants constituted a violation of ILO conventions (see Part II, Ch. I, below).

6. We must, however, start the exploration of modern British labour law at the beginning. This Introduction describes for those with no background knowledge the general features of the country, its political and legal systems and economy; some definitions of basic concepts; a brief historical sketch; a description of the main institutions, industrial tribunals and courts, and of the sources of labour law. There is also a short account of how British law deals with the problems which arise when more than one legal system may be relevant. Part I considers the law and practice of the individual employment relationship, and Part II collective labour relations and the law.

§2. Geography and Population

A. The countries

7. The island of Great Britain comprises England (total area including inland water 130,367 sq. km.), Wales (20,763 sq. km.) and Scotland (including its many inhabited islands 78,773 sq. km.). Separated from Northwestern Europe by the natural 'moat' of the English Channel, the island has avoided foreign invasion since 1066. To the West, across the Irish Sea, lies Ireland which the British have colonised since early times.

8. England was united as a Kingdom 1,000 years ago and Wales became part of this Kingdom during the middle ages. The thrones of England and Scotland were dynastically united in 1603 and in 1707 a single Parliament was established for the whole of Great Britain. In 1800 the United Kingdom was completed by a union joining the Irish Parliament and that of Great Britain. In 1922 Southern Ireland (now the Republic of Ireland) became a self-governing country. The six counties of Northern Ireland had in 1920 been given their own subordinate Parliament and they have remained within the United Kingdom. (*This monograph is concerned only with Great Britain. Northern Ireland and the Republic of Ireland are the subject of separate monographs in this series.*)

9. When studying British statistics it is important to note whether they refer to England alone, to England and Wales, to England, Wales and Scotland (*i.e.* Great Britain) or to the United Kingdom as a whole. United Kingdom statistics and other data sometimes include the Isle of Man (558 sq. km.) and the

Channel Islands (194 sq. km.) which strictly are not part of the United Kingdom but are dependencies of the Crown.

B. The people[1]

10. In mid-1983, the estimated population of Great Britain was 54.8 million (with a further 1.6 million in Northern Ireland), compared with 54.7 million in mid-1973 (with 1.5 million in Northern Ireland). This can be contrasted with the figure of 38.2 million in the whole of the UK in 1906. The majority (about 46.8 million) live in England. On the basis of present trends in the birth and death rates, the population of Great Britain is expected to reach 55.38 million in 1993, 56.14 million in 2003 and 56.38 million in 2013. The percentage of the population over retirement age has increased from 14.8 per cent in 1963 to 17.9 per cent in 1983, a figure of major importance in the allocation of resources.

1. These and other demographic statistics are derived from *Social Trends*, Central Office of Statistics, London (annual) and *United Kingdom in Figures*, Government Statistical Service, 1985 edition.

11. The people of Great Britain are relatively homogeneous, with none of the linguistic, cultural or religious divisions which characterise either Northern Ireland or parts of Continental Europe. Living in a unitary state, whose boundaries have remained stable for centuries, the inhabitants share the English language (although in Wales there has been a revival in recent years of Welsh which now enjoys the status of an official language) and there is a fairly uniform system of free secular popular education up to the age of 16. The Anglican Church has been a state church since the 16th Century (as is the Presbyterian Church in Scotland) subordinate to the ruling political class; dissenting minorities secured rights to equal treatment during the 19th Century and non-conformism has had an important influence on sectors of the working-class, particularly in Wales. The British traditions of religious and cultural tolerance have meant that groups of political refugees, such as the Huguenots in the 17th Century, the East European Jews in the late 19th Century and the post-war Polish and Hungarian exiles, have been readily integrated. So Britain has escaped the phenomenon of religious, linguistic or racial divisions in the trade union and labour movements.

12. Race relations have, however, become an important factor in social and industrial life as a result of the influx, since the late 1950s, of economic migrants from the 'New Commonwealth' countries such as the West Indies, India and Pakistan. At the last census (1981) 4.5 per cent of the usually resident population were living in households whose head was born in the new Commonwealth or Pakistan, and in 1983, an estimated 2.39 million people described themselves as being of an ethnic origin other than white.[1] Most black Britons are born or educated in Britain, and many are concentrated in the decaying 'inner cities' in poor housing and doing the worst jobs in a relatively small number of industries. Ethnic minorities are permanent residents in

Britain and cannot be compared to migrant workers elsewhere in Europe. The period of immigration is over, largely due to the tightening of immigration controls, but Britain must now be characterised as ethnically heterogeneous. The pressure of these ethnic groups has sharpened awareness of the age-old problems of poor housing, low pay and law enforcement. Black workers are, however, playing an increasing part in the general trade union movement.

1. *Labour Force Survey* 1983 (issued Dec. 1984). This figure is qualified by the fact that 952,000 did not state their ethnic origin.

§3. POLITICAL AND LEGAL SYSTEM

A. Constitution

13. The British Constitution is not to be found in a basic document or set of documents. It has evolved over the centuries and consists of Acts of Parliament and other legislation, judge-made common law and precepts and practices known as constitutional conventions. These conventions are political usages, not directly enforceable in courts of law. The most important feature of the constitution is parliamentary sovereignty. Parliament (which means effectively the democratically elected House of Commons because the largely hereditary House of Lords has only a delaying power) can enact any law on any subject; even the rules and conventions of constitutional law can be changed by ordinary legislation. This means that there are not the formal restraints against encroachment on individual liberties which exist in other liberal democracies – there is no entrenched bill of rights – and there are no constitutional 'rights' to strike or to associate in trade unions. Concern over issues such as the denial of the right to belong to trade unions at the Government Communications Headquarters by the Conservative Government in 1984, and earlier legislation by a Labour Government permitting compulsory trade union membership (the closed shop) has led in recent times to pressures for some limitation on executive and parliamentary power and for the formal entrenchment of certain individual rights. The United Kingdom Government is a party to the European Convention on Human Rights, but the terms of the Convention have not been enacted as part of domestic law.

14. Parliamentary government does not, however, mean government by Parliament. The public or civil service is non-partisan and serves the Government in office; its members enjoy security of employment irrespective of the political complexion of the party in power. The Government consists of members of both Houses of Parliament (mostly drawn from the Commons). The Cabinet is collectively responsible to the Commons; a Government that lost the support of a majority in the Commons would have to resign or call an election. The Government is not, however, the delegate of Parliament. Because of the way in which the two party system operates, the Government is generally able to command Parliamentary support for the implementation of its policies. Those who are baffled by the apparently sudden reversals of legislative policies – such as the repeal of the Industrial Relations Act in 1974 only three years after its enactment – should remember that apart from times of war or national emergency (as in 1931) there has not been a Coalition Government in Britain. Where major policy differences exist between the Conservative and Labour parties, it can be expected that the party with a parliamentary majority will be able to reverse the legislation initiated by its predecessor, as happened in the case of the Industrial Relations Act. At various times, however, the largest party in the Commons has had to rely on the parliamentary support of the small Liberal Party and the Scottish and Welsh Nationalists. For example, the minority Labour Government's labour relations legislation introduced in March 1974 could not be carried in full because of the absence of support from these smaller parties, and also because of the use of their delaying powers by the House of Lords in which there is a permanent majority of hereditary Conservative peers. The emergence of a Social Democratic Party, in 1980, in alliance with theLiberal Party, makes it possible that future labour legislation will have to command the support of more than one political party.

B. Trade unions and the political system

15. An understanding of the relationship between collective bargaining and legislation enacted by Parliament is impossible unless two vital facts are borne in mind. The first, which Professor Sir Otto Kahn-Freund has emphasised,[1] is that British trade unions won minimum labour standards, without the aid of legislation, before the franchise was extended to the town artisan in 1867 and to the country operative and miner in 1885. The suffrage never assumed the same importance in the formative period of the British unions as it did elsewhere in Europe; and the British unions came to rely on their industrial strength rather than the parliamentary struggle. The second fact is that the trade unions had given birth to their own leaders and their own pragmatic, reformist organisations, long before the Socialist movement assumed importance. The socialists who formed the Marxist Social Democratic Federation (SDF) in 1884 and the less orthodox Independent Labour Party (ILP) in 1893, faced an already established trade union leadership, predominantly Liberal in outlook. In 1900 a number of unions affiliated to the Trades Union Congress (TUC) combined with the SDF, ILP and Fabian Society to establish the Labour Representation Committee from which emerged the Labour Party. British trade unions are the products of the practical organisation of wage earners and are not the creation of political parties nor are they the outcome of a socialist critique of society as in some other European countries.

1. O. Kahn-Freund, *Law and Opinion in the Twentieth Century* (ed. M. Ginsberg), London, 1959; *Selected Writings*, London, 1978.

16. There is no organisational link between the TUC and the Labour Party, although there is a regular liaison. Individual trade unions, representing about half the total affiliated membership of the TUC, are affiliated to the Labour

Party. Trade union block votes exercise a decisive influence on Labour Party conferences and shifts in the political balance between right and left in unions can therefore be reflected in shifts in Labour Party policy. Unions 'sponsor' (*i.e.* help with expenses) a considerable number of Labour MPs.

C. Legal systems

17. England and Wales, on the one hand, and Scotland, on the other, have different systems of law, different legal professions and a different judiciary as well as different education systems and different local government organisation. In order to extend this devolution of decision-making from London, there have been moves for the establishment of elected assemblies with limited law-making powers for Scotland and Wales. At present, Acts of Parliament do not extend to Scotland and Wales, unless they are expressly stated to do so. In practice nearly all labour legislation does expressly extend to the whole of Great Britain and it is only a few old Acts which are peculiar to a single law district. The English Common Law, by which is meant here all the law that is not the result of legislation, differs in some important respects from Scots law. One practical example is that in Scotland third parties may directly acquire rights under collective agreements, whereas the *jus quaesitum tertio* does not exist in English law. Scots law today is a hybrid system with roots in the Roman (civil) law as well as being under the living influence of the English Common Law. A brief description of the court system in each country, so far as relevant, will be found in para. 81. (*In this monograph only the rules of the English Common Law will be described and in general, not any special features of Scots law.*)

D. European Economic Community (EEC)

18. Britain has been a member of the EEC since 1 January 1973. The effect on the British Constitution and the legal systems of England and Scotland is profound. Legislative power has been transferred from London to Brussels, in certain important matters, and the decisions of the European Court of Justice in Luxembourg on questions arising under the Treaty of Rome are binding on British courts. Above all, English lawyers are having to familiarise themselves with laws and practices expressed in the Continental legal idiom. Industrial relations are being affected not only by the generally higher social standards in other Member States, but also by regulations and directives made by the Community organs. The most important of these so far are the regulations made under article 48 of the Treaty providing for the freedom of movement for workers within the Community, and under article 51 relating to social security for migrant workers and a series of directives relating to equal pay and equal treatment for men and women (under article 119), on harmonisation of the laws of Member States on collective redundancies, on safeguarding employees' rights in the event of transfers of undertakings, and on the protection of workers in the event of bankruptcy of the employer (under articles 100 and 117).

19. The foundation of Community law is a set of treaties. It is a general principle of British law that a treaty entered into by the Government does not in itself affect British domestic law. Domestic law and international law are regarded as separate legal orders. In view of this the effect of Community law is specially defined in an Act of Parliament, the European Communities Act 1972. The Act provides three principal methods by which Community law may be given effect.

(1) Section 2(1) provides that directly effective or directly applicable Community law is binding in the UK. This includes secondary Community law and future Community law. The question whether a particular provision is 'directly effective' or 'directly applicable' is determined by Community law but it is for national courts to decide how to give effect to such rights. Articles 48,[1] 52,[2] 59[3] (freedom of movement) and 119[4] (equal pay) have been held to be directly effective, but articles 117 and 118 (harmonisation and co-ordination) are not.[5] Regulation 1612/68 on freedom of movement of workers is directly applicable,[6] as is Directive 63/221 on the same subject.[7] Directive 75/117 on equal pay has been held by the European Court of Justice to facilitate the practical application of article 119,[8] which is directly effective, but the Court has said that Directive 76/207 on equal treatment of men and women is not sufficiently precise to be relied upon in the absence of national implementing measures by an individual seeking a specific remedy for its infringement when such a remedy is not provided for under a national law.[9] There has, as yet, been no definitive decision on the direct effectiveness of other Directives relevant in the labour law field.

(2) Section 2(4) requires a court or tribunal to construe 'any enactment passed or to be passed' in the UK so as to be consistent with Community law. After considerable controversy, the House of Lords (the highest court) has favoured the use of this provision, rather than the creation of an independent legal right under section 2(1), in order to give effect to article 119 and the Directives on equal pay and equal treatment.[10] In other words, the British Equal Pay Act 1970 and Sex Discrimination Act 1975 are construed subject to the overriding effect of Community law, as interpreted by the European Court of Justice. Questions as to the scope of Community law may be referred to the European Court by courts and tribunals under article 177 of the treaty.

(3) Section 2(2) enables the Government to implement Community obligations which are not directly effective by means of subordinate legislation made by Ministers of the Crown subject to parliamentary approval. This procedure was used to give effect to Directive 77/187 on safeguarding employees' rights in the event of transfers of undertakings,[11] and to remedy the infringement by the UK of article 119[12] in respect of equal pay for work of equal value. The use of this procedure, rather than legislation by Parliament itself, has been severely criticised because it allows only for

short debates and the ministerial order has to be accepted or rejected *in toto* without the possibility of amendment.

1. *Van Duyn* v. *Home Office*, Case 41/74 [1974] ECR 1337 (ECJ).
2. *Reynders* v. *Belgian State*, Case 2/74 [1974] ECR 631 (ECJ).
3. *Van Binsbergen*, Case 33/74 [1974] ECR 1299 (ECJ).
4. *Defrenne* v. *Sabena* (Defrenne II), Case 43/75 [1976] ECR 455 (ECJ).
5. *Defrenne* v. *Sabena* (Defrenne III), Case 159/77 [1978] ECR 1365 (ECJ).
6. *Van Duyn* v. *Home Office*, Case 41/74 [1974] ECR 1337 (ECJ).
7. *Ibid.*
8. *Jenkins* v. *Kingsgate Clothing*, Case 96/80 [1980] ECR 911 (ECJ); *Worringham* v. *Lloyds Bank Ltd* Case 69/80 [1981] ICR 558 at 589 (ECJ).
9. *Van Colson and Kamann*, Case 14/83 [1984] ECR 1892; *Harz*, Case 79/83 [1984] ECR 1921 (ECJ).
10. *Garland* v. *British Rail Engineering Ltd* [1982] ICR 420 at 438.
11. Transfer of Undertakings (Protection of Employment) Regulations 1981 (SI 1981 No. 1794).
12. In *Commission of the European Communities* v *United Kingdom*, Case 61/82 [1982] ICR 578, the ECJ held that the UK had failed to provide equal pay for work to which equal value is attributed as required by art. 119. In a second infringement proceeding, *Commission of the European Communities* v. *United Kingdom*, Case 165/82 [1984] ICR 192, the ECJ held that the UK was not in compliance with art. 4(b) of the Equal Treatment Directive 76/207. At the time of writing, amending regulations are awaited. See para. 350, below.

§4. THE ECONOMY[1]

A. General

20. The outstanding feature of the British economy over the last hundred years has been its decline from the manufacturing workshop of the world to the status of a thoroughly second-rank economic power. Output per head is the most basic indicator of a country's productive power. A recent authoritative account of the pattern of productivity explains that 'the UK appears as the leader at the beginning of the period [1870], but is overtaken by the United States in the next decade, by Sweden between the wars, by France and Germany around 1960, by Italy around 1970 and Japan probably in the late 1970s'.[2]

1. This section on the Economy has been contributed by Andrew Glyn, Fellow and Tutor in Economics at Corpus Christi College, Oxford.
2. R. C. O. Matthews, C. H. Feinstein and J. C. Oddling-Smee, *British Economic Growth 1856–1973* (Oxford 1982), p. 33.

21. The UK's agricultural sector is small and highly productive, and some service sectors are relatively efficient. It is in manufacturing industry, crucial because of its importance in overseas trade, that the situation is particularly dire. In 1980 output per person in manufacturing in the UK was about half that in France, Italy, Japan and Belgium and only 40 per cent or so of that in the US, Netherlands and Germany. This has been reflected in a disastrous decline in the UK's share of world manufacturing trade – from 25 per cent in 1950 to 8 per cent by 1985. Imports of manufactures now exceed exports.

22. Two factors have helped to mask this disastrous decline. First the great post-war boom of the 1950s and 1960s in the advanced capitalist countries dragged the UK along. Between 1951 and 1973 UK production grew by 2.8 per cent per year, faster than in any previous peacetime period of comparable length. But behind this, UK manufacturing productivity grew at half the rate of the main European economies and one-third of the rate in Japan. Unlike its rivals the UK failed to catch up with the technical level achieved in the US This has left the UK economy extremely exposed in the more difficult economic conditions faced by the advanced countries in the 1970s and 1980s. But the full impact of this weakened position has been cushioned by the entirely fortuitous discovery of North Sea Oil. By 1985 the government was receiving nearly 7 per cent of its revenue from this source, some £10 billion, enough to pay the enormous social security costs of more than 3 million unemployed. Paid for out of increased income tax this would have meant an extra 10p in the pound on the standard rate. In the context of the Conservative Government's deflationary policies, however, even North Sea Oil turned into a mixed blessing. For the impact on the balance of payments (£11 billion extra exports or reduced imports) was allowed to push the value of the pound up, making British manufacturing industry even less competitive.

23. Looking for causes of the UK's economic failures has been a major pre-occupation of UK economists. It would be generally agreed that the low level of UK investment has been of crucial importance. For it is investment in new machinery and factories which increases the productivity of labour by incorporating new technology. During the 1950s and 1960s the stock of capital in UK manufacturing grew at around $3\frac{1}{2}$ per cent per year, only two-thirds of the rate in Europe and one-third of that in Japan. But this immediately invites the question why was UK investment so much lower? One answer might be low profits, and indeed by the early 1970s the profit rate in British manufacturing, around 10 per cent, was less than that in Europe and far below that of Japan. But this cannot be the fundamental explanation, for in the early 1950s the profit rate in Britain was around 20 per cent and the investment rate was even lower then. Indeed, the decline in profitability over the period has been attributed to low investment and the declining competitiveness which it brought.

24. The involvement of the City in overseas investment has often been blamed for starving British industry of finance. But there is little evidence that it has been shortage of finance which has constrained British firms. What does seem to be clear is that British industry, early in the post-war period, became locked into a low investment pattern from which it has been unable to break out. This is despite the greatly increased competition it has faced, both at home and from imports and in its export markets. Much energy has been dissipated on mergers, whose benefits in increased efficiency have been severely limited. The banks have never taken it upon themselves to develop and implement strategic plans for individual industrial sectors and governments' efforts have been limited to a few general investment incentives.

25. Not only has investment been low in total, but its effectiveness has not been up to international standards. The amount of output derived from each unit of investment has been as much as one-third below that of France and Germany. Studies of the motor industry in particular have suggested much lower productivity in British plants of identical design than those in Europe. Bad organisation and management, poor training and bad industrial relations are favourite explanations. The latter finds some support in the fact that some large UK plants have been abnormally strike-prone by international standards. The fact that British unions entered the 1950s in an entrenched position (unlike those in most of Europe and Japan), but without a strong modernising ethos, may have reinforced the negative effects of sluggish and complacent management. It is striking, however, that a recent government survey into the implementation of new technology found workforce opposition to be a factor of negligible importance in comparison to factors such as low expected profitability, doubts as to whether the equipment would be fully used and lack of technical expertise.[1]

1. D. Armstrong, A. Glyn, J. Harrison, *Capitalism since World War II*, London, 1984, p. 424.

26. The recent history of the British economy has to be viewed in this context. The Labour Government of 1974–1979 was elected on a policy of industrial interventionism. But these plans were abandoned in the teeth of hostile opposition from business (the Director-General of the CBI recently admitted that the employers' organisation had contemplated launching an 'investment strike'). In the context of deflationary policies and wage limitations the government supported firms in trouble and attempted to strengthen trade union rights in relation to employment preservation. The Conservative Government pursued the opposite policy of attempting to force rationalisation of industry by more deflation, high interest rates and a rise in the pound. Productivity grew rapidly in 1981–1982 as unemployment rose by about 2 million. But much of this productivity growth was 'degenerate' in the sense of increasing the average of those in work simply by closing down the least productive plants. There has been fierce rationalisation in the public sector, especially in steel and the coal industry where bitter strikes ended in defeat for the trade unions and sweeping job losses. But it seems that this weakening of the trade union movement is limited to the public sector. In the meantime manufacturing investment is at an all-time low. The capital stock is hardly growing, having shrunk by perhaps 10 per cent during the recession of the early 1980s. As pointed out by a 1985 House of Lords Report of the Select Committee on Overseas Trade[1], the UK economy is facing the prospect of North Sea oil's decline in the early 1990s with the manufacturing base in an even more dilapidated state.

1. House of Lords, paper 238, sessions 1984–1985, July 1985.

B. The changing structure of the labour force

27. In 1984, there were approximately 23.63 million people in employment (including self-employed), about 43 per cent of the total population.[1] The most prominent characteristic of the years since 1979 has been the accelerated increase in unemployment figures, partly as a result of the strict monetary policies of the incumbent Conservative government. Unemployment reached 3.35 million (13.8 per cent of all employees) in September 1985, according to official figures, or 3.82 million (15.8 per cent of all employees) if calculated on the official basis used before November 1982 when certain persons previously classified as unemployed were excluded. This can be contrasted with the 20 years prior to 1967, when the general unemployment level in Britain was among the lowest in the western world – usually between 1 per cent and 2 per cent of the working population. Although unemployment has been growing since 1967, the peak figure in the 1970s was only 1.47 million (excluding students). The growth of long-term unemployment has been particularly prominent; the number of people unemployed for over 3 years grew by 38 per cent between January 1984 and January 1985, to reach a total of 429,000. The statistics also indicate that the young are disproportionately represented among the unemployed.

1. All figures in this section are taken from statistics published in the *Employment Gazette* and in *Labour Research* (Labour Research Department, London).

28. For those in work there have been several significant changes in the structure of employment. Of particular importance has been the shift of the working population away from production industries to service industries. Employment in the manufacturing sector fell from 7.28 million in 1976 to 5.5 million in 1984. More than 60 per cent of total employment is now in the service sector, accounting for half of all working men and more than three-quarters of working women. These trends are reflected in the changing occupational structure of employment, which displays a marked shift away from manual towards non-manual occupations. By 1984, more than half the workforce were employed in non-manual occupations.

29. A second important change in the structure of the workforce has been the increase in the number of women workers. The female workforce has grown by more than 2 million since 1959, reaching 9.25 million in December 1984, and accounting for about 40 per cent of those in employment. The increase in working women has been parallelled by an increase in part-time work. There were almost 5 million part-time workers by 1984, as against about 3.2 million in 1971. This represents the highest proportion of part-time workers in the EEC, apart from Denmark. (In the same period, full-time employment decreased by 2.5 million.) The part-time workforce is predominantly female, with married women accounting for three-quarters of all part-time employees (as against one-quarter of full-timers) (see further, para. 127 below).

30. Another feature of the labour force is the relatively disadvantaged position of the ethnic minority population (see para. 337, below). About three-quarters of the white male labour force are employees. Fewer of the minority groups, about 60 per cent of West Indians and about 65 per cent of other groups are employees, and for Pakistani/Bangladeshi this proportion is only half. On the other hand, relatively large proportions of the male Asian labour force are self-employed. Only three-fifths of the Pakistani/Bangladeshi female labour force are in paid employment, and four-fifths of females in other ethnic minority groups, compared to nine-tenths of white females.[1]

1. The information in this paragraph is derived from the *Employment Gazette*, December 1985, pp. 467–477.

31. Employment in the public sector constitutes a significant portion of the workforce.[1] In March 1984, about 6.8 million people were employed in the public sector, of whom 1.6 million were employed by public corporations, 2.3 million by central government and 2.9 million by local authorities. The total number of public employees has, however, fallen since 1978, particularly in public corporations and in the civil service. The majority (nearly 60 per cent) of those employed in central government in mid-1984 were women, but women formed only 40 per cent of full-time employees. This reflects the large number of women working part-time in education and health. By contrast in public corporations women form less than one-sixth of the workforce; there are few part-time jobs in public corporations. The number of non-industrial civil servants, employed by central government departments of State, fell from 511,800 in 1974 to 504,300 in 1984 as a result of cuts in public expenditure.

1. Central Statistical Office, *Economic Trends*, March 1985.

32. Britain is sharply distinguished from other Western European and industrialised countries by the small proportion of the population engaged in agriculture. In 1984, 340,000 people were employed in agriculture, fishing and forestry, or 2.5 per cent of those in employment.[1]

1. *Monthly digest of statistics*, June 1985.

II. Definitions and Notions

§1. INDUSTRIAL RELATIONS

33. The reader who seeks any clear or explicit definition in Britain of basic notions, such as *industrial relations* and *labour law* will be disappointed. The subject of *industrial relations* has become an accepted area of academic study. But the scope of the subject has been determined empirically with attention being concentrated on the collective bargaining activities of trade unions.[1] Allan Flanders, elaborating Dunlop's analysis[2], has defined industrial relations as a system of rules which appear 'in different guises in legislation and in statutory orders; in trade union regulations; in collective agreements and arbitration awards; in social conventions; in managerial decisions; and in "accepted custom and practice". In other words, the subject deals with certain regulated or institutionalised relationships in industry.'[3] Flanders' emphasis was on the *institutions of job regulation* excluding 'personal' and 'unstructured' relationships from the system of *industrial relations*. Since the 1960s, however, the prevailing conception of industrial relations has broadened to include the informal, largely unstructured relationships on the factory or shop floor which modify or even contradict the official institutions. The emphasis has increasingly been on the impact of informal work group relations, and unofficial 'custom and practice' as means of controlling jobs. An important landmark in this new approach was the Report of the Royal Commission on Trade Unions and Employers' Associations (1968)[4] which distinguished the formal system of industrial relations embodied in official institutions, from the informal system 'created by the actual behaviour of the trade unions and employers' associations, of managers, shop stewards and workers'. Since then, there have been a number of major empirical studies of industrial relations[5], and a lively debate has developed about the virtues and vices of 'industrial pluralism' which is the dominant theory of British industrial relations.[6]

1. Notably in H. A. Clegg, *The Changing System of Industrial Relations in Great Britain*, Oxford, 1979.
2. J. T. Dunlop, *Industrial Relations Systems*, New York, 1958.
3. A. Flanders, *Industrial Relations: What is Wrong With The System?*, London, 1965.
4. Cmnd. 3623, 1968.
5. *E.g.* W. Brown (ed.), *The Changing Contours of British Industrial Relations*, Oxford, 1981; W. W. Daniel and N. Millward (eds.), *Workplace Industrial Relations in Britain*, London, 1983.
6. *E.g.* in Lord Wedderburn, R. Lewis and J. Clark (eds.), *Labour Law and Industrial Relations: Building on Kahn-Freund*, Oxford, 1983; H. Clegg, *op. cit.* (note 1, above), chap. 11; compare A. Fox, 'Industrial relations – a social critique of pluralist ideology' in J. Child (ed.), *Man and organization*, London, 1973; R. Hyman, *Industrial Relations – A Marxist Introduction*, London, 1975, and, generally, H. Arthurs, 'Understanding Labour Law: The debate over "industrial pluralism" ', *Current Legal Probems* 38 (1985), p. 83.

§2. Labour Law

34. This changing emphasis has also had an influence on the study of the law relating to industrial relations. Right down to 1939, legal studies were almost exclusively concerned with the common law of 'master and servant' (the earliest book on this subject by Matthew Dutton was published in Ireland in 1723)[1], and with legislation on safety and welfare and workmen's compensation for accidents. This *law of master and servant*, concerned exclusively with common law and, less often, legislation affecting the *individual employment relationship* has developed into what is today generally called *'employment law'*. This includes the rights and duties of individual employer and employee and is sometimes extended to such matters as the employer's vicarious responsibility to third parties for the torts (delicts) of his employees.

    1. Matthew Dutton, *The Law of Masters and Servants in Ireland*, Dublin, 1723.

35. The legal aspects of relations between trade unions and employers and internal trade union matters were, however, little studied before 1939 and then only concerning specific legislation or case law. Books on *trade union law* usually focussed on the judicial interpretation of Acts of Parliament defining the legal status of trade unions and the protection of acts in so-called 'trade disputes'. There were also a few studies of the *practice of conciliation and arbitration*. This particularly narrow focus and the neglect of *collective labour law* can only be understood in the light of two factors. First, the pragmatic case by case orientation of English lawyers, who generally eschew the broader conceptual and doctrinal study of the subject; and secondly, the neglect of the sociology of law by English academic writers.

36. It was in this situation that Otto Kahn-Freund, a pupil of Hugo Sinzheimer, the great German exponent of industrial relations 'pluralism', arrived in England in 1933. He found in the London School of Economics the intellectual environment in which he was able to combine his experience as a judge of the Berlin labour court, his wide understanding of the sociology of Marx, Weber and others, with his study of English law and the British practice of collective bargaining. It is to him that the scientific study of *collective labour law* in Britain, a study filled with valuable comparative insights, owes its origin. Where English lawyers thought collective agreements not worth studying because they were never directly enforced in courts, Kahn-Freund found them a fascinating subject precisely because of the apparent 'abstention' by the law. He was able to generalise this into a theory of the absence of an intention to create legal relations (itself a Continental rather than English notion) in collective bargaining. In studying the legal support given to collective bargaining he expounded general principles such as that of 'voluntarism' – the aim of the law is to help the parties reach a settlement not to impose it – and that of the 'priority of autonomous institutions' – the law intervenes only if the parties' own machinery has failed to produce a result.[1]

    1. A Bibliography of the writings of the late Professor Sir Otto Kahn-Freund (1900–1979) will
      be found in his *Selected Writings*, London, 1978. Many of his most important ideas are

crystallised in his *Labour and the Law*, 2nd ed., London, 1977 (also available in German and Italian translations), and *Labour Relations: Heritage and Adjustment*, London, 1979. A 3rd ed. of *Labour and the Law*, ed. by P. L. Davies and M. Freedland, was published in 1983. Appraisals of his work will be found in F. Gamillscheg *et al.* (eds.), *In Memoriam Sir Otto Kahn-Freund*, Munich, 1980, and Lord Wedderburn, Roy Lewis and Jon Clark (eds.), *Labour Law and Industrial Relations: Building on Kahn-Freund*, Oxford, 1983. For his earlier period in Germany, see Roy Lewis and Jon Clark (eds. and Introduction), *Labour Law and Politics in the Weimar Republic. Selected German Writings of O. Kahn-Freund* (translated by J. Clark), Oxford, 1981.

37. The elaboration of general principles such as these, and the Continental and the United States influences, have resulted in a change of scope and emphasis of legally-based studies. The scope of what since the 1960s has tended to be called *labour law* (although the term *industrial law* is still not infrequently used to describe the same subject) is now defined in terms of the law which is used '*to regulate, to support and to restrain the power of management and the power of organised labour*'[1].

1. O. Kahn-Freund, *Labour and the Law*, 3rd ed., p. 15.

38. Labour law may now be understood in this way in academic studies, but legislation still uses a bewildering variety of descriptions of the same subject matter. For example, there was an Industrial Relations Act in 1971, but the repealing legislation dealing with some of the same topics is called the Trade Union and Labour Relations Acts 1974 and 1976. The Employment Protection Act 1975 covered not only a diverse range of individual employment rights (now consolidated in the Employment Protection (Consolidation) Act 1978), but also set up new institutions and gave legal support to trade unions and collective bargaining. The Employment Acts of 1980 and 1982 dealt with the rights of trade union members, picketing and industrial action as well as individual employment rights. The labour courts are known as 'industrial tribunals' and from them there is an appeal on questions of law to an Employment Appeal Tribunal.

§3. Social Law

39. This lack of uniformity is also reflected in the absence of any clear dividing line between labour law and *social law*. The latter concept is not even generally recognised in academic studies. In a wide sense it includes all studies of the operation of law in society; more narrowly it concerns the law affecting the working population as a whole, as distinct from those at work; more narrowly still it covers only *social security law*, that is the law relating to the administration of contributory and non-contributory state benefits for income maintenance. The term *welfare law* usually covers both social security and the law relating to personal welfare services. Legislation on contributory state benefits has, since 1946, been known as the National Insurance Acts, but in 1975 these were consolidated in the Social Security Act. An employer wishing to know the statutory obligations relating to sick pay may be bewildered to find that set out in an Act called the Social Security and Housing Benefits Act 1982!

§4. COLLECTIVE BARGAINING

40. The absence of agreed or statutory definition of the scope of study is matched by the lack of any precise definition of some of the main subjects of study. For example, the term 'collective bargaining' (which is said to have been invented by Mrs. Beatrice Webb in 1891)[1] was for many years regarded as the collective equivalent of industrial bargaining in the labour market:

> 'Instead of the employer making a series of separate contracts with isolated individuals he meets with a collective will, and settles, in a single agreement, the principles upon which, for the time being, all workmen of a particular group, or class, or grade, will be engaged.'[2]

1. In *The Co-operative Movement in Britain*, London, 1891, and subsequently developed by her and Sidney Webb, *Industrial Democracy*, London, 1898.
2. Sidney and Beatrice Webb, *Industrial Democracy*, p. 173.

41. This analysis was criticised by Allan Flanders[1] as being inadequate because it suggests that collective agreements commit someone to buy and sell labour, whereas in fact, collective agreements simply lay down the *terms* upon which individual workers sell their ability to work. This led Flanders to develop the alternative theory of collective bargaining as an 'institution for the joint regulation of labour management and labour markets'.[2] Against this view Alan Fox has argued that in collective bargaining there is
'(1) a bargaining process during which the parties deploy arguments, present evidence and issue threats; this may or may not end in
(2) an agreement which adjusts the antithetical interests of buyer and seller. This may or may not be embodied in
(3) a contract into which both parties decide to enter . . . In practice these elements often appear to be fixed in a single process . . . But it is important to distinguish them for analytic purposes.'[3]
Whatever the relative merits of these theories for understanding the phenomenon of collective bargaining, it has to be stressed that for certain legal purposes (such as trade union recognition) 'collective bargaining' has a much more limited definition excluding certain subjects such as bargaining about investment plans (see below, Part II, Ch. IV).

1. *British Journal of Industrial Relations*, 6 (1968), p. 1.
2. *British Journal of Industrial Relations*, 6 (1968), p. 1; for a defence of this definition against a Marxist criticism, see Clegg, *The Changing System of Industrial Relations in Great Britain*, Ch. 11.
3. *British Journal of Industrial Relations*, 13 (1975) p. 151.

§5. Negotiation and Consultation

42. A distinction has often been drawn in Britain between 'negotiation' and 'consultation'. The former refers to matters within the power of joint regulation by management and trade unions; the latter refers to subjects within the scope of managerial prerogative. The distinction is fluid and controversial. The scope of managerial prerogative has traditionally been wide in Britain, including matters such as health and safety and pensions. But these matters for 'consultation' have in several industries now become matters for 'negotiation'. In legal contexts, workers' participation in decision-making in Britain has generally been limited to 'consultation' (*i.e.* the right to be heard) before management decides (*e.g.* redundancy consultation, see Part I, Ch. VII).

§6. Procedural and Substantive Agreements

43. The 'dynamic' structure of collective bargaining (see below para. 44) in Britain does not lend itself to any sharp distinction between *procedural* and *substantive* collective agreements. The Trade Union and Labour Relations Act 1974, s. 29(1)(g) lists as a possible subject of 'collective bargaining' (for certain legal reasons) 'machinery for negotiation and consultation, and other procedures, relating to any of the foregoing matters including the recognition by employers or employers' associations of the right of a trade union to represent workers in any such negotiation or consultation or in the carrying out of such procedures'. The world of industrial relations has borrowed this concept to describe *procedural* agreements. It covers both collective procedures and procedures to deal with individual grievances and individual discipline. *Substantive* agreements on the other hand relate to wages and other terms and conditions of employment.

§7. Disputes of Rights and Disputes of Interest

44. Britain is probably the only industrial country in which the distinction between disputes of rights and disputes of interest is not recognised. The reason for this is to be found in the dynamic method of collective bargaining, as distinguished from the contractual or static method, which is characteristic of British industrial relations. This typical British method, in Kahn-Freund's words:

> 'consists in the creation of a permanent bilateral body, known as a joint industrial council, a conciliation board, or a joint committee, on which both sides are represented by an equal number of members, sometimes (in a minority of cases) with an independent chairman presiding. To this body the parties give a constitution and a · code of procedure, but they leave it to the body thus created by

unanimous resolutions to settle the wages and the substantive conditions of the industry. . . .

. . . Since the "dynamic" or "institutional" method consists in the passing of resolutions by a joint body which is always free to modify its own decisions, provided it does so unanimously, it encourages "open ended" agreements and discourages the fixing of time limits. More important, the body which lays down the conditions is often also the body which interprets is own resolutions. Over a large area of British industrial relations, the rule-making and the decision-making processes, the, as it were "legislative" and "judicial" functions are as indistinguishable as they were in the constitution of medieval England. Within these processes of institutional bargaining every dispute about existing "rights" can be turned into a dispute about "interests" by the simple device of solving it through a new and possibly retrospective resolution."[1]

Although the ambiguity of procedures has tended to decrease since Kahn-Freund first described this 'common law' model of collective bargaining and the location of procedures has shifted from national to company or workplace level in the private sector, little else has changed in the practice of collective bargaining.[2]

1. *Labour and the Law*, 3rd ed., pp. 70–72.
2. K. Sisson and W. Brown in *Industrial Relations In Britain* (ed. G. Bain), Oxford, 1983, p. 150.

45. It is the absence of any clear distinction between these two types of dispute that goes a long way to explain why collective agreements in Britain are generally not regarded as contracts. Where English lawyers talk about 'disputes of right' in labour law they usually have in mind not disputes arising out of collective agreements, but the determination of rights arising from legislation.

§8. VOLUNTARY AND COMPULSORY METHODS

46. The voluntary nature of much of the disputes settlement machinery in Great Britain is often cited as a distinctive feature of British industrial relations. The extent to which this reflects reality is discussed in the section on Historical Background (below, para. 49). At this point, it is necessary to analyse what 'voluntary' and 'compulsory' mean. At one end of a spectrum the word 'voluntary' suggests that disputes are resolved entirely by the parties themselves, using agreed procedures or industrial action without any third party intervention; at the other end of the 'voluntary' spectrum are negotiated settlements reached after third parties have assisted the employer and unions, with their consent, through means such as conciliation or mediation.

47. The anonym of 'voluntary' is 'compulsory' but as Kahn-Freund explained,[1] 'compulsory' is used in at least four different senses in Britain. (1)

The parties must use a particular procedure prescribed by law, such as compulsory arbitration. In the 20th century this has applied only in time of war. (2) One of the parties may invoke a particular procedure without the consent of the other side. The most prominent example is unilateral arbitration. From 1940 to 1980, in various forms, it was possible for representative trade unions or employers' organisations to invoke arbitration to oblige employers in otherwise well-organised industries to observe employment terms established by collective bargaining in that industry. The Employment Protection Act 1975 utilised unilateral arbitration of terms of employment as the final sanction against employers who failed to recognise independent trade unions or to disclose information to unions, once recognised, for purposes of collective bargaining. With the repeal of the extension and recognition provisions by the Employment Act 1980 (see Part II, Ch. IV), all that remains of unilateral arbitration is the almost unused provision relating to disclosure of information. (3) The results of a process (*e.g.* a collective agreement or arbitration award) are binding on one or both parties. As will be seen later, collective agreements are presumed not to be intended to be legally enforceable between the collective parties, but some of their provisions may take effect as binding obligations in individual contracts of employment (see Part I, Ch. II); only to this extent are they 'compulsory', and in this connection it should be remembered that it is possible (in theory, at least) for the individual employee and employer to opt out of the terms of the collective agreement. The awards of arbitrators are not legally enforceable, unless they take effect through individual contracts of employment (see Part I, Ch. II). This is expressly provided for in the case of unilateral arbitration, but may occur by implication in other cases. (4) No industrial sanctions may be used by either side during a defined period. This was the case under the Industrial Relations Act 1971 when a 'cooling-off' period could be imposed in certain emergency disputes but this was repealed in 1974. The Trade Union Act 1984 has achieved a similar objective by requiring pre-strike ballots in respect of virtually all 'official' (*i.e.* union-backed) strikes, and the effect of this is a compulsory delay until a ballot has been held. In a wider sense, the removal of immunities from many traditional forms of industrial action by the Employment Acts of 1980 and 1982 and the Trade Union Act 1984 has removed the key element of freedom to impose social sanctions, which underpinned the so-called 'voluntary' system (see Part II, Ch. V).

1. Kahn-Freund, *Labour and the Law*, 3rd ed., p. 147.

§9. Conciliation, Arbitration, Mediation and Inquiry

48. Conciliation and arbitration are not defined by law in Britain, although machinery is provided by statute to implement these methods of dispute settlement (see below, paras. 460–463). However, these terms are a well-known part of industrial relations vocabulary.

Conciliation is a voluntary, informal process of dispute resolution, whereby an independent third party assists the parties to a dispute to clarify the points of disagreement and attempts to promote a settlement. No binding award is made and any agreement reached is the responsibility of the parties. *Arbitration* differs from conciliation in that reference is made to an independent third party to adjudicate on the dispute and come to a decision. In *voluntary arbitration*, the decision is not legally binding, but the parties have nevertheless embarked on the procedure on the understanding that they will abide by whatever decision is reached. In the case of *compulsory arbitration* (see above), the award is usually legally enforceable as an implied term in the contract of employment. *Mediation*, on the other hand, leads to a recommendation by the third party which the parties to the dispute are free to reject. In Britain, *arbitration* and *meditation* may involve the settlement of conflicts of interest and conflicts of right, a distinction which, as we have seen, is difficult to make in a British context. *Inquiry* or *investigation* of the facts of industrial relations matters by an individual or a committee (sometimes misleadingly called a 'court') and the making of recommendations for the settlement of a dispute is also known in Britain; this eventually leads to an agreement between the parties.

III. The Historical Background

§1. THE TRADITIONAL VOLUNTARY SYSTEM UNTIL THE 1960S

49. In order to understand modern labour law and industrial relations it is necessary to appreciate three features of the legal framework of industrial relations as it developed until the 1960s. The first is the tradition of individualism; the second is the tradition of support for voluntary collective bargaining; and the third is the selective nature of regulatory or 'protective' legislation.

A. The individualist tradition[1]

50. The notion of the individual contract of employment is central to the legal analysis of industrial relations. This fragmentation of industrial relations into millions of individual relationships, is not an accidental or modern phenomenon. It is deeply rooted in social and legal tradition. The conception of the reciprocal rights and duties of the parties flowing from their free exchange of promises arrived relatively late on the legal scene in Britain in comparison with the continental countries influenced by Roman law. The reason was the tradition of the Statute of Labourers passed by Edward III in 1351, following an Ordinance of 1349, later reinforced by the Elizabethan Statute of Artificers of 1563, and the tradition of the Poor Law Act 1601. Under these laws the 'servant's' status determined the obligation to work at wages arbitrarily fixed by justices of the peace, usually themselves masters. Servants were liable to punishment for not accepting the work, for not doing it according to directions, or for deserting the master. As late as 1850 Blackstone's definition of the master-servant relationship was still in vogue among lawyers and, according to that definition the relationship need not be based on contract: for example, a labourer could be compelled to serve by justices of the peace; a parish apprentice indentured under the Poor Law had to serve a master with whom he had no contract; and the mere condition of 'having no visible effects' could give rise to a direction to compulsory work.[1] The sanctions were criminal. When the Elizabethan statute fell into disuse, the legal basis for prosecutions against workers were the 19th-century Master and Servants Acts. It was the trade unions which were largely responsible for the modification and repeal of these penal laws by the Master and Servant Act 1867 and the Conspiracy and Protection of Property Act 1875 respectively. Trade union agitation arose primarily because of the effect of the laws on the freedom to strike: 'it was a recognised tactic of the employers, particularly in dealing with smaller strikes, to cause all the strikers to be arrested for breach of contract and then to confront them with the alternatives of returning to work on the employer's terms or suffering up to 3 months' imprisonment. Furthermore, as the law stood, a troublemaker might be silenced not just once but repeatedly'.[2]

Between 1858 and 1875 an average of 10,000 prosecutions of workmen for breach of contract took place each year in England and Wales.[3]

1. This section draws extensively on B. Hepple, Chap. 16 in *Industrial Relations in Britain* (ed. G. S. Bain), Oxford 1983.
2. P. S. Bagwell, *Industrial Relations in 19th Century Britain*, Dublin 1974, p. 30.
3. D. Simon, 'Master and Servant' in *Democracy and the Labour Movement*, London 1954, p. 160.

51. The repeal of the Master and Servant Acts removed a major impediment to the development of the notion of freedom of contract between equal contracting parties by civil sanctions alone. However, the intellectual backwardness of the legal analysis of 'master and servant' relationships has had a lasting impact on the modern law. One consequence has been the patchy and inadequate coverage of labour law (see Part I, Ch. I, below). Another has been the inordinate complexity of labour law. The bulk of labour legislation in the 19th century developed outside the framework of the contract of employment. This 'atrophy' of the contract of employment, as Kahn-Freund called it,[1] is largely attributable to the absence of an explicit and flexible contract model in the formative period of labour law. The most important consequences of the heritage of ideas evolved over centuries under the influence of the Statute of Labourers, the Statute of Artificers, and the Poor Law is that the form of contract which emerged in the 19th century effectively guaranteed the rule-making powers of the employer. When the worker at the factory gate accepts an offer of employment, neither he nor the employer may be conscious that they have concluded a binding contract of service. In law they have done so although nothing was said about wages or hours of work, let alone such matters as holidays, sick pay, pensions or what is to happen if there is a stoppage of work due to a power failure. If there is no legislation in point, and no express agreement, it is left to the courts and tribunals to make sense of the contract by implying terms as to these matters. As indicated later (Part I, Ch. II), where there is collective bargaining the courts may be prepared to fill in the gaps by incorporating the relevant terms of the collective agreements as implied terms of the individual contract. The great success of collective bargaining in many industries has meant that the courts have rarely been called upon to imply terms. In reality, where there is no collective agreement or arbitration award or legislation, the superior economic power of employers enables them to dictate terms of the contract which the individual employees are in no position to contest through the courts, least of all when they are still working for the employer. The law of contract was developed by the courts, and the principal conceptual instrument they use to fill the gaps left by the parties is the implied intention of the parties. In a few extreme cases (such as contracts in restraint of trade) public policy is used to nullify a contract, but never to mould it. This means that the idea of positive legal regulation of the contract by imperative forms is alien to the common law approach: parties are even free to 'contract out' of protective legislation unless and until Parliament says they cannot do so. This is quite different from the continental legal systems which for two centuries have applied general imperative norms to all contracts and special norms to the contract of employment. Moreover, when British judges have sought to imply terms they have relied heavily on custom and practice. The task of discovering the custom is greatly simplified, as indicated later, when there is a collective agreement. Where none exists everyday obligations, such as the speed of work, the conditions of labour, and the subjection to discipline, are implied from what the parties do in practice, and that means in effect what the employer has laid down and applied in works rules, even informally. Some obligations, such as fidelity, the maintenance of mutual trust and confidence, and obedience to the employer's reasonable commands, are regarded as fundamental. They are implied as a matter of law from judicial precedents which have been influenced from the traditions of the law of 'master and servant'. The judicial perspective, even in recent times, has been unitary rather than pluralist, although under the impact of modern legislation there are some signs of change.

1. O. Kahn-Freund, 'Blackstone's neglected child: the contract of employment' *Law Quarterly Review* 93 (1977) 508 at p. 524.

B. Support for voluntary collective bargaining

52. The traditional British system of industrial relations until the 1960s rested on a social consensus that the state's role should be minimal. Trade unions and strikes emerged from illegality in a series of statutes from 1824 to 1906. As pointed out earlier (para. 3, above) no positive rights to organise and strike were established but only a number of negative 'immunities' from the judge-made common law. The recognition of trade unions for collective bargaining was achieved without the aid of legislation or any significant demand for such legislation. Robson noted,[1] in 1935, that 'England is the home of trade unionism; it was on her soil that the practice of combined bargaining first arose; yet here alone is the collective contract still denied the elementary right of legal enforcement in the courts of law despite the fact that it is the recognised method of determining the conditions of employment of the vast majority of wage earners'. However, there was a certain amount of 'auxiliary' legislation designed to promote and support voluntary collective bargaining. This included the minimum wage-fixing machinery established in selected 'sweated' trades where collective bargaining was non-existent, originating with the Trade Boards Act 1909, the successive Fair Wages Resolutions of the House of Commons, from 1891, which imposed obligations on government contractors to pay 'fair' wages, of which collectively agreed terms were a primary guide, and the machinery established in 1896 and 1919 to encourage the use of voluntary conciliation and arbitration.

1. W. Robson, 'Industrial law' *Law Quarterly Review* 51 (1935), p. 204.

53. It is a striking feature of Britain's war-time legislation, and of the policy of the first twenty years after the Second World War, that this served to consolidate the traditional voluntary system. The Conditions of Employment and National Arbitration Order No. 1305 severely restricted strikes and lock-outs and made it compulsory to submit disputes to arbitration. In practice, however, the peacetime system of voluntary collective bargaining remained intact. Moreover, the unions were more deeply involved in carrying out war-time measures such as the allocation of labour and paying out unemployment benefits for the Ministry of Labour. At plant level, joint production commit-tees distributed work and administered discipline. Labour benefitted from this policy of 'tripartite corporatism'. Average earnings in real terms were 24 per cent higher in 1944 than in 1938 (due to extra overtime and bonuses) and membership in trade unions rose by about one-third during the War to bring it up to 8 million (45 per cent of the workforce). When a Labour government was elected with a massive majority in 1945, the unions did not seek any major changes in the traditional system. The only immediate measure was the repeal of the Trade Disputes and Trade Union Act 1927, which a Conservative government had imposed in the aftermath of the 1926 General Strike to outlaw 'political' sympathy strikes, to restrict financial support by union members for the Labour Party, and to forbid civil servant unions from affiliating to outside bodies such as the Trades Union Congress (TUC). The war-time Order 1305 remained in force, with union consent, until 1951 when it was repealed as the result of withdrawal of trade union support following the prosecution of some strikers. It was replaced by Order 1376 of 1951 which restored the freedom to strike and lock-out and allowed representative organisations to invoke unilateral arbitration in order to extend collective agreements; when the Order was replaced by permanent legislation in 1959 (under a Conservative administration) a modified form of such extension remained a feature of the law until 1980. Other legislative changes in the immediate post-war period also aimed to improve support for the traditional voluntary system. These included a new and amended Fair Wages Resolution of 1946, and a Wages Councils Act of 1945. The latter replaced the earlier trade boards legislation and enabled the renamed 'wages councils' to recommend that the Minister made a wages order not only where there was no collective bargaining machinery but also where such machinery was inadequate, as, for example, where it had collapsed leaving workers unprotected in times of depression. Trade union acquiescence in the consolidation of the voluntary system was closely linked to the implementation of Beveridge's proposals for a reformed comprehensive system of social security.

54. The welfare state, together with the voluntarist system of industrial relations, was part of the policy not only of the post-war Labour Government but also was accepted by the Conservative administrations from 1951–1964. In retrospect, it is possible to see that this 'rested upon a middle-class acquiescence in the current balance of industrial power'.[1] There was a stable economic basis for the social consensus. In the 1930s, despite high levels of unemployment, wage and salary earners in employment enjoyed relative prosperity, and Britain was cushioned from the economic crisis by its foreign assets. During the War Britain lost £7,000 million, a quarter of its national wealth, but the sporadic post-war economic crises were held in check by loans from the United States. Britain had not suffered military occupation or physical destruction as other European countries had, and there was no significant pressure for the renewal of industry and the 'modernization' of industrial relations. In that climate it is not surprising that there were no moves towards restructuring labour law, for example by introducing forms of co-determination of the kind which the British occupation forces, with British trade union advice, fostered in Germany. Even in the industries which the Labour Government nationalised (civil aviation, cable and wireless, coal, railways, long-distance road transport, electricity, gas, iron and steel and the Bank of England), the legislation went no further than to require the boards of the new public corporations to 'consult' with 'appropriate organisations' with a view to establishing and maintaining negotiation and arbitration procedures, provisions which have proved to be largely symbolic. Co-partnership or even more radical notions of workers' control formed no part of the traditional consensus.

1. K. W. Wedderburn, 'Labour Law and Labour Relations in Britain' *British Journal of Industrial Relations* 10 (1972) p. 270 at p. 275.

C. The selective nature of regulatory legislation

55. The primacy of voluntary collective bargaining meant that regulatory legislation, directly laying down rules of employment on matters such as wages, hours, health and safety, has tended to take second place. The policy of the law has been not to regulate by statute the terms of employment of those who are considered capable of protecting themselves. Legislation applied primarily to children and women and not to adult men. In the 20th century, the principle has been to cover by direct regulation only those who are not protected by collective bargaining and to deal only with those subjects which do not appear to lend themselves to collective bargaining. Even where there is regulatory legislation, it has often been designed to allow for its replacement by approved collective agreements, which are at least as good in content as regulatory legislation. In any event, legislation can always be supplemented by collective bargaining on the same subject. The most important consequence of the approach has been the absence of the kind of comprehensive regulation that is to be found in other industrial countries of such matters as hours and holidays for all employees. Significantly, apart from the mining industry, the 8-hour day in Britain was achieved by collective bargaining rather than legislation. There is specific regulation of the hours of women and young persons in certain activities (see Part I, Ch. III), but with a few exceptions the hours of adult men are regulated by collective bargaining or by wages councils (above).

56. The reason for the selective use of the 'method of legal enactment' as a means of worker protection is to be found in the ebb and flow of struggle of unions and reform groups inside and outside Parliament, and the resistance by powerful groups of employers and intellectual supporters of *laissez-faire*. The earliest legislation, including the Regulation of Chimney Sweepers Act 1788 and the Health and Morals of Apprentices Act 1802, was concerned with child labour. The initial aim of the short-time committees from 1831 onwards was the 10-hour day for all employees, regardless of sex and age, but when the political reality of the time made this unattainable, the committees modified their aims to concentrate on the hours of work of women. The first major victory for the short-time committees was the Factories Act 1844 which equated women with young persons, restricted their hours, and required dangerous parts of machinery to be fenced, as well as strengthening the powers of the inspectorate which had been established by the Factories Act 1833. The opportunities for evasion were many and some loopholes were closed in 7 Acts passed between 1844 and 1856. Most important of all was the 'Ten Hours Act' of 1847 which conceded the main demand of the short-time committees. In the second half of the 19th century this legislation, which applied only to textile factories, was gradually extended to cover factories and workshops over a wide range of old and new manufacturing industries. At different times activities outside these industries were also regulated: mines from 1842 (but with effective inspection only from 1860), shops from 1886 (although the health and safety aspects of shop work were not covered until 1963), and standards comparable to factory legislation were not extended to agriculture until 1956. Surveying the scene in 1972, an official committee of inquiry, under the chairmanship of Lord Robens, found that there were 9 main groups of statutes supported by over 500 subordinate statutory instruments. These contained a mass of intricate and ill-assorted detail. Some 5 million workers worked in premises not covered by any occupational health or safety legislation. A result of the recommendations of the committee was the comprehensive Health and Safety at Work etc. Act 1974. The existing legislation relating to health, safety and welfare is very slowly being replaced by this new comprehensive system, which is based on the philosophy of self-regulation. This does not, however, mean that there has been a significant shift to collective bargaining over these matters in place of statutory regulation. The legislation is based on the concept of 'consultation' with safety representatives and safety committees rather than bargaining (see Part II, Ch. III below).

§2. THINGS FALL APART: THE 1960s AND 1970s

57. There were already signs in the late 1950s and early 1960s that the social consensus which had sustained the traditional voluntarist framework was under strain. The pressure of full employment had contributed to a shift of power to the workplace: employers anxious to retain and recruit labour did not need much prompting to accede to demands for pay increases made by shop stewards on behalf of workgroups. Shop stewards were increasingly identified by politicians and the media as the main cause of 'wages drift', increases in earnings not accounted for by central industry-wide negotiations, and so a serious impediment to the control of inflation which, together with the maintenance of full employment, was a major goal of successive governments from 1945. Trade unions were also blamed for their failure to control the relatively large number of unofficial ('wildcat') strikes in breach of agreed procedures, and for the inefficient use of manpower through the imposition of restrictive 'custom and practice' overmanning. The more deep-seated causes of Britain's post-war economic problems, such as the high levels of military spending and the insistence of the multinational enterprises on keeping Britain as an international financial centre and open economy with a high level of capital export and relatively little domestic investment, received much less attention in the public debate. Trade unions were unable to influence factors such as these, but they came to be seen as a major cause of Britain's relative economic failure. The preoccupation of successive governments was with the exchange rate and the balance of payments, and wage-induced inflation could be readily identified as a source of economic instability.

58. Two broad strategies were adopted to control this phenomenon. One was a succession of incomes policies, the other was the use of the law in order to influence the conduct of industrial relations. These strategies were not consistently applied, and, indeed, they were not infrequently discordant. The political parties, the trade unions and the employers were locked in ceaseless battle over these questions. In the period 1948 to 1979 there were no less than six different incomes policies: voluntary wage restraint under the Labour administration (1948–1950); a freeze on prices under the Conservatives (1956–1957); a 'pay pause' under the Conservatives (1961–1962); the Labour government's voluntary (1965) and later (1966–1967) compulsory incomes policy; the Conservative's Counter-Inflation Acts (1972–1974); and Labour's 'social contract' with the TUC (1974–1976), followed by a unilateral policy (1977–1979) and a 'concordat' with the TUC (February–May 1979). Each of these policies had distinctive features and used different institutional devices. Some were voluntary and some of them had statutory support. All of them ended in failure. However, it is important to note that, while 'encroaching very directly upon the autonomy of collective bargaining',[1] these policies did not reshape labour law itself.[2] The Prices and Incomes Acts of 1966 and 1967 and the Counter-Inflation Acts of 1972 and 1973 nominally rested upon criminal sanctions, but these were never enforced; the traditional 'immunities' in respect of industrial action were not removed and, indeed, the Act of 1966 actually widened them. Moreover, the policies exempted either wholly or in part the machinery designed to help the low paid and to achieve equal pay for men and women. The negative restraints on the results of collective bargaining were accompanied by a series of positive measures to encourage or promote trade union growth and recognition: in the period from 1948 to 1979 union density among manual workers grew from 50.3 per cent to 63.0 per cent, and among white-collar workers from 33.0 per cent to 44.0 per cent.

1. P. Davies and M. Freedland, 'Editors' Introduction' to *Kahn-Freund's Labour and the Law*, 3rd ed., p. 7.
2. Lord Wedderburn, 'Labour Law Now – A Nudge and a Hold' *Industrial Law Journal* 13 (1984), p. 73.

59. Indirectly, however, incomes policies did have a major impact on the conceptual framework of labour law. Successive governments always tried to

secure trade union consent to their incomes policies. This 'corporate bargaining' recognised the trade union interest in a wide range of policy issues outside the traditional 'economic' questions of terms and conditions of employment. In return for this political influence the unions were ready to accept periods of pay restraint and more state interference in 'free' collective bargaining. For example, during discussions with Prime Minister Heath in 1972 the unions demanded the repeal of the Industrial Relations Act (below) and some other legislation in return for agreement on pay restraint. Mr. Heath regarded this as too high a price, but the subsequent Labour government entered into a 'social contract' with the TUC. In return for a programme of social and legal reforms, the TUC agreed a policy of temporary pay restraint. The first stage of the reforms was the repeal of the Industrial Relations Act; the second was the enactment of a wide range of new legal rights for trade unions and workers in the Employment Protection Act 1975; the third stage was to have been an extension of workers' participation in the enterprise, but this did not get beyond the government policy statement on industrial democracy (1978) in response to the Report of a Committee of Inquiry under the chairmanship of Lord Bullock (1977). The government's attempts to continue some form of pay restraint after the social contract had collapsed led to a high level of industrial unrest in the winter of 1978–1979, widely regarded as a major reason for Labour's defeat in the 1979 elections. The most significant result of the incomes policies was the 'politicization' of industrial relations, the complete blurring of the distinction between economics and politics on which the traditional system was based. Government attempts to impose wage restraints and to restructure collective bargaining (below) forced the trade unions directly into the political arena. The traditional consensus that the state was essentially 'neutral' or 'abstentionist' could not survive. The boundaries between 'legitimate' economic 'trade disputes' and political action came under stress in a way which had not occurred since the abortive General Strike of 1926.

60. The second strategy which signalled the breakdown of the traditional voluntary system was that of direct legal intervention. Here policies both of reform and of the restriction of collective bargaining have been adopted and these have not always been consistent. On the side of reform, the first legislation on the contract of employment since 1875 had been introduced by a Conservative administration in 1963 and received 'without enthusiasm' by the unions. The Contracts of Employment Act 1963 laid down minimum periods of notice to terminate employment (these have been progressively increased since then but are still low by European standards), and to require employers to provide employees with written statements of their main terms of employment, largely in the hope that this would remove the causes of some disputes. The Redundancy Payments Act 1965, introduced by a Labour government, provided for lump sum payments based on age and length of service for those dismissed on grounds of redundancy after a minimum of two years' employment. The Conservative's Industrial Relations Act 1971 implemented the recommendation of the Royal Commission on Trade Unions and Employers' Associations (1965–1968) (chaired by Lord Donovan) that there should be a statutory right for employees not to be unfairly dismissed. This was re-enacted, with improvements, in Labour's Trade Union and Labour Relations Act 1974, and, as already mentioned, the Employment Protection Act 1975, as part of the 'social contract', created a number of other rights for individual employees, such as maternity pay and the right to return to work after pregnancy and confinement, guarantee payments by the employer when work is not available, and protection of wages on the insolvency of the employer. As already mentioned, a comprehensive Health and Safety at Work etc. Act was enacted in 1974. Starting with the Equal Pay Act 1970 and complemented by the Sex Discrimination Act 1975, action has been taken against discrimination on grounds of sex and marital status, and the Race Relations Act 1976 (replacing the earlier Act of 1968) deals with discrimination on racial grounds. The growing volume of legislation can be seen from the fact that compared with some five general Acts of Parliament regulating employment passed between 1950 and 1959, and 16 from 1960 to 1969, there were 30 such Acts from 1970 to 1979. Most of the new individual rights were enforced through the industrial tribunals, established in 1964 (see below, section V). The case law has spawned several specialist law reports and journals devoted to labour law.

61. The policy of reform has also been evident in the legislation on collective labour relations. The Donovan Commission wanted to introduce 'order' into the largely informal system of plant bargaining, in order to reduce wages drift, restrictive practices and strikes. They hoped that reform could be achieved 'if possible, without destroying the British tradition of keeping industrial relations out of the courts'.[1] However, the Conservative government, elected in 1970, saw legislation as the 'main instrument' in bringing about reform. The Industrial Relations Act 1971 contained a series of provisions designed to reform bargaining structures, to secure recognition of unions by employers, to encourage legally enforceable collective agreements and to reform union rules, in particular so as to make governing bodies responsible for controlling and disciplining their members. The immediate cause of the failure of the 1971 Act was the defeat of the Heath government in the February 1974 election which arose from the confrontation with the miners' union over incomes policy. However, the TUC's policy of non-co-operation with the Act had rendered it largely inoperable: the Act tried to bring about too drastic a change in existing institutions and behaviour by means of law, it was based on the mistaken assumption that employers would use the law, and the transplantation of legal institutions from the United States (*e.g.* bargaining units, cooling-off periods etc.) took insufficient account of the different economic and political climate in Britain.

1. Report of the Royal Commission on Trade Unions and Employers' Associations, Cmnd. 3623 (1968), para. 190.

62. The Labour government's 'social contract' legislation (1974–1976) returned to the path of reform by restoring the presumption that collective agreements were presumed not to be intended as legally enforceable contracts, and recreating extended immunities from legal action in respect of acts 'in contemplation or furtherance of a trade dispute'. An Advisory, Conciliation and Arbitration Service (ACAS) and a Central Arbitration Committee (CAC) were created and novel collective rights to trade union recognition and the disclosure of information for collective bargaining, as well as improved provisions for the extension of collective agreements to non-organised workers were granted. Consultation rights were enacted in respect of collective redundancies (this in response to an EEC Directive), health and safety and occupational pension schemes. The wages councils system (above) was strengthened and provision was made for encouraging collective bargaining in industries covered by those councils. Some 'individual' rights, such as those to time off work for trade union duties and activities and protection against victimization for trade union membership and activities, underpinned this reassertion, by legal means, of the primacy of the collective bargaining system.

63. Labour law policies, however, contained a strand of restriction of trade union power and collective bargaining. In 1969, Mr. Wilson's Labour government had unsuccessfully proposed penal sanctions against unconstitutional strikers who failed to observe a 28-day 'conciliation pause' as well as ballot requirements for certain official strikes and a power to control inter-union disputes over recognition. The Conservative's Industrial Relations Act, somewhat inconsistently with its support for collective bargaining (above), contained a strong element of individualist philosophy in its ban on the closed shop, with some limited exceptions, and the positive right not to belong to any trade union or to a particular union. This was an individual right capable of undermining the organisational strength and representativeness of trade unions. The Act also contained many restrictions on the right to strike, and civil liabilities for so-called 'unfair industrial practices'. These led to several confrontations between unions and the courts. The 'social contract' legislation was reformist in character, but some parts of it were restrictively interpreted by the courts and tribunals. For example, dislike of the consequences of the widening of the statutory immunities by Parliament led the Court of Appeal between 1977 and 1979 to impose novel limitations on these immunities; the statutory recognition provisions became largely inoperable because of restrictive judicial interpretations; and the protection for trade union activities proved to be very limited. For their part, employers were increasingly complaining that the new laws imposed undue burdens on them. The language and philosophy of individual rights, which had become increasingly pervasive, was also criticised from the Left on the grounds that this had strengthened managerial control over jobs giving an enormous impetus to unilateral rulemaking by management, in particular through the formalization of disciplinary procedures. The factors which most severely undermined the reformist legislation were economic and political. By 1979, unemployment was mounting, inflation remained at high levels, public expenditure was being cut, and there was acute discontent with the government's policies. In May 1979, the Conservatives led by Mrs. Thatcher were elected to power.

§3. LEGAL RESTRICTION AND MARKET INDIVIDUALISM: THE 1980s

64. The policies and legislation of Mrs. Thatcher's administration have fundamentally shifted the parameters of labour law. The solution to the major problems of the 1970s – inflation and the politicization of the unions – has been sought in the restoration of 'free' markets. The argument is that trade union 'coercion' has caused inflation and unemployment and fluctuating living standards. The unions' 'coercive powers' are said to rest upon their legal 'privileges'. Therefore, in the words of Professor F. A. Hayek, whose ideas have been extremely influential, 'there can be no salvation for Britain until the special privileges granted to trade unions three-quarters of a century ago are revoked'.[1] Trade unions and labour legislation are seen as a distortion of market relations between employer and employee. In order to make 'free' markets work, it is necessary to 'get the state off people's backs' and to 'deregulate'. It is also necessary to curb effective demand, so as to reduce inflation, and this involves weakening trade union power, and also severely reducing public expenditure. This ideology is reflected in the three main pieces of legislation introduced by the Conservative government: the Employment Acts 1980 and 1982 and the Trade Union Act 1984. This legislation has pursued four specific policies.

1. F. A. Hayek, *1980s Unemployment and the Unions*, London 1980, p. 58.

65. First, workers' rights of self-help through collective organisation and industrial action have been effectively restricted to their own employment units. For example, workers are now allowed to picket only outside their own place of work; sympathy and solidarity action between enterprises is effectively prohibited; the immunity from civil action in 'trade disputes' has been narrowed to disputes between workers and their own employer. Traditional union methods of preventing the supply of goods to an employer in dispute or banning the sending of work to non-union shops are now unlawful. Secondly, trade union funds have been placed at the mercy of the law. Previously only union officials could be sued for acts which fell outside the boundaries of permissible 'trade disputes'. Since 1982, union funds themselves are at risk. The increasing likelihood of confrontation with the courts has exposed the unions to the additional dangers of heavy fines for contempt of court and the sequestration of all or a substantial part of their assets to pay the fines and damages (see Part II, Chs. II and V, below). Thirdly, contrary to the public policy of the previous 100 years, in the new structure of labour law there is now a clear commitment to *restrict* collective bargaining. The government itself gave a lead by banning membership of trade unions at the Government Communications Headquarters (GCHQ) in January 1984 (see Part II, Ch. I, below). Statutory provisions for the recognition of trade unions by employers were repealed in 1980. The legislation of 1980, 1982 and 1984 has also been calculated to weaken trade union organisation. This has been done in part by the incentive of large penal awards against employers and trade unions in favour of those who leave a trade union and are then dismissed by the employer. Unions are now required to have secret ballots before industrial action which is approved or endorsed by the principal executive body of the union. These provisions give the union executives an incentive to disown local action. The contrast is obvious with the Industrial Relations Act 1971 which sought to make unions responsible for local action. Now the emphasis is on weakening, not strengthening, central union leadership. The law now makes pressures on an employer to engage only unionists and to negotiate and consult with trade unions unlawful, while at the same time it is lawful to induce an employer *not* to negotiate with a trade union.

66. Fourthly, central to the whole strategy has been the control of labour through the market. The most striking feature of the years since 1979 has been the accelerated increase in unemployment, partly as a result of the strict monetary policies of the Conservative government. A fall in employment by 8 per cent from 1979–1984 has been accompanied by a fall in trade union membership of 17 per cent (from 13.2 million members to 11 million). The spectre of unemployment has had a depressing effect on the labour market in general and this has been accentuated by official policies. Traditional supports for the low-paid are being removed: in 1983 the government secured the repeal of the Fair Wages Resolution (above); the machinery for fixing minimum wages in the road haulage industry was repealed in 1980, the provisions for extending collective agreements to unorganised sectors of a trade or industry were repealed in 1980; in 1986 the government proposes to 'slim down' the wages councils (above) so as to exclude young people under 21 from the statutory protection and to restrict the councils to setting only a minimum hourly rate and a single overtime rate for those aged 21 and over, and to replace the 150-year old Truck Acts with less onerous provisions on deductions from wages. Moreover, traditional tripartite bodies are now being used to place new restrictions on labour. For example, under the Youth Training Scheme operated by the tripartite Manpower Services Commission, employers are financially penalised if they pay young workers above certain low levels. Job security has been diminished by Orders which first (from July 1980) increased the qualifying period for unfair dismissal rights to one year from six months, and then (from June 1986) to two years. Welfare rights have been dismantled, for example abolishing earnings-related benefits for unemployment and sickness payments in 1982, reducing many other benefits in real value, replacing sickness benefit by an inferior system of statutory sick pay from the employer for the first 28 weeks' absence and imposing charges for a number of formerly free sevices. These cuts not only serve to reduce public expenditure but they also act as a powerful discipline on workers to hold down their jobs.

67. Measures such as these have had the effect of widening the gulf between an elite of relatively well-paid secure workers who have the good fortune to remain in full-time employment and a growing 'reserve army of labour' on the fringes of the 'core' labour market, many of these fringe workers being women, young persons and members of ethnic minorities. The trend since the 1970s has been for inequality to grow between those in full-time secure employment and

the various types of marginal workers such as outworkers, part-time workers, casual workers and temporary workers, most of whom fall outside the protection of the employment legislation. In such a climate, labour law has undergone a functional transformation. On the one hand, the trade unions weakened by unemployment and the movement towards the privatization of heavily-unionised public corporations are now exposed to a wider range of common law liabilities than at any time since 1906 and they have lost most of the traditional 'auxiliary' legislation which supported collective bargaining. On the other hand, the individual employment protection legislation now applies to a diminishing 'core' of the labour market, with workers fearful of unemployment.

IV. The Role of Governmental Institutions in the Shaping and Administration of Labour Law and Industrial Relations Policy

68. The growth of legal regulation (as described above) has been accompanied by the development of regulatory government agencies, most of them constituted on a tripartite basis, to administer labour law and control industrial relations policy. The main institutions are surveyed in this section. In section V (para. 80, below) the specialised courts, known as industrial tribunals, first set up in 1964 to adjudicate on most of the new statutory employment rights, are discussed, as is the role of the ordinary courts.

69. Despite the growth of these institutions, it remains true to say that most disputes are not processed through machinery provided by the state. They are settled informally through workplace procedures and joint industrial bodies. Parliament has actively encouraged the growth of voluntary procedures. For example, employers are obliged to give every employee a note specifying disciplinary and grievance procedures applicable to each employee.[1] Another example is that statutory rights of employees in respect of unfair dismissal[2] and redundancy payments[3] and guarantee payments[4] may be replaced by dismissal procedures voluntarily agreed by the collective parties with the approval of the Secretary of State. (In practice, however, few parties have attempted to obtain approval and rigorous criteria are applied before approval is given.) A final example is the requirement that officers of the Advisory, Conciliation and Arbitration Service (next para.) must have regard to the desirability of using voluntary procedures before intervening in individual or collective disputes.[5]

1. EPCA 1978, s.1(4).
2. EPCA 1978, s.65: only one agreement has been approved.
3. EPCA 1978, s.96: only two agreements have been approved.
4. EPCA 1978, s.18: 18 agreements have been approved.
5. EPCA 1978 ss.133(5), 134(4); SDA 1975 s. 64(3); RRA 1976 s. 55(3); and see generally C. Bourn, 'Statutory Exemptions for Collective Agreements' (1979) *Industrial Law Journal*, p. 85.

§1. ADVISORY, CONCILIATION AND ARBITRATION SERVICE (ACAS)

70. This service was established from 2 September 1974[1] as an essential element in the Social Contract package of statutory aids to collective bargaining.[2] It is charged with the general duty of promoting the improvement of industrial relations, which includes the extension, development and, where necessary, reform of collective bargaining machinery. It also took over from the Department of Employment the functions of conciliation, arbitration and mediation (see below). In recognition of the priority of autonomous institutions, the service must have regard to the desirability of using voluntary procedures before intervening in individual or collective disputes.[3] Moreover, ACAS has no powers of compulsion – it seeks to discharge its responsibilities through the voluntary co-operation of the parties concerned. A central characteristic of ACAS is its impartiality and independence from Government. Although it is required to report annually to the Secretary of State, it is independent of Government and is not subject to the direction of Ministers. Thus during the period of operation of incomes policies, the service made it clear that it did 'not act as an interpreter or an enforcement agency' for government incomes policies.[4] ACAS is directed by a tripartite Council consisting of a full-time independent Chairman, and 9 members: three nominated by the Confederation of British Industry (CBI), three by the Trades Union Congress (TUC) and 3 independent members (usually academics).

1. It replaced the former Commission on Industrial Relations which had somewhat different functions and structure.
2. It was placed on a statutory basis from 1976 by EPA 1975, Part I.
3. EPCA 1978, ss. 133(5), 134(4); SDA 1975, s. 64(3); RRA, s. 55(3).
4. ACAS Annual Report, 1976.

71. ACAS has nine principal functions:
(1) *Collective conciliation*: ACAS provides facilities for settling disputes by conciliation, either at the request of one or more of the parties or on its own initative where a 'trade dispute' (see para. 486) exists or is apprehended. Since its establishment, there seems to have been greater willingness to accept third party intervention in disputes.[1] In 1975, ACAS completed conciliation action in 2,017 collective disputes (with a success rate of 80 per cent), a sharp contrast with conciliation in the 1960s, when the Department of Employment took action in only about 400 cases annually. The rapid rise in the number of collective conciliation cases was partly due to the search for loopholes to income policies, as is evidenced by the fact that, having peaked at 2,891 in 1977, the number of completed cases dropped sharply with the relaxation of incomes policies in 1979. These figures continued to decline in the 1980s, reaching 1,621 in 1983 and 1,448 in 1984. However, despite the decrease in numbers, ACAS reports that cases tend to be longer, larger and more complicated.
(2) *References to Arbitration and Mediation*: (for definition, see para. 48). Where a trade dispute exists or is apprehended, ACAS may appoint one or more persons (who are not officers of ACAS) to arbitrate or mediate, provided at least one party requests such a reference, both parties consent, and ACAS is satisfied that agreed procedures have been exhausted and conciliation has failed. Disputes may also be referred to the Central Arbitration Committee (see below). Awards of *ad hoc* arbitrators are published only if the parties consent. ACAS is also responsible for servicing a number of standing boards of arbitration in the public sector, such as the Railway Staffs' National Tribunal, the Police Arbitration Tribunal, the Post Office Arbitration Tribunal and tribunals under the Remuneration of Teachers Act 1965 and the Education (Scotland) Act 1980. As in collective conciliation, the number of cases referred to arbitration peaked in 1978 at 421, an eight-fold increase on the 54 cases dealt with by the Department of Employment in 1973. Since then, the numbers have declined to 207 in 1983

and 202 in 1984. The majority of disputes have consistently been concerned with pay and conditions of employment, but the complexity and importance of issues referred have increased with the demise of incomes policy.

(3) *Conciliation in proceedings before industrial tribunals*: Conciliation officers designated by ACAS are required to promote a settlement of any complaint presented to an industrial tribunal (see below) in respect of statutory employment rights. This has proved to be a large part of ACAS's workload. From 29,100 cases received in 1975, this figure leapt to 41,930 in 1976, and has remained consistently high, peaking at 47,040 in 1981. In 1984, a total of 42,723 cases were received. The Service has proved highly successful in its task of promoting settlements; an average of two-thirds of cases received are cleared without reference to a tribunal. The vast majority of cases received concern unfair dismissal (about 87 per cent in 1984).

(4) *Advice*: ACAS provides free advice to employers, employers' associations, individual workers and trade unions on a variety of subjects. It regards its advisory function as the principal means of fulfilling its statutory duty to promote the improvement of industrial relations and devotes a considerable proportion of its resources for this purpose. Advice includes both short-term assistance on specific matters and long-term, in-depth assistance which the Service considers to be more likely to lead to lasting improvements in industrial relations.

(5) *Codes of Practice*: ACAS has general power to issue codes of practice containing practical guidance to promote the improvement of industrial relations. Under this power, a Code of Practice on Disciplinary Practice and Procedures has been issued. ACAS has also issued Codes of Practice, as it is obliged to do, in respect of the disclosure of information for purposes of collective bargaining, and time off for trade union officials and members. (The effect of a Code in legal proceedings is considered in para. 96 below.)

(6) *Wages Councils*: ACAS has miscellaneous duties in connection with wages councils (see Part I, Ch. IV, paras. 205–212).

(7) *Inquiry*: ACAS may inquire into any question relevant to industrial relations generally or in any particular industry. The findings may be published if ACAS considers it desirable. This power is not often used.

(8) *Disclosure of information for bargaining*: ACAS has specific duties in relation to this procedure (see Part II, Ch. IV below).

(9) *Equal pay*: ACAS has responsibility for designating independent experts to report on claims for equal pay for work of equal value when required to do so by an industrial tribunal (see Part I, Ch. VIII below).

1. All statistics are derived from ACAS Annual Reports, 1976–84.

§2. Central Arbitration Committee (CAC)

72. The Central Arbitration Committee was established in 1975 as a permanent tripartite arbitration committee maintained at state expense.[1] It consists of a Chairman and members with experience as employers' and

workers' representatives respectively. For hearings, the Chairman (or Deputy) sits with two other members, one drawn from each side. It is independent of ACAS and is not subject to governmental directions of any kind.

1. EPA 1975, s. 10 and Sch.1.

73. Compulsory arbitration has never been a central feature of British industrial relations, consistent with the primacy of voluntary disputes resolution mechanisms (see paras. 46 and 47 above). Voluntary arbitration facilities have, however, been provided by the state since 1919, in the form of the Industrial Court (renamed the Industrial Arbitration Board in 1971), to which the relevant Government Minister could refer a dispute for voluntary arbitration with the consent of both parties and if all voluntary procedures had been exhausted. The CAC took over the voluntary arbitration functions of the Industrial Arbitration Board. Thus, at the request of one or more parties to a trade dispute, and with the consent of all parties, ACAS may refer a dispute to arbitration by the CAC. When created, the CAC's powers extended further, to include the power of unilateral arbitration as a sanction for failure to comply with many of the 'statutory props' introduced as part of the Social Contract legislation.[1] These included claims for the extensions of terms of employment and for the observance of fair wages in industries which receive government contracts, subsidies, loans or licences; claims arising from failure to comply with ACAS recommendations for union recognition or to disclose information for collective bargaining; disputes on statutory joint industrial councils and claims in respect of equal pay under collective agreements.

1. From 1959 to 1975, the only provision for unilateral arbitration was in cases where an employer failed to observe recognised terms and conditions (s. 8 Terms and Conditions of Employment Act 1959).

74. These facilities were widely used in the first years of the existence of the CAC, primarily because they provided a means to correct anomalies created by the operation of incomes policies. Thus, the number of references received shot up from 132 in 1976, to 1,030 in 1977 and 1,065 in 1978, dropping back to 617 in 1979. With the repeal of many of the 'statutory props' by the Conservative Government since 1979, the CAC's unilateral arbitration jurisdiction has been narrowed, to include, in 1985, only the disclosure of information facilities (see below Part II, Ch. IV), under which a mere trickle of references is received each year (11 in 1984), and discriminatory pay provisions in collective agreements (see below Part I, Ch. VII), whose impact has all but dried up. The voluntary arbitration function remains and the CAC is anxious to develop this jurisdiction, although only 7 references were received in 1984. The CAC determines its own procedure. Decisions under its statutory jurisdiction are published, but voluntary awards are only published with the consent of the parties. Its general practice is not to give reasons for its decision, except in the case of failure to disclose information, in which case it has a statutory duty to give reasons.

§3. Equal Opportunities Commission (EOC) and Commission for Racial Equality (CRE)

75. The EOC and CRE follow the same model and so can conveniently be dealt with together. Consisting of 8 to 15 members appointed by the Secretary of State, each Commission is charged with the general duty to work towards the elimination of discrimination, to promote equality of opportunity between men and women (EOC) or persons of different racial groups (CRE) and to review the operation of the anti-discrimination legislation.[1] The Commissions function as an important supplement to the individual right of recourse to an industrial tribunal on a discrimination complaint. Many cases of unlawful discrimination may not reach a tribunal: an individual may lack the resources or courage to initiate an action: evidence of individual detriment may be difficult to amass; or an individual remedy may be of little assistance to others affected by discriminatory practices (there are no class actions). To remedy some of these weaknesses, each Commission has the power to assist an individual complainant and to institute its own proceedings in relation to discriminatory advertisements, instructions or pressure to discriminate, and discriminatory practices.

1. SDA 1975, Part VI; RRA 1976, Part VII.

76. More significantly, each Commission has the additional power to initiate and conduct a 'formal investigation' into cases of suspected unlawful discrimination. This power, which combines investigative and judicial functions, carries with it the ability to demand written or oral evidence and the production of documents. The aim of the investigation is to secure a change in the discriminatory practices, and to this end the Commission may make recommendations for changes in policy or practice, either during or after the completion of the formal investigation. Moreover, if unlawful discrimination is revealed, each Commission has its own sanction, in the form of a 'non-discrimination notice', which (subject to the right of appeal to an industrial tribunal) may require the respondent not to commit any further unlawful discrimination and to keep the Commission informed of any changes instituted to do so. Recourse to judicial sanctions is envisaged only as a last resort – if the notice is not overturned on appeal and there is persistent discrimination within 5 years, the Commission can take the respondent to the County Court and obtain an injunction. Formal investigations have not had the impact that might have been expected, partly because the procedures are cumbersome and the courts have implied procedural requirements which have enabled some respondents to avoid or seriously delay investigation. The CRE has placed more emphasis on formal investigations than the EOC, having begun 46 in its ten years of existence, as against ten by the EOC. Both Commissions also have powers to undertake and assist research or educational activities and to issue Codes of Practice: the EOC Code was issued in February 1985 and that of the CRE in April 1984 (see further Part I, Ch. VII).

§4. Manpower Services Commission (MSC)

77. Rising unemployment in the 1970s and 1980s has led to increased Governmental activity in planning and subsidising job creation and training. A central institution administering these policies is the Manpower Services Commission, established under the Employment and Training Act 1973 with the responsibility for 'assisting persons to select, train for, obtain and retain employment suitable for their ages and capacities' and to assist employers to obtain suitable employees. The MSC is a semi-autonomous body, subject to the residual power of the Secretary of State, and is composed of representatives of employers' and employees' organisations as well as members representing local authority and educational organisations. It is responsible for a plethora of administrative measures for job creation and training, including the granting of subsidies to employers for employing and training school-leavers, which has come to perform a central role in the employment field (see paras. 277–278, below).

§5. Certification Officer (CO)

78. The CO is an independent statutory officer, appointed under EPA 1975, who is responsible for supervising several aspects of the internal affairs of trade unions. The powers of the CO are far less interventionist than those of his immediate predecessor, the Registrar of Unions and Employers' Associations, who, as part of the legal interventionism of the Industrial Relations Act 1971, had extensive powers to scrutinise union rulebooks. Instead, the CO's primary function in scrutinising trade unions is to decide whether they are truly independent of employers and to issue a certificate of independence if appropriate (see Part II, Ch. II). He is also responsible for monitoring the annual returns and accounts of trade unions, as well as having a supervisory role in connection with trade union political funds, amalgamations and ballots for trade union elections (see below).

§6. Department of Employment (DE)

79. It is clear from the above that many functions exercised in other countries by Labour Ministries are, in Britain, entrusted to independent or semi-independent Government agencies. In fact, these functions were originally developed by the Department of Employment and its predecessors. The Labour Department of the Board of Trade was set up in 1886 mainly to collect information on trade unions, strikes and other matters. During World War I, a separate Ministry of Labour was established, exercising various functions in relation to conciliation and arbitration, functions which were retained by its successors, the Department of Employment and Productivity and finally the Department of Employment, until they were transferred to ACAS in September 1974 (see above). The Department retains a central role in the co-ordination and formulation of policy, research and consultation with employers' associations and trade unions, as well as having specific functions, such as the administration of several job creation and training programmes (complementing those of the MSC), the promotion of equal opportunities, the collection of labour statistics, and since 1985, responsibility for government policy on deregulation. It is also responsible for wages councils, industrial tribunals, the Employment Appeal Tribunal and Courts of Inquiry (on the latter see para. 505, below).

V. Industrial Tribunals and Courts

§1. JURISDICTION OF TRIBUNALS

80. A specialised system of labour courts, known as industrial tribunals, has only existed in the UK since 1964. They were first created, under the Industrial Training Act 1964, to deal with the relatively minor question of appeals by employers against levies imposed on them by industrial training boards. Since then, the jurisdiction has been expanded enormously, to cover almost all the statutory individual employment rights, including for example, unfair dismissal, redundancy compensation, equal pay, and sex and race discrimination in employment. The Donovan Commission suggested that industrial tribunals should be concerned with individual rights only, and not in collective matters, 'since these are matters which must be settled by procedures of, or agreed through, collective bargaining' (para. 576). While this is broadly the case (see, for example, the provision excluding claims for unfair dismissal during industrial action, para. 477, below), the distinction has not always proved easy to draw, as with the right not to be dismissed for trade union activities, and the right to have one's trade union consulted about impending redundancies. Since 1980, industrial tribunals have been given additional powers which have clear collective ramifications, particularly in closed shop cases[1]. Nor have industrial tribunals been given jurisdiction over all claims concerned with employment. An awkward separation of jurisdictions between tribunals and the ordinary civil courts remains. Jurisdiction for claims arising out of breach of contract, including the contract of employment, remains with the ordinary civil courts, as do actions for damages in tort, particularly for personal injury or death. Similarly, collective disputes, insofar as they give rise to civil action, are dealt with by the ordinary courts. Thus if an employee complains of unfair dismissal, he or she cannot also ask the tribunal to deal with a claim for arrears of holiday pay because this raises a question of breach of contract which must be taken before the ordinary courts. This is not to say that tribunals never have to decide questions of breach of contract, for example, in the case of 'constructive dismissal', an unfair dismissal claim is premissed on the tribunal making a preliminary finding of breach of contract (see Part I, Ch. VII). The Lord Chancellor (for England) and the Secretary of State (for Scotland) have the power, not yet exercised, to confer jurisdiction on industrial tribunals to deal with claims for damages for breach of the contract of employment and other related contracts, in limited circumstances, such as contractual claims arising or outstanding on the termination of employment.

1. For example, the right not to be unreasonably excluded or expelled from one's trade union, and the right to join a trade union as a defendant in unfair dismissal proceedings in closed shop cases (see further Part II, Ch. I, below).

§2. JURISDICTION OF COURTS

81. The ordinary courts have exclusive jurisdiction in respect of (1) actions for damages and other remedies arising out of breach of contract, and for arrears of pay, including holiday pay, due under a contract; (2) actions in tort (delict), the most important of which are for injunctions and damages in connection with industrial action (see Part II, Ch. V, below); (3) actions for damages for personal injuries in respect of a person's death. Where the amount of a civil claim is relatively small (£5,000 or less in 1985) the action in contract or tort may be brought in a county court in England and Wales or a sheriff court in Scotland, where it is heard by a full-time circuit judge (or registrar if for £500 or less) or sheriff. There is an appeal to the Court of Appeal (Civil Division) in England and Wales, or to the Sheriff Principal and then to the Inner House of the Court of Session in Scotland. Other cases, in particular those for injunctions arising out of industrial action, are brought before a single judge in the High Court in England and Wales (in either the Queen's Bench or Chancery Division) and the Court of Session (Outer House) in Scotland. There is an appeal to the Court of Appeal and the Inner House of the Court of Session respectively. The House of Lords is the final appellate court for both England and Wales and Scotland; appeals to this body require either leave of itself or of the court below. The High Court and the Court of Session also have a general supervisory jurisdiction over inferior tribunals and power to review administrative action.

§3. COMPOSITION OF TRIBUNALS

82. Industrial tribunals have a tripartite structure, consisting of a legal chairman (a barrister[1] or solicitor of at least 7 years' standing drawn from a panel of chairmen appointed by the Lord Chancellor[2]) and two lay members with industrial experience, drawn from panels appointed by the Secretary of State for Employment, one after consultation with the trades unions, the other after consultation with employers' organisations. This structure made industrial tribunals more acceptable to trade unions than the ordinary courts, which, as we have seen, had frequently been hostile to trade union interests. The lay members have full voting rights and it is not unknown for them to outvote the lawyer chairman, although they are generally reluctant to do so on points of law. The lay members are not intended to act as representatives of trade unions or employers' associations. Instead, they are expected to act as neutral arbiters, drawing on their experience of industrial relations to enhance the quality of their decision-making. Indeed, about 96 per cent of decisions are unanimous.

1. Advocate in Scotland.
2. Secretary of State for Scotland in Scottish tribunals.

83. As at March 1985, there were 66 full-time (permanent) chairmen and 132 part-time chairmen in England and Wales.[1] There is no professional civil service-type judiciary in Britain: chairmen usually come from the ranks of private practitioners in the ordinary courts and may have no special expertise in labour law when first appointed. At March 1985, there were 2,053 lay members for England and Wales. They are all part-time, and are usually practising trade union officials or personnel managers of companies.

1. All statistics in this section are derived from the Central Office of the Industrial Tribunals (England and Wales), Fact Sheet March 1985.

84. There are three separate Central Offices of Industrial Tribunals: one in London, for England and Wales, one in Glasgow, for Scotland, and one in Belfast, for Northern Ireland, each with its own President. In addition, there are 14 regional offices in England and Wales, each with a Regional Chairman. Permanent accommodation for hearing applications is provided at 24 centres in England and Wales, dealing with approximately 14,700 hearings per annum.

§4. PROCEDURE

84bis. Despite their structure, industrial tribunals retain many of the characteristics of ordinary courts. The adversarial system prevails, with each party responsible for presenting and proving its case and the tribunal having no investigative powers of its own. Furthermore, the tribunal itself has no power to promote or order a compromise, the function of conciliation being given instead to ACAS (see above, para. 70) at the pre-hearing stage. On the other hand, their enforcement powers are not as strong as those of ordinary courts. The ultimate sanction for breach of an order made by an industrial tribunal is payment of a sum of money; it has no power to issue injunctions or to fine or imprison for contempt of court. Instead, the county courts in England and Wales and the sheriff's court in Scotland have jurisdiction to enforce tribunal orders in the same way as other orders.

85. Nevertheless, tribunals have several advantages over the ordinary courts. They are much quicker – over three quarters (78 per cent) of all applications reach a first hearing in under 16 weeks, whereas a case in the civil courts can take years rather than months. Furthermore, tribunals are more accessible, sitting, as we have seen, all over the country. Although the basic adversarial procedure remains, tribunals are more informal than courts: there are no complicated pleadings and tribunals are not bound by the strict rules of evidence. It was initially envisaged that legal representation would normally be avoided in tribunals. A party can choose any representative or be unrepresented. State-funded legal aid is not available. Each party bears his or her own expenses and legal costs will only be awarded against a party who acts frivolously or vexatiously or otherwise unreasonably. In practice, legal representation has become common, particularly on the parts of employers. In 1983, 49 per cent of all respondents had legal representatives at the hearing, as against 37 per cent of all applicants. Applicants were represented by trade union officials in a further 16 per cent of cases. About 37 per cent of applicants and 40 per cent of respondents appeared in person. With respect to costs, a discretionary provision for a pre-hearing assessment was introduced in October 1980, to function as a filter for worthless claims, and a party who insists on pursuing a case despite a warning at the pre-hearing assessment may have costs awarded against him or her. In the year ending September 1984, assessments were arranged for just over 3,000 cases, but of the 40 per cent warned, only 79 eventually had costs (at an average of £136) awarded against them.

86. Tribunals have come to occupy a central position in labour law, as is evidenced by their workload. The number of applications registered jumped from 13,555 in 1972 to 43,066 in 1976 as the number and scope of tribunal jurisdictions increased. The intake declined thereafter until 1981 (as a result of the removal of certain short-service workers from protection: see Part I, Ch. VII below), when the numbers again increased to 40,042. Since then, numbers have again declined, but, with 35,640 applications registered in 1984, the workload remains substantial. Of those registered in 1984, about 73 per cent concerned unfair dismissal, 8.6 per cent consisted of claims for redundancy pay, and a small number concerned claims for equal pay, race and sex discrimination and other employment protection rights. Tribunals remain relatively inexpensive: the average cost to the tax-payer of a day's hearing was approximately £450 in 1983–1984, while expenditure on salaries, fees and directly related expenses in 1985 is expected to be about £10 million.

§5. EMPLOYMENT APPEAL TRIBUNAL (EAT)

87. The EAT was established by the Employment Protection Act 1975, replacing the National Industries Relations Court which had been established to administer the unpopular Industrial Relations Act 1971 (see Introduction, § III). The EAT adjudicates on appeals on questions of law from decisions of industrial tribunals in most of their jurisdictions[1], and on questions of fact and law in appeals on decisions relating to exclusion or expulsion from a trade union (see Part II, Ch. I below); and has original jurisdiction to assess compensation in some of the latter cases. The EAT can entertain appeals on questions of both fact and law from certain decisions of the Certification Officer (e.g. listening and independence) (see above, para. 78). In its earlier years, the EAT went to some lengths to establish guidelines and standard criteria for application by tribunals, but in recent years, it has been more inclined to refuse appellate jurisdiction by classifying issues as questions of fact, on which no appeal lies, rather than questions of law. The rationale for thus limiting possible points of appeal has been to discourage legalism and technicality, retaining the tribunals' character as quick, cheap and accessible means of resolving disputes. This stance has, however, been criticised as leading to inconsistencies in the application of legislative provisions by different tribunals. There is a further appeal on questions of law from the EAT to the Court of Appeal (CA) in England and Wales and to the Court of Session

(Inner House) in Scotland, but the leave of either the EAT or the higher court must first be obtained. From these courts, there is a final appeal, with leave, on questions of law to the House of Lords, the highest court. In practice, most appeals do not go beyond the EAT.

1. Appeals on a few questions of law, such as under compensation schemes for displaced local authority employees and industrial training levies, go from industrial tribunals to the High Court in England and the Court of Session in Scotland.

88. Unusually for an appellate body, the EAT has a tripartite composition, consisting of a judge, drawn from a panel of High Court and Court of Session judges, and either two or four lay members, drawn from a panel of persons appointed because of their special knowledge and experience of industrial relations. As in the case of industrial tribunal proceedings, in any case there is an equal number of persons with experience as representatives of employers and workers respectively, again the aim being to draw on industrial relations expertise, rather than to adopt a partisan approach. In the period April 1983 to March 1984, the EAT registered 935 appeals from decisions of industrial tribunals in England and Wales, approximately 6 per cent of cases determined at a tribunal hearing. Of the cases that were heard on appeal during this period, the EAT dismissed 51.7 per cent, allowed 6.2 per cent and remitted 12.6 per cent to the tribunal for rehearing. A further 29.5 per cent were withdrawn. The majority of these appeals (58.6 per cent) were lodged by employees.

89. The doctrine of precedent, by which lower courts and tribunals are bound by the *ratio decidendi* (or grounds) of decisions of higher courts, applies equally to the industrial tribunals and the EAT. Thus, industrial tribunals are bound by the decisions of the EAT and of all the higher courts. The EAT is in turn bound by decisions of the Court of Appeal and the Court of Session (Inner House), and, at the top of the pyramid, the House of Lords. The EAT is considered to be of equal jurisdiction to the Queen's Bench Division of the High Court and the Court of Session (Outer House); therefore decisions of these latter courts will have persuasive but not binding force in the EAT. This system of precedent means that law reporting is a matter of some importance. Since tribunal decisions are binding only on the parties, reports of these decisions are of interest only as illustrations of the practice of tribunals. Reports of decisions of the EAT and superior courts are, however, potential precedents. The main series of reports are listed at the end of this book.

VI. Sources of Labour Law

90. Legal norms regulating employment relationships are derived from a variety of sources, including the common law, legislation, codes of practice and voluntary or autonomous sources.

§1. COMMON LAW

91. At common law, the focus of legal analysis is the relationship between the employer and each individual employee. This relationship is characterised as a contract, the assumption being, as in other contractual relationships, that there is a 'personal and voluntary exchange of freely bargained promises between two parties [employer and employee] equally protected by the civil law alone'.[1] In practice, however, the terms and conditions of employment of most employees are not negotiated individually and on an equal basis with the employer. In the vast majority of cases, terms and conditions are either unilaterally imposed by the employer, or are laid down in a collective agreement between the employer or employers' organisation and the relevant trade unions. Nevertheless, industrial relations continues to be characterised by lawyers as a mass of individual contracts of employment and it is through the mechanism of contract that most rights and obligations take effect. For example, terms and conditions laid down in a collective agreement are only given legal effect if they can be shown to be incorporated into an individual contract (see Part I, Ch. II).

1. K. W. Wedderburn, *The Worker and the Law*, 2nd ed., London, 1971, p. 77.

92. The common law has also been a source of legal norms regulating collective relationships. A series of civil wrongs regulating industrial action was developed by the courts (for example, the tort of inducing breach of contract) and although these have been overlaid by a complex system of statutory immunities (see Part II, Ch. V), the foundation remains the common law. The relationship between trade unions and their members is construed as one of contract (see Part II, Ch. II).

§2. LEGISLATION

93. In the absence of a written constitution (para. 11, above), the major legislative impetus comes from Parliament. Although voluntary collective bargaining was the primary source of protection for employees until the 1960s, certain aspects of industrial relations have been regulated by the State since the nineteenth century. This included legislation protecting children and women, regulating some aspects of health and safety and establishing mechanisms for setting minimum wages in certain industries. More recently, there has been a rapid increase in employment legislation, with 54 general Acts of Parliament regulating employment being passed between 1960 and 1985 (see section III, above). To these must be added numerous statutes applying to specific sectors of employment.

94. In addition to Parliament, other bodies such as Ministers, Departments of State, public corporations and local authorities have limited law-making powers, subject to repeal or alteration by Parliament. There are several hundred pieces of subordinate legislation of this kind, covering matters as diverse as the employment of children, levies for industrial training, minimum wages orders, the licensing of employment agencies and the procedure of industrial tribunals. There is also a large number of regulations applying to specific employments. A peculiar feature of law-making in the UK is that regulations governing the terms and conditions of employment of civil servants (in central government) are made by the Minister for the Civil Service under the ancient prerogative powers of the Crown. It was only in 1984 that it was established, for the first time, that the exercise of these powers is subject to judicial review on grounds of illegality, irrationality or procedural impropriety, but the extent and significance of such reviews remains doubtful[1].

1. *Council of Civil Service Unions* v. *Minister of the Civil Service* [1984] 3 All ER 935, HL; see Part II, Ch. I.

§3. RELATION BETWEEN LEGISLATION AND COMMON LAW

95. Because legislative intervention developed in parallel and often independently of the common law concept of the contract of employment, the relationship between statutes and the contract is complex:
(1) Some statutory rights operate wholly outside of the contract of employment. For example, a breach of an employer's statutory safety duties may be the subject of criminal prosecution or administrative enforcement under the Health and Safety at Work Act 1974 or, in some cases, a civil action for damages by an injured employee in tort.
(2) In some cases, both statutory and contractual rights exist, as in the case of statutory rights to guarantee payments for employees who are laid off work, maternity pay and payment for time-off (see Part I, Chs. IV and V). In such cases, overlap is avoided by express provision in the statute either for the set-off of sums of money awarded under the statute against amounts due under the contract, or vice versa, or by the creation of 'composite' rights enabling the employee to claim those features of the contractual and statutory rights which are most favourable.
(3) Some recent legislation expressly provides that the duties they impose are to take effect as terms of the individual contract. An example is the Equal Pay Act 1970 which provides that an 'equality clause' is deemed to be included in the contract of every man and woman employed at an establishment in Great Britain.
(4) Other statutes are silent on this point, leaving the courts and tribunals free

to decide whether or not rights arise under the contract. This has on occasion led to the employee being deprived of statutory protection (*e.g.* protection against unfair dismissal is lost if the contract is illegal because of an agreement to defraud the Revenue of PAYE tax).

(5) Arbitration awards made by the CAC under its statutory jurisdiction take effect as compulsory terms of the contracts of employment of the employees concerned (see Part II, Ch. IV).

§4. CODES OF PRACTICE

96. Codes of Practice are issued under statutory powers to provide guidance to industrial relations practitioners on the application of various statutory provisions. The Codes do not have the same status as statute or subordinate legislation: failure to observe the provisions of a Code does not of itself render a person liable to legal proceedings. But a Code is admissible in evidence in proceedings before an industrial tribunal or the CAC or court and any provision of the Code which appears to be relevant to any question arising in the proceedings must be taken into account by the tribunal or CAC or court in determining that question.[1] Several bodies now have powers to issue Codes, which have to be approved by both Houses of Parliament.

   1. EPA 1975, s. 6; EA 1980, s. 3(8)

97. A code of Industrial Relations Practice was issued under the Industrial Relations Act 1971 and this has been retained in force despite the repeal of the Act in 1974. It covers a wide range of issues, such as employment policies, collective bargaining and grievance and disputes procedures. It may eventually be replaced by Codes to be issued by ACAS. Thus far, ACAS. has issued 3 Codes, dealing with (i) disclosure of information for collective bargaining; (ii) time off for trade union duties and activities, and (iii) disciplinary practice and procedures.[1] The Commission for Racial Equality and the Equal Opportunities Commission have issued Codes for the elimination of race and sex discrimination respectively,[2] while the Health and Safety Commission has issued a Code in respect of safety representatives and safety committees.[3] In 1980, the Secretary of State for Employment was given power to issue Codes[4] and has issued two: one on Picketing (17 December 1980) and one on Closed Shop Agreements and Arrangements (18 May 1983, replacing an earlier version of 17 December 1980). The latter have proved contentious, and some critics have argued that since they do not reflect a consensus view of industrial relations practice, these Codes should have obtained full Parliamentary approval through the legislative process. This is particularly so since the Code on picketing appears to have influenced police conduct with respect to picketing.

   1. A draft revised Code was circulated for consultation by ACAS in October 1985.
   2. RRA 1976, s. 47(1); SDA 1975, s. 56A.
   3. Health and Safety at Work etc. Act 1974, s. 16.
   4. EA 1980, s. 3.

§5. VOLUNTARY SOURCES

98. As we have seen, it is a distinctive characteristic of British labour law that the parties themselves have wide scope for creating norms which in practice govern working relationships. These norms are not always given legal effect even if they function in practice as a code governing important aspects of behaviour, the preference being for non-legal means of enforcement (such as disciplinary or industrial action). Where such norms are given legal effect, it is generally at the individual rather than collective level, via incorporation into the individual contract of employment. The most important 'voluntary' sources of terms and conditions of employment are (i) works' rules, notices and other documents issued by management to employees; (ii) collective agreements; and (iii) 'custom and practice', a more informal source of regulation, whereby working conditions are determined by force of tradition or by informal arrangements between workers and employees. Custom and practice is also an important source of norms supplementing the rulebook which governs the relationship between trade unions and their members.[1] These norms may be emanations of either unilateral management decision-making or joint regulation, or even unilateral worker action. Thus works' rules are examples of unilateral government by management of the workplace. Collective agreements are important examples of joint regulation, as are resolutions of joint negotiating bodies such as the Whitley Councils (see Part II, Ch. IV). While custom and practice is frequently an example of joint regulation, albeit informal, it may also be a result of unilateral management decision-making which has become the accepted status quo. The methods of incorporation of these sources into the individual contract of employment are considered in Part I, Ch. II.

1. *Heatons Transport (St. Helens) Ltd.* v. *TGWU* [1972] ICR 308 (HL).

VII. Private International Labour Law

§1. SCOPE AND SOURCES

99. The increasing international migration of labour gives rise to three distinct problems. (1) The limits of the jurisdiction (*i.e.*, the power to hear and determine issues) of national courts and tribunals. (2) The choice of the system of law to be applied in determining cases with a foreign element. (3) The law as to nationality and the minimum standards to be applied to workers of foreign nationality. In England and Scotland, the terms 'private international law' and 'conflict of laws' are synonymously applied to the first two of these problems. Rules as to nationality and the treatment of foreign workers are considered as part of constitutional and administrative law, and in this monograph are dealt with briefly in paras. 143–145. Since England and Wales, Scotland, and Northern Ireland have separate legal systems, it follows that English private international law rules are distinct from those of each of the other law-countries within the United Kingdom: thus Scots law and the law of Northern Ireland are as 'foreign' in England as the law of Italy or France. Scottish private international law rules are markedly similar to those of the English and Northern Irish legal systems, and the following brief account of the English rules may be taken to be generally similar to the Scottish and Northern Irish rules.

100. Judge-made case law is the most important source of the law in this field. The rules have been developed piecemeal by the judges on the basis of principles of justice, comity and convenience. The 'choice of jurisdiction' question is treated entirely as a question of procedure. Whether or not a court or tribunal is competent to try an issue depends solely upon procedure, and not upon nationality, domicile or residence. So far as proceedings in the High Court are concerned so long as a writ of summons has been served upon a person, who is present within the jurisdiction, in accordance with the rules of procedure he or she is subject to the power of the court even though he or she is a foreigner and the cause of action has no factual connection with England. This basic common law rule has been modified by Acts of Parliament and rules of court, which give a discretionary power to a judge to authorise service of a writ of summons upon a defendant abroad in a limited number of cases. For example, where a contract was made within the jurisdiction or a breach of contract was committed within the jurisdiction it may be possible to obtain leave to serve process abroad in an action affecting that contract and by so doing create an 'assumed jurisdiction'. The details fall outside the scope of this monograph. The scope of the jurisdiction of the industrial tribunals, which deal with various statutory employment rights, is dealt with above, para. 80.

101. The problem as to which national labour law to apply depends upon (1) the English and Scottish private international law rules, as developed by the judges, which determine whether a contract or tort (delict) is governed by a particular system, and (2) the express or implied territorial scope of Acts of the United Kingdom Parliament and of subordinate legislation. These are matters which have received little attention from the courts and legal writers.[1] These problems are particularly important in the context of the freedom of movement guaranteed by Art. 48 and the freedom of establishment guaranteed by Art. 51 of the Treaty of Rome. The EEC Convention on the Law Applicable to Contractual Obligations (1980) which seeks to harmonise the rules applying to all cases having a foreign element, whether or not they have any connection with the EEC, makes special provisions in Article 6 for the choice of law in the case of employment contracts. But this has not yet been implemented, and so will not be discussed here.[2]

1. For a more detailed treatment than is possible here see Hepple and O'Higgins, *Employment Law*, 4th ed. by B. A. Hepple (London, 1981) Ch. 21; and for an earlier account O. Kahn-Freund, 'Notes on the conflict of laws in relation to employment in English and Scottish law', *Rivista di Diritto Int. e Comp. del Lavoro*, 3 (1960) 307; *Selected Writings* (London, 1978), p. 259.
2. See C. G. J. Morse, 'Contracts of Employment and the EEC Contractual Obligations Convention' in *Contract Conflicts* (ed. P. M. North) 1982, pp. 143–173, and B. A. Hepple, 'Conflict of Laws on Employment Relationships within the EEC' in K. Lipstein (ed.), *Harmonisation of Private International Law by the EEC* (London, 1978), pp. 39–49 for a detailed critique.

§2. Choice of Law Rules

102. One must distinguish three questions: (a) which is the law that applies to the contract or tort (delict)? (b) if English (or Scottish) law is the applicable law, is there a statute which, within that law, restricts its application in space, *i.e.* is there a self-limiting statute such as a statute restricted to the contracts of employees who ordinarily work under the contract in Great Britain, or excluding those who under an English or Scottish contract ordinarily work abroad? (c) is there a statute which by its terms applies irrespective of what is the law applicable to the contract or tort in question, for example on the ground that the employee ordinarily works under the contract in Great Britain, thus including those who do so under a contract governed by foreign law *i.e.* 'is there a true *loi d'application immédiate* which, on proper analysis, is a crystallised rule of *ordre public*'?[1] In regard to question (a) the English and Scottish courts apply the 'proper law of the contract', by which is meant the law that the parties intended to govern the contract. Where their intention has not been expressed and cannot be implied from the circumstances, the 'proper law' is the legal system with which the contract is most closely connected. In this latter case the judge puts himself in the position of the 'reasonable person' in order to discover the law with which the contract has the 'closest and most real connection'. There is no rigid rule as to which connecting factors must be applied. In the case of high-level management, advisory staff and specialists it is likely that the proper law (in the absence of express or implied choice by the parties) will be the law of the place where the undertaking has its centre of control and management because such employees are an integral part of the organisation's management. Lower-level employees are usually engaged in the State where they reside and where they are required to work and so the proper law (in the absence of express or implied choice by the parties) is likely to be the law of the place of residence of the employee or the law of the place where the contract is to be performed. However, the rules are flexible and other factors such as the connection with the place of contracting may also be relevant. Some issues arising out of the employment relationship are classified as questions of tort (delict) and not of contract. A work accident may be classified either as a breach of contract or as a tort (delict).[2] If it is treated as a tort and the accident occurred in a foreign country it will be actionable in England only if it satisfies the so-called double actionability rule: the act must be both (a) actionable as a tort according to English law, had the act occurred in England, and (b) actionable according to the law of the foreign country where it was done. The second limb of this rule appears to mean that if the injured employee is entitled only to social security or analogous state benefits by way of compensation for injuries received under the foreign law it will not be possible for the employee to succeed in a tort action in England.[3] Where there is an exception clause in the contract of employment limiting or excluding the employer's liability, it is first necessary to ask whether the law governing the tort would regard the defence as admissible, and then whether the clause is valid by the proper law of the contract.[4]

1. O. Kahn-Freund, *Selected Writings* (London, 1978), p. 271.
2. *Matthews* v. *Kuwait Bechtel Corpn.* [1959] 2 QB 57 (an English contract with a Panamanian company to work in Kuwait: held claim arising out of work accident in Kuwait could be pleaded in contract or tort for purposes of obtaining leave to serve a writ of summons out of the jurisdiction)'.
3. See comment on *Coupland* v. *Arabian Gulf Petroleum Co.* [1983] 3 All ER 226, CA, by C. G. J. Morse (1984) 33 *International and Comparative Law Quarterly* 449.
4. *Ibid*,; see too, *Sayers* v. *International Drilling Co. NV* [1971] 1 WLR 1176, criticised by L. Collins (1972) 21 *International and Comparative Law Quarterly* 320.

§3. APPLICATION OF STATUTES

103. An important feature of judicial interpretation of statutes in Britain is that the courts have refused to apply to statutes the ordinary criteria of private international law. In other words, instead of regarding the territorial scope of statutes as being co-terminous with the proper law of the contract, labour legislation has generally been confined in its operation to work done within the territorial boundaries of Great Britain. (In this connection, it is to be noted that most labour legislation extends to the whole of Great Britain, including Scotland; in a few exceptional cases, such as agricultural wages and teachers' remuneration, there is separate Scottish legislation.) For example, the Factories Acts have been judicially interpreted as applying only to work within Great Britain,[1] and most modern employment protection legislation is expressed to apply only to those employees who under their contracts of employment 'ordinarily work' within Great Britain. This is the case, for example, with the right to complain of unfair dismissal, various other rights arising in the course of employment, maternity rights, and rights upon the insolvency of the employer.[2] The criteria for applying the Equal Pay Act 1970, the Sex Discrimination Act 1975 and the Race Relations Act 1976 are that the work must be 'at an establishment' in Great Britain and, subject to a number of exceptions, this covers all those who are not proved to do their work 'wholly or mainly' outside Great Britain.[3] In regard to redundancy payments, an employee who ordinarily works outside Great Britain is not entitled to a redundancy payment unless on the 'relevant date' (*i.e.*, the date when the dismissal takes effect) he is in Great Britain in accordance with instructions given to him by his employer. An employee who is outside Great Britain on the 'relevant date' is entitled to a redundancy payment only if he ordinarily works inside Great Britain.[4]

1. *Yorke* v. *British & Continental Steamship Co.* (1945) 78 LlLR 181 (accident in Gibraltar to employee under contract governed by English law: held dock regulations made under Factories Act 1937 did not apply); *Tomalin* v. *S. Pearson Ltd.* [1909] 2 KB 61 (Workmen's Compensation Acts applied only to accidents arising out of and in the course of employment in Great Britain); see now Social Security Act 1975, s. 131 and regulations thereunder.
2. EPCA 1978, s. 141(2).
3. Equal Pay Act 1970, s. 1(1); SDA, ss. 6, 10; RRA, ss. 4, 6, 8, 9, 37.
4. EPCA 1978, s. 141 (3) (4) (5). Generally speaking, for the purposes of calculating a person's period of continuous employment (upon which eligibility and the amount of payment depends) no account may be taken of weeks during which he was employed outside Great Britain and no social security contributions were being made).

104. The criterion used to determine the territorial application of legislation is usually whether the employee 'ordinarily works' outside Great Britain. The Court of Appeal was held[1] that the correct approach is to examine the relevant terms of the contract of employment, express or implied, over the whole period of the contract. If the contract expressly or impliedly requires the work to be wholly or substantially done outside Great Britain, no problem arises. Similarly, there is no problem if the contract expressly or impliedly requires the work to be wholly or substantially done inside Great Britain. The difficulty arises where the contract leaves it to the employer's discretion where the work shall be carried out. In such a case, the Court of Appeal has said[2] that it must be asked where the employee's base was to be, and in the absence of special factors leading to the contrary conclusion the country where his base was to be is likely to be the place where he is to be treated as 'ordinarily' working. This is so, even if he spends a considerable amount of time working abroad. In ascertaining the 'base' all the relevant express and implied terms of the contract must be considered, including those which define where the employee's headquarters were to be, indicating where his travels would begin and end, where his orders came from, where his residence was and in what currency he was to be paid. It seems that an employee cannot have a 'moving' base and cannot during the whole period of his contract be ordinarily working both inside and outside Great Britain.[3] In general, British labour legislation affords an example of *loi d'application immédiate*, or crystallised *ordre public*. For example, the Employment Protection Act 1975, the Employment Protection (Consolidation) Act 1978 and the Equal Pay Act 1970, apply irrespective of the proper law of the contract.[4] A similar result has been achieved by judicial interpretation in respect of the Truck Acts which regulate deductions from wages of manual employees.[5] An English or Scottish court will, in these cases, apply the British statute, insofar as the statute has territorial application (*e.g.*, to a person ordinarily working inside Great Britain), to a person working under a contract governed by foreign law. This approach may be justified on the ground that labour legislation is part of the public policy of the *lex fori* (Great Britain), and employers should be prevented from abusing their superior bargaining power by obtaining the employee's agreement to apply a less socially advanced system of law.

1. *Wilson* v. *Maynard Shipbuilding Consultants A.B.* [1978] ICR 376; *Todd* v. *British Midland Airways Ltd.* [1978] ICR 959; *Janata Bank* v. *Ahmed* [1981] ICR 791, CA.
2. *Wilson's* case at p. 387; *Todd's* case at pp. 964, 967.
3. *Wilson's* case at p. 384, overruling *Portect (UK) Ltd.* v. *Mogensen* [1976] ICR 396.
4. EPA 1975, s. 126(8); EPCA 1978, s. 153(5); Equal Pay Act 1970, s. 1(11).
5. *Duncan* v. *Motherwell Bridge & Engineering Co. Ltd.* 1952 SC 131 (held by Inner House of Court of Session that Truck Act 1831 applied if deductions made from wages paid in Scotland irrespective of proper law).

§4. Collective Labour Relations

105. A collective agreement is conclusively presumed by section 18 of the Trade Union and Labour Relations Act 1974 not to have been intended by the parties to be a legally enforceable contract unless the parties expressly agree in writing that it shall be enforceable (see Part II, Ch. IV). The Court of Appeal has held that this provision is not a material consideration in determining the proper law of the collective agreement.[1] This was in the context of a case in which Maltese shipowners claimed damages from the International Transport Workers' Federation (ITF), based in London, on grounds *inter alia* of their failure to issue a certificate, that the crew of a ship flying a Maltese flag and manned by a Spanish crew were engaged on terms acceptable to the ITF. The undertaking to issue the certificate was contained in a 'special agreement' on a printed form issued by ITF in London, but executed in Bilbao, Spain. It contained no statement of enforceability under section 18 of the British Act. On a preliminary point, it was held that the proper law of the 'special agreement' was Spanish law and not English law. This was because the agreement, intended to be used worldwide, had been entered into in Spain and affected the recruitment of Spanish crews and so had its 'closest and most real connection' with Spanish law. Section 18 of the British Act was treated as substantive and not merely procedural in effect: hence it was the proper law, rather than the *lex fori* which should govern the issue.

1. *Monterosso Shipping Co. Ltd.* v. *ITF* [1982] ICR 675, CA. No reference was made in this case to TULRA 1974, s. 30(6) which provides that for purposes of the Act 'it is immaterial whether the law which (apart from this Act) governs any person's employment is the law of the United Kingdom, or of a part of the United Kingdom, or not'.

106. So far as industrial action is concerned, trade unions and others who take international solidarity action with workers in other countries risk legal liability in tort (delict) in British courts. There have been several instances of such action leading to the grant of injunctions. This has been because the statutory immunity afforded to any person who commits certain torts 'in contemplation or furtherance of a trade dispute' (Part IV, Ch. V), has been held not to apply.[1] The re-definition of a 'trade dispute' in the Employment Acts 1980 and 1982 and the severe restrictions on most forms of secondary action now make it likely that most types of action will fall foul of the law (Part II, Ch. V). Moreover, the territorial scope of the immunity was specifically narrowed by the Employment Act 1982. There is a 'trade dispute' only so long as the person whose actions in the UK are said to be in contemplation or furtherance of a trade dispute relating to matters occurring outside the UK are likely to be affected in respect of one or more of a list of specified subjects by the outcome of the dispute.[2]

1. In particular on a variety of grounds in a series of cases involving action by the ITF against 'flags of convenience', and also solidarity action by communications workers against apartheid in South Africa.
2. TULRA 1974, s. 29(3) as amended. The subjects are those which fall within the permitted scope of a 'trade dispute' so presumably excluding a strike over the investment plans of a multinational enterprise.

Part I. The Individual Employment Relationship

Chapter I. Formation of the Relationship

§1. Categories of Workers

A. Introduction

107. The coverage *ratione personae* of British labour law is not consistent. As we have seen (para. 50, above) the contract of 'service' was slow in overtaking the pre-industrial characterization of the employment relationship according to status and the nature of the employment (*e.g.* 'servant in husbandry', 'artificer', 'labourer'). In the nineteenth century the law struggled to develop a general notion of a contract of service regardless of the type of work. Unlike the civil law systems of Continental Europe which moved from a general theory of contract towards a specific concept of an autonomous contract of employment, British labour law only slowly conceptualised the contract of employment on a case by case basis utilising pre-industrial conceptions of 'service'. The common law developed a distinction between those under a contract for services (self-employed workers) and those under a contract of service (employees), which does not correspond exactly to the civil law distinction between *locatio conductio operis* and *locatio conductio operarum*. The English common law category of 'employee' is frequently narrower than the range of persons under a contract of employment in a civil law system. Scots law, despite its civil law roots, has broadly speaking the English approach. Statute law, since the nineteenth century, has usually been limited in coverage to those under contracts of service, but the tests for determining whether the contract is one of service has been left to the common law. By 1951, Kahn-Freund could say that the common law had 'fallen into a maze of casuistry'.[1] This tendency has become even more pronounced in the past 35 years. The changes in the labour force[2], from the pattern of full-time employment in the core of the labour market, towards part-time, temporary and homework (including the expanding 'cottage' technological industry), and the expansion of self-employment and of employment in the twilight area between employment and self-employment, have highlighted the uncertain, inconsistent and inadequate coverage of the common law concepts. There are many workers who in reality fall within the category of dependent labour, such as those on the 'lump' in the building industry, who are not always regarded as working under contracts of service. There is ample scope for the avoidance of labour legislation. Quite apart from the inadequacies of the common law tests of the contract of employment, legislation is sometimes confined to employees in specific employments (*e.g.* merchant seamen, teachers, agricultural workers) or to certain types of contract of service, with complex exclusions in particular statutes of different categories such as part-time workers, casuals and domestic servants in private households.

1. (1951) 14 *Modern Law Review* 504.
2. See generally G. Clark, 'Recent developments in working patterns' (1982) 90 *Employment Gazette* 284; P. Leighton, *Contractual Arrangements in Selected Industries*, DE Research Paper No. 39, February 1983; 'Employment contracts: a choice of relationships' (1982) 90 *Employment Gazette* 433; 'Employment and self-employment' (1983) 91 *Employment Gazette* 197.

B. Contract of service or contract for services

108. The criteria for distinguishing between a contract of service and a contract for services have been developed by the courts on a casuistic basis. For this purpose, several tests have been expounded. The early cases, emphasising the elements of command and subordination inherent in the employment relationship, established a test based on the employer's power to control the manner in which the work is done.[1] A contract of service, on this test, is one under which an employer 'can not only order or require what is to be done, but how it shall be done'.[2] The test yields straightforward answers in some cases, but is difficult to apply where the employee's skills surpass those of the employer and the employer is a corporate entity. Thus more recent cases have held that control cannot be the determining test when dealing with a professional person or a person with skill and experience.[3] 'The greater the skill, the less significant is control in determing whether the employee is under a contract of service'.[4]

1. *Performing Rights Society Ltd.* v. *Mitchell and Baker Ltd.* [1925] 1 KB 762; *Mersey Docks and Harbour Board* v. *Coggins and Griffiths Ltd.* [1947] AC 1.
2. *Collins* v. *Hertfordshire County Council* [1947] KB 598 at 615, *per* Hilberry J.
3. *Cassidy* v. *Ministry of Health* [1951] 2 KB 343 at 579; *Morren* v. *Swinton and Pendlebury Borough Council* [1965] 2 All ER 349; *Market Investigations* v. *Minister of Social Security* [1969] 2 QB 173.
4. *Beloff* v. *Pressdram Ltd.* [1973] 1 All ER 241 at 250.

109. A second test, which has been applied in only a few situations, is whether the person forms part of the employer's organisation. Denning L.J. (as he then was) explained this as follows: 'Under a contract of service, a man is employed as part of the business, and his work is done as an integral part of the business; whereas under a contract for services, his work, although done for the business, is not integrated into it but is only accessory to it.[1] This test has been applied, for example, to determine whether a regular contributor to a newspaper is an employee,[2] but it has failed to provide a comprehensive test, particularly in cases where the worker provides some equipment or is paid on a piece-rate basis.

1. *Stevenson, Jordan & Harrison Ltd.* v. *Macdonald & Evans* (1925) 1 TLR 101.
2. *Beloff* v. *Pressdram Ltd.* [1973] 1 All ER 241.

110. The courts have therefore moved to a more complex test, the so-called multiple or mixed test, in which a multiplicity of factors are considered, none of which is necessarily determinative. The starting point of this approach is to ask whether there is a sufficient degree of control to make the worker an employee, and then to ask whether the provisions of the contract are consistent with its being a contract of service. This is a somewhat question-begging approach, because if it were asked whether the contract is consistent with a contract for services, precisely the opposite result could be achieved. Moreover, everything depends upon the weight which is given to a particular 'inconsistency'. A series of recent cases have emphasised, as the most significant 'inconsistency' with a contract of employment, the entrepreneurial character of self-employment, asking the question: Is the person in business on his or her own behalf?[1] Factors to be considered in this context include the extent to which the person takes the chance of profit or risk of loss by investing money or equipment in the business.[2] Although this was at one time considered to be the 'fundamental test'[3], the Court of Appeal has rejected the notion that any single test is fundamental.[4] Thus, in any case, consideration should be given to all the factors, including degree of control, the risk of loss and the chance of profit, the provision of equipment, the methods of tax and national insurance payment, and the parties' intentions. The industrial tribunal should 'consider all aspects of the relationship, no single feature being in itself decisive and each of which may vary in weight and direction'.[5]

1. *Ready-Mixed Concrete (SE) Ltd.* v. *Minister of Pensions* [1968] 2 QB 497.
2. *Market Investigations Ltd.* v. *Minister of Social Security* [1968] 3 All ER 732.
3. *Per* Cook, J. in *Market Investigations Ltd.* v. *Minister for Social Security,* [1969] 2 QB 173 approved in *Ferguson* v. *John Dawson* [1976] 1 WLR 1213, and *Young & Woods* v. *West.* [1980] 1 IRLM 201.
4. *Addison* v. *London Philharmonic Orchestra Ltd.* [1981] ICR 261; *Midland Sinfonia Concert Society Ltd.* v. *Secretary of State for Social Services* [1981]) ICR 454; *Warner Holidays Ltd.* v. *Secretary of State for Social Services* [1983] ICR 440.
5. *O'Kelly* v. *Trusthouse Forte (plc)* [1983] ICR 728 at 743.

111. There has been much debate as to whether the classification of a contract is a question of fact or law, appeals to the higher courts only being available on points of law. The most recent authorities have held that although the question is one of law, the answer includes questions of degree and fact which it is for the tribunal of first instance to determine. 'The precise quality to be attributed to various individual facts is so much a matter of degree that it is unrealistic to regard the issue as attracting a clear legal answer'.[1] Appellate courts will therefore only interfere with a first instance decision if there has been a misdirection in law or if the decision is one which no tribunal properly conducting itself on the relevant facts could have reached.[2] As a result, each decision tends to depend on its own balance of factors and the outcomes of cases are difficult to predict.

1. *O'Kelly* v. *Trusthouse Forte plc* [1973] ICR 725, at 759, per Fox, L. J.

2. *Ibid.*; followed in *Nethermere (St. Neots) Ltd.* v. *Gardiner* [1984] ICR 365.

112. One of the major sources of difficulty concerns marginal workers, such as homeworkers, casual workers and agency workers. None of these could be said to be entrepreneurs and yet they do not fit comfortably in the traditional categories of workers employed under a contract of service. In this connection, the courts have stressed the 'irreducible minimum' of a contract of service, namely, that the worker is under a contractual obligation to work if so required by the employer. Where the worker has the option of declining to work on any specific occasion, then he or she cannot be said to be employed under a contract of service. This is so even if, in practice, economic need obliges the worker to accept the work. Thus it has been held that regular casual waiters[1] or secretaries working as temporary workers for an employment agency[2] were not employed under a contract of service because they were not contractually obliged to work. Since many employment protection rights depend on being employed under a contract of service, the consequence is that some of the most vulnerable workers remain unprotected. However, in one important case, the Appeal Court was willing to imply the existence of such a contractual obligation on the basis of a course of dealing, so that a homeworker who had regularly worked for an employer was held to be working under a contract of service.[3]

1. *O'Kelly* v. *Trusthouse Forte plc*, above.
2. *Wickens* v. *Champion Employment* [1984] ICR 365. See Employment Agencies Act 1973; Hepple and Napier, 'Temporary Workers and the Law' (1978) 7 *Industrial Law Journal* 84.
3. *Nethermere (St. Neots) Ltd.* v. *Gardiner* [1984] ICR 612 (CA); see also *Airfix Footwear (Ltd.)* v. *Cope* [1978] ICR 1210.

113. Another area of difficulty concerns cases where one or both parties to the employment relationship choose to place themselves in one category rather than another in order to reap the benefits of a particular tax or social security regime. In strict contract theory, the parties' agreement should be conclusive. However, the courts have been willing to look beyond the label given by the parties to the substance of the relationship. For example, an employer could not escape liability for breach of a statutory safety duty owed to a building worker by pleading that the worker had agreed to be self-employed simply in order to mislead the Inland Revenue.[1] But where there is a detailed written contract which explicitly carries out the genuine intentions of the parties to create a status of self-employment, that contract has been regarded as 'the best material from which to gather the true relationship between them'.[2]

1. *Ferguson* v. *John Dawson & Partners (Contracts) Ltd.* [1976] 1 WLR 1213.
2. *Massey* v. *Crown Life Insurance Co.* [1978] ICR 590 at p. 594.

C. Specific categories of worker

I. Employees

114. The statutory definition of employee is based on the common law contract of service. Thus an employee is defined as 'an individual who has entered into or works under (or where the employment has ceased, worked under) a contract of employment, otherwise than in the police service'. A contract of employment, in turn, means 'a contract of service or apprenticeship, whether it is express or implied and (if it is express) whether it is oral or in writing'.[1]

1. TULRA 1974 s. 30(1); EPCA 1978, s. 153(1); see below for apprenticeship.

115. Most employment rights are limited to employees. For example, rights to complain of unfair dismissal[1], to claim compensation for redundancy[2], to be given a written statement of employment terms[3], and a variety of other individual employment protection measures are confined to employees. Similarly, some collective rights, such as legally binding recommendations by ACAS for disclosure of information to trade unions, may be enforced only through the contracts of employment of employees.[4]

1. EPCA 1978, s. 54(1).
2. EPCA 1978, s. 81(1).
3. EPCA 1978, s. 1(1).
4. EPA 1975, s. 21.

II. Workers

116. Some statutes extend beyond employers to those who work under contracts personally to execute work or labour. The earliest example is the definition of 'workmen' in the Truck Acts 1831–1940. In the Trade Union and Labour Relations Act 1974, a 'worker' is defined to include those who normally work or seek work under a contract of employment or under any other contract whereby the worker undertakes to do or to perform personally any work or services for another party to the contract who is not a professional client.[1] This definition is wide enough to cover all employees, those who are temporarily unemployed and workseekers, as well as those under contracts of services to personally perform work. It excludes the contract for the sale of a completed work (*e.g.* by an author[2]) and those such as solicitors who work for a 'professional client'.[3] Parliament has, however, expressly provided that individuals providing general medical, pharmaceutical, dental or ophthalmic services under the National Health Services are to be treated as workers.[4] Inclusion in the category of 'workers' is important to secure certain collective rights, such as listing as a trade union (which must consist of workers). Similarly, the Race Relations Act and Sex Discrimination Act[5] apply to those employed under a contract of service or apprenticeship as well as those employed under a contract personally to execute any work or labour. A contract which entitles a person to delegate all the contractual duties to others to perform does not qualify as a contract personally to execute work.[6]

1. TULRA 1974, s. 30.
2. *Writers' Guild of Great Britain* v. *BBC* [1974] ICR 234.
3. *Carter* v. *Law Society* [1973] ICR 113.

4. TULRA 1974, s. 39(2)(*a*).
5. RRA 1974, s. 78(1); SDA 1975, s. 82(1).
6. *Mirror Group Newspapers Ltd.* v. *Gunning* [1986] IRLR 27; *Tanna* v. *Post Office* [1981] ICR 374; *cf. Hitchcock* v. *Post Office* [1980] ICR 100.

II. Public employees

117. Although this monograph is primarily concerned with workers in the private sector, the fact that 6.8 million people, or 28.5 per cent of the total employed labour force in 1984 were employed in the public sector makes it important to give a brief account of their legal status. Public sector employment includes: (i) those who are employed by public corporations, such as the Post Office, British Steel Corporation, British Rail and the National Coal Board (1.6 million in 1984); (ii) those employed by local authorities, including education, the social services, fire services, and police (2.9 million); and (iii) central government employees, including the National Health Service and the armed forces (2.3 million).[1] Apart from the police and civil service, there are relatively few legal distinctions between public and private employees.[2] Local authorities and public corporations have the power to enter into contracts of employment and, provided this power is properly exercised, the resulting contracts are treated in the same way as private sector contracts of employment. Most employment protection rights apply to employees of local authorities, public corporations and the National Health Service. The police are appointed and may be dismissed by local police authorities, and are subject to administrative control by the Home Secretary. Their terms and conditions of employment are regulated by statute and they are subject to statutory disciplinary codes. Similarly, the definition of 'worker' referred to above includes government employees, except the Armed Forces.

1. Economic Trends No. 377, March 1985 p. 91.
2. See Hepple and O'Higgins, *Public Employee Trade Unionism in the UK*, Ann Arbor, 1971.

118. The most important distinct group of public sector employees are civil servants, or 'Crown Servants'. The legal framework governing Crown servants harks back to the personal retinue of the monarch rather than the complex bureaucratic structure of the modern civil service. Crown servants may be dismissed at will, and it is debatable whether they have contracts of employment. The source of the power of the State as employer is the Royal Prerogative, 'the residue of the discretionary power left at any moment in the hands of the Crown'.[1] This power has been delegated by the Sovereign on the advice of Ministers by successive Orders in Council, by virtue of which the Minister for the Civil Service may determine the terms and conditions of employment of civil servants.[2] In contrast to their tenuous legal position, civil servants have traditionally enjoyed a relatively protected *de facto* status. A formalised collective bargaining system, the Whitley Councils, has been in operation since 1919; trade unionism was actively encouraged until 1979 and established civil servants have greater security of tenure than most private employees.[3] On the basis of the tradition of negotiation and consultation between Government and Civil Service trade unions, it has been held that the Minister should consult trade unions before making important changes to terms and conditions of employment, unless the Minister considers that national security would thereby be imperilled.[4] Failure to do so may result in a ministerial decision being set aside by the High Court on procedural grounds, but there is no judicial review of the substance of Civil Service regulations. Legislation does not bind the Crown unless there is a specific provision to that effect. For example, the Crown is therefore not bound to supply Crown employees with written statements of terms of employment. However, the unfair dismissal provisions do apply to civil servants, unless the Minister certifies that such protection is withdrawn in the interests of national security. This power was exercised in 1984 when trade union rights were withdrawn from civil servants employed at Government Communications Headquarters (see para. 375, below).

1. Dicey, *Law of the Constitution* (8th ed.), p. 421.
2. The most recent is the Civil Service Order in Council of 1982.
3. D. Winchester in *Industrial Relations in Britain* (G. S. Bain ed.), London, 1983, pp. 155–178.
4. *Council of the Civil Service Unions* v. *Minister for the Civil Service* [1984] 3 All ER 935 (HL).

IV. Office holders

119. The concept of an 'office' is sometimes applied to those in positions of authority in various public and private institutions. For example, there are the Fellows of Oxford and Cambridge Colleges and the steward and bailiff appointed by the Lord of a manor. Historically, offices such as these were distinguished from the 'contract of service', and the proprietary interests attaching to these offices were specially protected by the common law. In modern times tax legislation specifically applies to 'office-holders'. In other cases the mere fact that an individual holds an 'office' does not preclude him or her from belonging to the category of *workers* or that of *employees*. In these cases it all depends on factors such as whether he or she is a member of the corporate body in question, whether the office is a permanent one created by an enactment, whether the office continues to exist whether or not it is occupied at any particular time, and how the office-holder can be removed. The most important example of an office-holder in modern law is the director of a limited liability company. If he or she is also a working (*i.e.* executive) director then he or she will have a service contract with the company.

V. Manual workers

120. In general labour legislation applies equally to manual (or 'blue-collar') workers and non-manual (or 'white-collar') employees. However, some 19th-century legislation was limited in coverage to those engaged in *manual labour.* The last of this legislation, the Truck Acts (see Ch. IV, below) is expected to be repealed in 1986.

VI. Domestic servants

121. In the 19th century, special rules applied to those 'whose main or general function is to be about their employer's person, or establishments, residential or quasi-residential, for the purposes of ministering to their employer's needs or wants, or to the needs or wants of those who are members of such establishments or those resorting to such establishments'.[1] The Truck Acts excluded such employees from their coverage. This pattern has been continued by some modern legislation, despite the fact that such employees tend to be particularly vulnerable. The most important examples are the Sex Discrimination Act 1975 and the Race Relations Act 1976 which do not apply to employment in a private household except where the discrimination is by way of victimisation.[2] However, the European Court has held that the exclusion of such workers from the sex discrimination legislation constitutes a breach by the UK Government of its obligations under the EEC Treaty.[3] The Government is expected to amend the legislation in 1986.

    1. *Re Junior Carlton Club* [1922] 1 KB 166.
    2. SDA, s. 6(3); RRA, s. 4(3).
    3. *Commission of the European Communities* v. *UK* (1984) IRLR 29 ECJ.

VII. Specific employments

122. Among the groups of workers to whom specific legislation applies are: agricultural workers, bakers and confectioners, building and engineering workers, hotels and catering workers, civil aviation employees, docks and harbours employees, drivers, teachers, electricity and gas workers, firemen, hairdressers, laundry workers, court officials, local government officers, merchant seamen, national health service employees, oil-rig workers, shop and office workers, postal workers, railway workers, share fishermen and some transport workers.[1]

    1. For further details see *Encyclopedia of Labour Relations Law* (ed. B. A. Hepple and P. O'Higgins), London, 1972, Part 3.

VIII. Apprentices and trainees

123. A contract of apprenticeship is one under which the employer agrees to instruct and teach the apprentice his or her trade, profession or business and to maintain him or her during the existence of that relationship. The apprentice in turn agrees to serve and to learn from the employer. The apprentice may leave only if the employer's conduct indicates that the employer is unwilling to teach the apprentice and the employer may only dismiss the apprentice if the latter's conduct makes it impossible to instruct him or her. A wrongfully dismissed apprentice may claim damages not only in respect of loss of earnings but also for the value of lost future prospects. Employment protection legislation usually applies to apprentices,[1] but an apprentice who comes to the end of a fixed term apprenticeship cannot claim a redundancy payment or complain of unfair dismissal if he or she is not kept on as a journeyman.[2] Those who work as trainees under the Government's Youth Opportunities Programme (YOP) do not qualify as apprentices or as employees.[3] Nor do police cadets.[4]

1. For example, EPCA 1978, s. 153(1).
2. *Northeast Coast Shiprepairers Ltd.* v. *Secretary of State for Employment* [1975] ICR 755.
3. *Daley* v. *Allied Suppliers Ltd.* [1983] IRLR 14. This meant that the trainee could not invoke the protection of the Race Relations Act. Subsequently the legislation was extended to such trainees by departmental order on 21 July 1983. See too Health and Safety (Youth Training) Regulations 1983 (SI 1983 No. 1919).
4. *Wiltshire Police Authority* v. *Wynn* [1980] ICR 649.

IX. Casual or short-term workers

124. There is no separate legal category of casual workers. During the 20th century there has been important progress towards the decasualisation of labour, notably through a special regime of job and income security for registered dockworkers.[1] However, a significant part of the workforce, particularly in seasonal trades and services, work for relatively short periods of time, or with frequent breaks in continuity of service, for a particular employer. The effect of this is usually to deprive them of employment protection rights. First, their freedom to choose whether or not to work on a particular occasion, and the employer's freedom to deny them work may lead to a finding that there is insufficient 'mutuality of obligation' to constitute a contract of employment.[2] Secondly, even if they are employees, they may have insufficient continuity of employment to qualify for particular statutory rights.[3]

1. Under the Dock Workers Employment Scheme 1967 (SI 1967, No. 1252).
2. *O'Kelly* v. *Trusthouse Forte plc, supra.*
3. See para. 279, below on continuity of employment.

X. Temporary workers supplied by an intermediary

125. Distinct from casual workers of the kind just described are those commonly known as 'temporary' workers because their services are supplied by an intermediary (the employment agency or business) for the benefit of a third party (the hirer) for a limited period of time. The activities of fee-charging employment agencies and businesses are regulated under the Employment Agencies Act 1973. A distinction is drawn between the 'employment agency' which supplies workers for placement with employers, and the 'employment business' which supplies the services of workers it itself employs. The system of regulation applies to both, and is not limited to those supplied on short-term assignments, although in practice this is a major part of their activities. It is a criminal offence to carry on an employment business or agency without a licence. Detailed regulations[1] lay down standards for the conduct of employment businesses and agencies and provide, as a sanction, for the withdrawal of the licence. Workers may not be charged fees by an employment business or agency, save in exceptional circumstances, but there is no regulation of the fees charged to hirers. The workers supplied by an employment business or agency have relationships with both supplier and hirer. The legal nature of these relationships is ambiguous. It has been held that 'where A contracts with B to render services exclusively to C, the contract is not a contract for services (or of service) but a contract *sui generis*, a different type of contract from either of the familiar two'.[2] More recently, the absence of an obligation on the part of the worker to accept any particular assignment has been held to indicate the absence of a contract of service between the supplier and the worker.[3] The temporary worker almost certainly also has no contract of service with the hirer, and probably does not have a contract of any kind with the hirer.[4] The relationship between the worker and the supplier is to a limited extent governed by the regulations (*e.g.* the employment business must supply a written statement of employment terms to the worker, and the supplier is responsible for deducting social security contributions). The hirer may be responsible, under health and safety legislation, for work accidents to the worker. A draft EEC directive, which would have enhanced the protection of temporary workers, has been opposed by the UK Government, on the ground that employment agencies and businesses in the UK are significantly different from their counterparts elsewhere in the Member States and would be severely handicapped if the Directive were given effect.[5]

1. Conduct of Employment Agencies and Employment Businesses Regulations 1976 (SI 1976, No. 715), and related regulations; for further discussion see B. Hepple and B. Napier, 'Temporary Workers and the Law' (1978) 7 ILJ 84.
2. *Construction Industry Training Board* v. *Labour Force Ltd.* [1970] 3 All ER 220, *per* Cooke J.
3. *Wickens* v. *Champion Employment* [1984] ICR 365.
4. *O'Sullivan* v. *Thompson-Croom* (1973) 14 KIR 108.
5. House of Lords Select Committee on the European Communities Session 1982–83, 6th Report (HMSO, January 1983).

XI. Homeworkers

126. A further important category of workers is that of outworkers, usually working at home rather than at the employer's establishment, or working from home as a base (*e.g.* market research). These are well established working practices, dating back to the times of 'sweated labour' in the early 20th century. Recent estimates suggest that the number of home-based workers is increasing. In 1981, as many as 250,000 people in England and Wales worked at home and a further 407,200 worked from home as a base, together accounting for 4 per cent of the workforce.[1] Homeworking has traditionally been common in the manual trades, such as sewing, and it is popularly considered to consist largely of manufacturing done at home. In fact, by 1981, less than one-third of those who worked at home (723,000 people) were engaged in manufacturing homework. Instead, white-collar and service work now form the predominant type of home-based work, with further additions in the areas of new technology, such as punch card operation and word processing. Homeworkers tend to fare less well than their counterparts working at the workplace. Even if the rate paid for the job is similar, allowances for overheads are the exception rather than the rule and holiday pay is a rarity.[2] The vast majority are employed by non-unionised establishments. Despite their vulnerability, homeworkers do not form a separate legal category. There are some statutory protective measures relevant to homeworking, such as the requirement that the employer observes minimum safety requirements,[3] while some types of homeworking fall into the jurisdiction of Wages Councils[4] which set minimum wages. However, these regulations are inadequate and often unenforced. Furthermore, employment protection rights, as we have seen, depend on being able to establish both a contract of service and the necessary continuity of service. The employment status of homeworkers is ambiguous: some recent cases have held that homeworkers may be employed under a contract of service[5] but these are confined to their own facts. A recent survey found that while 51 per cent of home-based workers believed themselves to be self-employed, as many as 16 per cent had doubts about their correct employment status.[6]

1. All figures in this paragraph are to be found in 'Homework and Outwork' by C. Hakim (1984) 92 *Employment Gazette* January, pp. 7–12. See generally K. Ewing, 'Homeworking, a Framework for Reform' (1982) 12 ILJ 94.
2. C. Hakim, 'Employers' Use of Homework and Outwork and Freelances' (1984) 92 *Employment Gazette* 146.
3. Factories Act 1961, s. 133.
4. Wages Councils Act 1979, s. 28.
5. *Airfix Footwear Ltd* v. *Cope* [1978] ICR 1210; *Nethermere (St. Neots) Ltd.* v. *Gardiner* [1984] ICR 365.
6. Hakim, *op. cit.* (note 2).

XII. Part-time workers

127. Part-time workers form an increasingly important sector of the workforce. By 1984, almost 5 million employees worked part-time, forming 21 per cent of the workforce, an increase of about 1.8 million since 1971 and the largest proportion in the EEC, apart from Denmark.[1] Of these, 4.3 million were women, constituting about 45 per cent of all women in employment, as against 4 per cent of all employed men. Indeed, part-time work has been the only source of increase in the overall level of employment in Great Britain since 1951.[2] Part-time work is heavily concentrated in the service industries, particularly distribution, hotels and catering, although a significant number of part-timers work in manufacturing.

1. Manpower Services Corporate Plan 1985–1989; Labour Force Survey (1985) 93 *Employment Gazette*, p. 177; New Earnings Survey 1984.
2. O. Robinson and J. Wallace, *Part-time employment and sex discrimination legislation in Great Britain*, Department of Employment Research Paper No. 43, *1984*, from which most of the figures in this section derive.

128. Part-time work is associated with relatively low levels of pay and the absence of important fringe benefits. In 1984, about 56 per cent of part-time workers in the distributive trades earned less than £1.80 per hour. Although this is in some cases due to part-timers being paid less per hour than full-timers in the same job, the main reason for the earnings differential between full-time and part-time workers is the fact that part-time working is concentrated in the lowest paying occupations, with fewer opportunities to supplement earnings with overtime premia. In fact, recent years have witnessed a deterioration in the relative position of part-timers, especially since 1977. For example, hourly earnings of women in part-time manual work fell from 65.4 per cent of that of full-time male manual employees in 1977 to only 60 per cent in 1982.

129. There is no statutory definition of part-time work, but many employment protection rights depend on the number of hours worked per week. Thus a minimum working week of 8 hours is a prerequisite for eligibility for rights relating to redundancy, unfair dismissal (except if the dismissal is due to trade union activities), guarantee pay, maternity pay and the right to return to work after confinement. For those who work at least 8 but less than 16 hours per week, the qualifying period for most of these rights is 5 years rather than two, as is the case for full-time employees. Although the definition of part-time work in official statistics usually applies to those who work less than 30 hours a week, a growing number of part-timers fall outside of the statutory limits. Thus, 6.5 per cent of part-timers worked fewer than 8 hours in 1982, compared with 3.9 per cent in 1975, while the numbers working between 8 and 16 hours per week increased 5.5 per cent to 21 per cent in the same period.

130. The most important rights for which hours of work are irrelevant concern sex and race discrimination, with the result that these Acts are the primary source of protection for part-time women. It has recently been established that payment of lower hourly wages to part-timers may indirectly discriminate against women and so contravene the Equal Pay Act 1970 unless the employer can justify the discrepancy.[1] It may also be discriminatory to make part-timers redundant before full-timers, regardless of length of service,[2] and to refuse to allow a woman to return to work in a part-time capacity after maternity leave.[3] In each of these cases, however, it is open to the employer to argue that his or her action is justifiable on reasonable commercial grounds.

1. *Jenkins* v. *Kingsgate (Clothing Productions) Ltd.* [1981] ICR 715 and see Part I, Ch. VIII below.
2. *Clarke* v. *Eley (IMI) Kynoch Ltd.* [1983] ICR 165, but see *Kidd* v. *DRG* [1985] ICR 405.
3. *Home Office* v. *Holmes* [1984] ICR 678.

131. Collective bargaining practice in relation to part-timers is not consistent.[1] Some agreements apply differential hourly rates of pay to full-timers and part-timers,[2] but most pay the full-time rate *pro rata*. Many agreements give full-timers and part-timers the same leave entitlement, while some reduce the part-timers' entitlement according to day normally worked. Few agreements appear to provide sick pay for part-timers. Part-timers may be denied access to occupational pension schemes solely because they work part-time, and even where they have access the benefits may be less favourable than for full-time workers. Some agreements provide that part-timers should be declared redundant before full-timers, but in a recent case, this practice was held to amount to sexual discrimination.[3] The UK Government has opposed a draft EEC Directive, which seeks to apply the principle of equal treatment between full-time and part-time workers.[4]

1. A full survey will be found in Income Data Services Part-time Work Study no. 118, London, March 1976.
2. Since *Jenkins* v. *Kingsgate (supra)*, the legality of this must be in doubt.
3. *Clark* v. *Eley Kynoch (supra)*.
4. House of Lords Select Committee on the European Communities Voluntary Part-time Work Session 1981–1982 19th report (1982).

§2. WRITTEN STATEMENT OF EMPLOYMENT TERMS

132. The employer is obliged to provide every employee with a written statement reflecting the main terms of employment.[1] The aim of this provision is to 'ensure for the benefit of an employee that the terms of his (or her) contract of employment are set out in writing so that the employee knows his legal rights in terms of the contract and can, if need be, insist upon them by legal action against the employer'.[2]

1. EPCA 1978, s. 1.
2. *Owens* v. *Multilux Ltd.* [1974] IRLR 113 at p. 114.

133. The statement must be given to the employee not later than 13 weeks after the beginning of his or her employment with the employer and must reflect the terms of employment at a specified date not more than one week before the statement is given. The statement should identify the parties, specify the date on which the employment began and state the date on which the employee's period of continuous employment began (taking into account any employment with a previous employer which counts towards that period). It should also give particulars of the following terms of employment:
  (i) The scale or rate of remuneration, or the method of calculating remuneration (including for example, any terms on piece-rates, or overtime pay).
  (ii) The intervals at which remuneration is paid (that is, whether weekly or monthly or some other period).
  (iii) Any terms and conditions relating to hours of work (including any terms and conditions relating to normal working hours).
  (iv) Any terms and conditions relating to:
      (a) entitlement to holidays, including public holidays, and holiday pay (sufficient to enable the employee's entitlement, including any entitlement to accrued holiday pay on the termination of employment, to be precisely calculated);
      (b) incapacity for work due to sickness or injury, including any provisions for sick pay;

    (c) pensions and pension schemes (employees who are covered by special statutory pensions schemes and whose employers are already obliged by law to provide information about them are excepted).

  (v) The length of notice of termination which the employee is obliged to give and entitled to receive, stating the date when the contract expires if the contract is for a fixed term.

 (vi) The title of the job which the employee is to do.

The statement may refer to some other document, in which these particulars are to be found but the employee must have reasonable opportunities for reading that document in the course of his employment, or it must be made reasonably accessible to him in some other way.

134. In addition the Act of 1978 requires the statement given to the employee to include a note which must:

  (i) specify any disciplinary rules (other than those relating to health and safety at work) which apply to the employee or refer to a document, reasonably accessible to the employee, which specifies the rules;

 (ii) specify by description or name the person to whom the employee can apply and the manner in which such applications should be made:
    (a) if he is dissatisfied with any disciplinary decision relating to him, or
    (b) for the purposes of seeking redress of any grievance relating to his employment; and

(iii) where there are further steps which follow from an application under (ii)(a) or (ii)(b), explain those steps or refer to a document which explains them and is reasonably accessible to the employee;

(iv) whether the employer has an occupational pension scheme which has a certificate that it is 'contracted-out' of the state pension scheme under the Social Security Pensions Act 1975.

135. The obligation to provide a written statement under the 1978 Act does not apply to certain categories of employees, *viz.* (i) employees whose normal hours are less than 16 (and, in some cases, 8) weekly; (ii) registered dock-workers engaged in dock work; (iii) masters and seamen on certain British ships; (iv) Crown servants; (v) employees who ordinarily work for their employers abroad during any period when these employees are engaged in work wholly or mainly outside Great Britain; (vi) an employee who is re-engaged by the same employer within 6 months of the ending of the last period of employment; (vii) an employee who has a written contract of employment covering each of the particulars listed in section 1 of the 1978 Act.

137. It is essential to note that the statement is not the contract itself, and may be an inaccurate reflection of the terms to which the parties actually agreed. 'The document is a unilateral one merely stating the employer's view of what those terms are. . . In the absence of an acknowledgement by the parties that the statement is itself a contract and that the terms are correct, the statutory statement does not itself constitute a contract in writing.'[1] While the statement is strong *prima facie* evidence of the terms of the contract, it is by no means conclusive.[2] Nor does the fact that an employee has signed acknowledgement of receipt necessarily mean that she or he has signed a contract or accepted the accuracy of the terms in it. It is only a contract if the parties acknowledge it as such.[3]

1. *System Floors Ltd.* v. *Daniel* [1982] ICR 54 at 58.
2. *Ibid.*, approved in *Robertson* v. *British Gas Corporation* [1983] ICR 351.
3. *Gascol Conversions Ltd.* v. *Mercer* [1974] ICR 420.

138.   Any changes in the listed particulars must be given to the employee not more than one month after the change. A statement of change does not in itself vary the terms of the contract; at most, it may provide evidence of an agreed variation. Nor does the fact that an employee continues working without objection mean that he or she has impliedly agreed to the change, especially where the variation relates to a matter which has no immediate practical application.[1] The statutory obligation to notify all changes can be avoided in cases in which the particulars refer to another document (such as a collective agreement), provided that, in the original statement, the employer indicates that future changes will be entered up in that document.

1. *Jones* v. *Associated Tunnelling Company Ltd.* [1981] IRLR 477.

139.   Where no statement has been given, or a statement is incomplete or its accuracy is in doubt, the employee may complain to an industrial tribunal, which will determine any missing particulars or confirm, amend or substitute for inaccurate particulars.[1] The tribunal should attempt to discover what the parties have in fact agreed, taking into account all the circumstances, including the parties' subsequent conduct. In this exercise, the tribunal is not confined to the tests applicable in deciding the terms to be implied in a commercial contract. If the tribunal cannot ascertain the agreed terms, it may imply a reasonable term. 'Section 11 would seem to impose upon the tribunals a statutory duty to find the specified terms and in the last resort to invent them for the purpose of literally writing them into the contract.'[2] This is an important departure from the traditional means of discovering contractual terms (see Part I, Ch. II, below). The effect of this determination is that the employer is deemed to have supplied a statement in the corrected form. However, the tribunal cannot enforce the terms of the contract; the employee's remedy for breach of contract is in the County Court or High Court (see para. 80, above).

1. EPCA 1978, s. 11.
2. *Mears* v. *Safecar Security Ltd.* [1982] ICR 626, CA.

§1. Capacity to Contract and Restrictions on Employment

A. Minors

140.   Persons under the age of 18 have limited capacity to contract. A minor may obtain benefits under an employment contract, but the general rule is that he or she is bound only if the obligations are on the whole beneficial to him or her. It seems that simple financial advantages are enough to make the contract 'beneficial'.[1]

1. *Chaplin* v. *Leslie Frewin (Publishers) Ltd.* [1966] Ch. 71.

141. There are statutory restrictions on the employment of children under the school-leaving age of 16.[1] The minimum age at which a child may be employed is 13, and between the ages of 13 and 16 children may not be employed at all in any factory, mine, transport undertakings or United Kingdom registered ship. They may be employed in industrial undertakings only if members of the same family are employed there. Previously, local authorities had the power to regulate the employment of children under 16, but this was replaced in 1973 by an enlarged power for the Secretary of State to restrict their employment. Local authorities have power to require information concerning children's employment and may prevent employment in ways or for periods which are unsuitable. There is specific control over the employment of children during the last year of compulsory schooling in work experience schemes and special regulations apply to the employment of children in the entertainment industry.

1. The principal Acts are: Employment of Women, Young Persons and Children Act 1920, s. 1; Children Act 1933; Mines & Quarries Act 1954, s. 124; Factories Act 1961, s. 167; Children & Young Persons Act 1963, ss. 37–44; Employment of Children Act 1973; Education (Work Experience) Act 1973; Merchant Shipping Act 1970, s. 51.

B. Women

142. Both single and married women have the same capacity to contract as men, and sex discrimination on grounds of marriage has been outlawed since 1975 (below, Ch. VIII). However, no women may be employed in a job the duties of which ordinarily require her to spend a significant proportion of her time below ground in a mine,[1] and there are restrictions on night and shift work by women in factories.[2] Legislation is expected in 1986 to repeal the latter restrictions.

1. Mines & Quarries Act 1954, s. 124(1).
2. Factories Act 1961, Part VI.

C. Foreign workers

143. In the face of rising unemployment, British governments have imposed increasingly stringent limitations on the rights of foreigners to work in the United Kingdom. Immigration controls are for the most part found in a complex set of non-statutory regulations administered with a large measure of discretion.[1] Only a very brief description is possible here.[2]

1. The main statutory source is the Immigration Act 1971, supplemented by Statements of

Changes of Immigration Rules: House of Commons Paper 169, 9 February 1983; House of Commons Paper 293, 26 March 1985; House of Commons Paper 503, 15 July 1985. See also the Parliamentary Statement on behalf of the Secretary for Employment, 14 November 1979, House of Commons debates vol. 973 written answers col. 609.
2. These paragraphs have been compiled with the assistance of Philip Trott, solicitor.

144. Only British citizens[1] have the unrestricted right to work in the United Kingdom. Anyone else may only work in the United Kingdom in accordance with the immigration rules. The principal categories are as follows: (i) Commonwealth citizens between the ages of 17 and 27 on holiday may work in the UK provided that such work is incidental to their holiday. They may be admitted in that capacity for an aggregate period of two years. (ii) No permission is needed to engage in certain occupations ('permit-free' occupations). These include ministers of religion; representatives of overseas firms which have no branch, subsidiary or representative in the UK; and representatives of overseas newspapers, news agencies and broadcasting organisations on long-term assignments to the UK. Doctors and dentists were removed from this category in March 1985.[2] (iii) Permission may be granted to establish a business provided certain criteria are met, including a minimum investment of £150,000 and the ability to demonstrate that the business will be successful and will create jobs. (iv) A work permit may be issued by the Department of Employment on application by the prospective employer. The permit is issued for a specific job and a named worker only. In recent years, very strict criteria have been applied to the issue of work permits. (v) Writers and artists may work in that capacity provided that they can maintain themselves without recourse to public funds from their earnings as writers or artists (or their savings in their first year of being in the country in this capacity). (vi) Indefinite leave to remain and work without restriction may be granted to anyone who has been in categories (ii), (iii), (iv) and (v) above for 4 years. Spouses and dependants are similarly eligible. In addition, indefinite leave to remain may be granted to anyone who has been admitted as a person of independent means (*i.e.* requiring a minimum of £150,000 capital) and has remained for 4 years. (vii) Nationals of other Member States of the European Economic Community, subject to restrictions in the case of Greece, Portugal and Spain, have the right to seek or take up employment or set up in business.[3] (viii) Students and dependants may also work in limited circumstances.

1. The British Nationality Act 1981 contains the definition of a 'British citizen'.
2. See House of Commons Paper 293, 26 March 1985.
3. This category is governed by the provisions of the EEC Treaty, Title III, Ch. 1 on the free movement of persons and the regulations and directions of the EEC.

145. There are some further restrictions including the prohibition on employment of non-British subjects in the civil service without a certificate[1] and as regards military employment. The recruitment of workers from outside the United Kingdom by private employment agencies and businesses is regulated, for example to ensure that the worker obtains full written details of the employment in a language he or she can understand.[2] Discrimination against EEC workers is prohibited by EEC regulations which are directly applicable in the United Kingdom,[3] and discrimination against any person on grounds of race, colour, ethnic or national origins or nationality is prohibited by the Race Relations Act 1976, insofar as this is not specifically authorised by legislation.[4]

1. Aliens Employment Act 1955.
2. Conduct of Employment Agencies and Employment Businesses Regulations 1976, SI 1976 No. 715, reg. 6.
3. In particular, Council Regulation 1612/68 of 15 October 1968; arts. 7, 8, 9 as amended.
4. See Pt. I, Ch. VIII, below. An example of specific statutory authority for discrimination is the Race Relations (Prescribed Public Bodies) Regulations 1984, SI 1984, No. 218, which allows certain public bodies to discriminate on grounds of birth, nationality, descent or residence when making appointments.

Chapter II. The Sources of Terms of the Contract of Employment

§1. Express and Implied Terms

146. The reciprocal rights and duties of employer and employee depend upon the express and implied terms of the contract of employment. Where the parties have not expressly dealt with any matter, the courts are willing to imply terms in order to make the contract a workable one. These terms are sometimes treated as resting upon the presumed intentions of the parties (terms *implied in fact*), sometimes as based on *custom and practice* (see para. 157, below) and sometimes as a legal incident of the relationship or status of employer and employee (terms *implied in law*). Two particular approaches from the law of commercial contracts have traditionally been adopted by the courts in deciding whether to imply terms in accordance with the presumed intentions of the parties. The first is 'to give such business efficacy to the transaction as must have been intended'.[1] The second is to imply 'something so obvious that it goes without saying; so that if, while the parties were making their bargain, an officious bystander were to suggest some express provision for it in their agreement they would testily suppress him with a cry of "Oh, of course!"'.[2] More recently, the courts have acknowledged that implied terms may involve judicial norm-making rather than reflecting the actual intentions of the parties. According to this approach, the relationship of employer and employee requires that there should be some kind of agreed term on certain matters, such as sick pay or the place of employment. Where that term has not been agreed and the parties would not have agreed had they been asked at the time of contracting what that term should be, the court has to imply the term.[3] In this type of case, all the facts and circumstances of the relationship, including the way in which the parties have worked the contract since it was made, must be considered. Recent decisions differ as to whether such a term should be upheld as a legal incident only if 'necessary' to the relationship,[4] or whether the more flexible 'reasonableness' test is appropriate.[5] The most important terms which have been implied in law as 'necessary' incidents of the relationship are (i) the reciprocal duty of *co-operation*; (2) the employee's duty of *faithful service*; and (3) the employer's duty to take *reasonable care* for the health and safety of his employees, and the employee's duty to take reasonable care about his employer's business. These are discussed in Ch. III, below.

1. *The Moorcock* (1889) 14 PD 64 at 68.
2. *Shirlaw* v. *Southern Foundries Ltd.* [1939] 2 KB 206 at p. 227.
3. *Lister* v. *Romford Ice and Cold Storage Co. Ltd* [1957] AC 555 (House of Lords); *Mears* v. *Safecar Security Ltd.* [1982] ICR 626 (Court of Appeal).
4. *Mears* v. *Safecar Security Ltd.* at pp. 650–651 *per* Stephenson L. J.
5. *Howman & Son* v. *Blyth* [1983] ICR 416 (EAT) at p. 420; *Jones* v. *Associated Tunnelling Co. Ltd.* [1981] IRLR 477 (EAT).

147. The scope of implied terms is important for several reasons. Many of them were developed in the context of the employer's right at common law to dismiss an employee without notice. Where the breach of the term is sufficiently serious, the employee may be said to have repudiated the contract so entitling the employer to dismiss him or her without notice. Conversely, the employee may be able to claim damages for breach of contract where the employer repudiates a contractual obligation (see para. 298, below). Legislation on redundancy payments and on unfair dismissal has incorporated the contractual notions into the statutory definition of 'dismissal'. This is particularly important in the context of 'constructive dismissal' where the employer's repudiation may entitle the employee to terminate the contract without notice (see para. 299, below). Moreover, in determining the reasonableness of an employer's actions, tribunals are strongly influenced by the express and implied contractual obligations of the parties. The legislation has therefore spawned an important body of case law on implied terms, particularly those implied in law. We must next examine the judicial techniques for incorporating collective agreements, works rules and notices and custom and practice into individual contracts. The use of statutory provisions as terms of contract is discussed in the Introduction, para. 95, above.

. *148.* Two preliminary points must be stressed. The first is the optional nature of implied terms (including custom). A term will not be implied if it is contrary to an express term; and a custom may not be proved if it is contrary to an express or implied term. These principles of the common law distinguish it sharply from the civil law systems: there are no *imperative* norms in the legal relationship between employer and employee. In particular, implied terms can always be replaced by express ones, even if these are less favourable to the employee. This is particularly important in relation to collective agreements (para. 149, below). The second preliminary point is that the written statement of particulars of terms of employment (para. 132, above) may facilitate proof of the express and implied terms of the contract, although this is not conclusive evidence of those terms.

§2. Terms Incorporated from Collective Agreements

149. In practice, the main terms and conditions of employment of the majority of employees in Britain are determined by collective bargaining rather than by individual negotiation. A recent survey indicated that in 1980 pay increases for 58 per cent of manual and 50 per cent of non-manual workers were the direct result of collective agreements.[1] The pay and conditions of (probably) another 25 per cent of employees are indirectly influenced by collective bargaining. Nevertheless, British labour law remains rooted in the notion that terms and conditions are a matter of contract between individuals. Collective agreements are presumed not to be intended to be enforceable as contracts between the trade union and employer parties unless an intention to be so bound is expressed in writing.[2] However, the terms of collective agreements may achieve legal effect if they are incorporated into individual contracts of employment. Incorporation is not automatic, not even as minimum terms, and express agreement always takes precedence. In this respect, British labour law stands in sharp contrast to that of other countries, such as France, where the clauses of collective agreements apply to employment contracts except where there are provisions more favourable to the worker. The seriousness of this gap in British labour law has become apparent in times of recession when employers have been able to cut wages by the simple expedient of terminating contracts of employment and offering re-employment on revised terms and conditions less favourable than those laid down in the collective agreement.

1. W. W. Daniel and N. Millward, *Workplace Industrial Relations In Britain*, p. 179.
2. TULRA 1974, s. 18(1). See Pt. II, Ch. IV, below.

150. Under what circumstances will a term of a collective agreement become legally enforceable as a term of the individual contract? Unfortunately, attempts to construct a theory of incorporation which is both consistent with contractual principle and reflects reality have not been wholly successful. There are several difficulties. First, collective agreements usually apply to all workers of a particular category, whether or not they are members of a trade union which is party to the agreement, and even if they subsequently join or leave the union. Many workers may not even know of the existence of the agreement. This is difficult to reconcile with the contractual principle that parties should consent to the terms of their contract. Secondly, collective agreements contain procedural terms which may not be amenable to individual enforcement, or may not have been intended to create individual rights. Thirdly, collective bargaining may take place on several different levels at once, with a national or industry-wide agreement being supplemented by local or plant level agreements. The courts have to decide which of these should be incorporated. It should be noted that a worker cannot sue directly on the collective agreement, since he or she was not a party to it.[1]

1. But this may be possible in Scots law: J. Casey, *Juridical Review* (1973) p. 22 at p. 39.

151. The first major issue in any attempt at incorporation is that of 'bridging' the gap between the collective agreement and the individual contract. Several principles of incorporation have emerged:
(a) *Express Incorporation*: This will occur where employer and employee expressly agree that the individual contract is subject to a particular collective agreement or agreements. Proof that such agreement has been reached may be facilitated by express reference to the collective agreement in the written statement of employment terms which the employer is obliged to provide.[1]
(b) *Incorporation by Custom*: It is a well-recognised contractual principle that a contract can be taken to include terms which are sanctioned by custom unless the parties clearly specified otherwise. To become a term of a contract, a custom must be certain, reasonable and well-known, although the individual worker may be ignorant of its existence. Kahn-Freund characterised collective agreements as 'crystallised custom', arguing that this was the basis of incorporation.[2] This explains much of the reality of

employment conditions, particularly the fact that collective agreements refer to all workers, regardless of their knowledge or approval. But it does not explain how new or varied collective agreements come to be incorporated.

(c) *Implied Incorporation*: In practice industrial tribunals and courts are very willing to find even in the absence of express agreement or proof of custom, that the terms of collective agreements have become impliedly incorporated into contracts of employment, almost to the point of a presumption of fact that such agreements apply unless the contrary is shown. The principles used are those described in para. 146, above.

1. EPCA 1978, s. 1; see above, para. 132.
2. Kahn-Freund, *System of Industrial Relations in Great Britain* (ed. Flanders and Clegg), Oxford, 1954, pp. 58–59; see *e.g. Donelan* v. *Kirby* [1983] IRLR 191 (EAT).

152. The 'bridging' problem is resolved by these techniques of express or implied terms or custom and practice. In general, the trade union negotiating a collective agreement is not treated as the agent of its members even if it purports to act as their 'representative'. The only exceptions to this might be where the number of workers involved is very small and the issues are local or are personal to those workers. English law has not favoured the agency approach because, in Wedderburn's words, 'a hundred legal puzzles would emerge'.[1] For example, the fact that collective agreements are generally regarded as applicable to non-unionists as well as trade union members is incompatible with the concept of the union as agent only for its own members. Another problem would arise with workers who joined the enterprise after the agreement was concluded. By the doctrines of the English law of agency, only those who were themselves capable of contracting at the time the agent made the contract may subsequently ratify the agent's action. This would mean that workers below the contractual capacity (18 years) at the time the collective agreement was made could not be bound by it. The most difficult question of all would be whether a member may revoke an agent's authority at any time in the same way as a principal may revoke an agent's authority. If this were possible, stable bargaining arrangements could be upset by individual withdrawals of authority.[2]

1. Wedderburn, *The Worker and the Law*, 2nd ed., p. 185.
2. *Land* v. *West Yorks CC* [1979] ICR 452; *Singh* v. *British Steel Corporation* [1974] IRLR 131.

153. Several problems remain, common to all the above theories. The courts have not fully worked out the principles governing the 'translation problem', that is the question of which terms are appropriate for individual enforcement and which are solely collective in nature.[1] It is the accepted wisdom that disputes procedures, recognition agreements or redundancy selection arrangements are usually ill-suited for individual enforcement and are intended by the parties to be resolved in the collective arena by negotiation or industrial action.[2] Some recent cases have, nevertheless, held that a disputes procedure and a shop stewards recognition agreement may be incorporated.[3] Such a term will not, however, survive the termination of the contract of employment or the suspension of the employee from duties.[4] Nor have the courts developed clear-cut principles to deal with collective bargaining at both national and local level.[5] Some collective agreements do, however, make specific provision by their own terms as to what is to happen in case of conflict with other agreements. A further complication arises if an employer or union unilaterally withdraws from a collective agreement. Contractual theory requires consent by both parties to a variation; it has thus been held that, once a collective agreement has been incorporated into the individual contract, its terms cannot be removed by the employer's or union's unilateral withdrawal from the collective agreement.[6] The employee's consent may however be implied if he or she continues to work without objection. Moreover, it remains open to the employer to terminate the conditions incorporated from the collective agreement by terminating the individual contracts and offering to re-employ the relevant workers on the new terms.[7] If the collective agreement is varied with the consent of the trade union, individual contracts will usually be varied accordingly, on the basis of an express or implied term that the individual contract is subject to collective agreements *for the time being in force.*

1. *British Leyland* v. *McQuilken* [1978] IRLR 245.
2. See *e.g. Tadd* v. *Eastman* [1985] IRLR 121 (CA).
3. *Irani* v. *Southampton and South West Hampshire Health Authority* [1985] IRLR 203 (ChD); *City and Hackney Health Authority* v. *National Union of Public Employees* [1985] IRLR 263 (CA).
4. *City and Hackney HA* v. *NUPE, supra.*
5. Compare *Clift* v. *West Riding CC, The Times* 10 April 1964 (local agreement prevailed) with *Gascol Conversions Ltd.* v. *Mercer* [1974] ICR 420 (national agreement prevailed).
6. *Robertson* v. *British Gas Corporation* [1983] ICR 351; *Gibbons* v. *Associated British Ports* [1985] IRLR 376.
7. *Burdett Coutts* v. *Hertfordshire CC* [1984] IRLR 91 (QBD).

§3. Terms Incorporated from Works Rules and Notices

154. The terms of individual contracts of employment may also be found in rules, notices and other documents issued by management to employees either at the time of engagement or subsequently. In some cases, such rules are collectively agreed, in which case the methods of incorporation are as set out above. Frequently, however, they are unilaterally imposed. In that case, they become terms of the contract in one of the following ways.

155. Unilaterally imposed rules may become part of the contract of employment:
(1) By *express* incorporation, for example by the worker signing an acknowledgement, at the time of making the contract or subsequently, that the rules are binding upon him, or if reasonable notice is given to the worker of the existence of the rules and he works under them without objection.
(2) By *implied* incorporation, for example where the worker has accepted

employment of the 'usual conditions', which would be taken to include the works rules.
(3) By proof that the rules were recognised by *custom and practice* (see below, para. 157).

Express rules take precedence over the second and third categories.

156. Works rules in British industry are of so many different kinds that no general statement can be made about their function as contractual terms. But it needs to be stressed that not all works rules are contractual in character. For example, the Court of Appeal[1] decided in 1972 that the British Railways Rules Book setting out the duties of railway employees were not terms of the contracts of employment of those employees. They were simply 'instructions to a man as to how he is to do his work'. This meant that they could be unilaterally altered by the employer without the employee's consent, at any time. The employee, on the other hand, was obliged to obey the rules, as altered from time to time, because of his duty of obedience to the lawful instructions of the employer. In cases like this therefore, works rules will be treated simply as instances of lawful managerial commands. In other cases, they may be construed as being contractually binding on both parties.

1. *Secretary of State for Employment* v. *ASLEF* [1972] 2 QB 443.

§4. Terms Incorporated from Custom and Practice

157. The custom and practice of a trade or industry has traditionally been an important source of terms and conditions of employment, although this form of regulation has become less frequent with the greater formalization of conditions of work, encouraged by the obligation to supply a statutory statement of terms (see para. 132, above). A somewhat different type of custom and practice developed in manufacturing industry during the 1950s, in the form of informal workplace bargaining, displacing national agreements. This was increasingly recognised as an important source of terms of the contract. In the past decade, however, workplace bargaining has itself become increasingly formalised, and informal workplace bargaining is less prevalent. To become a term of a contract, a custom or practice must be certain, reasonable and well-known. Even if an individual worker is ignorant of the particular custom, he or she may be taken to know of local customs.[1]

1. The classic example is *Sagar* v. *Ridehalgh* [1931] 1 Ch. 310. But see now *Bond* v. *CAV Ltd.* [1983] IRLR 360, where the requirement of notoriety was more strictly applied.

Chapter III. The duties of Co-operation, Fidelity and Care

158. Three of the most important duties implied in law into every contract of employment (see para. 146, above) are discussed in this Chapter. These are (1) the duty of mutual co-operation; (2) the duty of faithful service; and (3) the duty of reasonable care.

§1. THE DUTY OF MUTUAL CO-OPERATION

A. The employee's duty to obey lawful and reasonable orders

159. One of the most important terms implied by the common law into the contract of employment is the employee's duty to obey lawful and reasonable orders. This reflects a judicial endorsement of the employer's 'managerial prerogative' and of the notions of command and subordination inherent in the employment relationship. This has sometimes been treated as an aspect of the duty of faithful service (see below, para. 166). But recent case law suggests that the rationale of such an implied term lies in the duty not to frustrate the commercial objectives of the employer,[1] a perspective which assumes a unity of purpose between employer and employee in contrast with the pluralist premise of an intrinsic conflict of interest between the two sides. Thus it has been held to be an implied term that 'each employee will not, in obeying lawful instructions, seek to obey them in a wholly unreasonable way, which has the effect of disrupting the system, the efficient running of which he is employed to ensure'.[2]

1. *Secretary of State for Employment* v. *ASLEF* [1972] 2 All ER, 949 at pp. 971–972, *per* Buckley L. J.
2. *Ibid.*, at p. 980 *per* Roskill L. J.; see too Lord Denning MR at p. 965.

160. The scope of this implied term is of particular importance in determining the extent of the employer's common law right of summary dismissal. In the 19th century, a single act of disobedience was treated as entitling the employer summarily to dismiss an employee, provided the order was 'lawful'. Thus a refusal to allow an employee to visit her sick mother was held to be lawful,[1] as was an order to remain in a zone of danger so long as there was no *immediate* threat of violence or disease to the employee. More recent cases have held that one act of disobedience can only justify a dismissal if it in effect amounts to a repudiation by the employee of the contract.[2] It was judicially stated in 1974 that 'many of the decisions which are customarily cited date from the last century and may be wholly out of accord with current social conditions. . . . We have by now come to realise that a contract of service imposes upon the parties a duty of mutual respect'.[3]

1. *Turner* v. *Mason* (1845) 14 M&W 112
2. *Laws* v. *London Chronicle (Indicator Newspapers) Ltd.* [1958] 1 WLR 698 (CA).
3. *Wilson* v. *Racher* [1974] ICR 428 at 430.

161. Several recent cases have concerned the reasonableness of an order that the employee transfer to a new place of work. Where there is no express obligation to transfer, the courts have been willing to imply a reasonable term, taking into account such factors as the nature of the employer's business and whether the employee had been moved before.[1]

    1. *Jones* v. *Associated Tunnelling Co. Ltd.* [1981] IRLR 477 (EAT).

B. The employer's duty to take steps to achieve the purposes of the employment relationship

162. In contrast to the extensive nature of the employee's implied duties, the employer's implied obligations have traditionally been limited to the duty not to prevent or hinder the occurrence of an express condition upon which the performance of the contract by the employee depends (*e.g.* the provision of piece-work to a worker paid on piece rates). Under the influence of the law of unfair dismissal (see below, Ch. VII), this duty has been developed into an implied duty of mutual trust and confidence.[1] Although this does not extend to a requirement that the employer should treat employees reasonably,[2] it does require that the employer should not behave in a manner calculated to damage the relationship of trust and confidence[3] and should be good and considerate to employees.[4] The employer should take positive steps to achieve the purposes of the employment relationship, not only with regard to the material conditions of employment such as pay and safety, but also in respect of the psychological conditions which are essential to the employee's performance. For example, it has been held that the employer is under a positive duty to protect the employee from harassment by fellow employees,[5] to refrain from severely criticizing a supervisor in the presence of subordinates,[6] to investigate the employee's genuine grievances,[7] and generally to treat the employee with dignity and respect.[8] The employer must not falsely accuse the employee of serious misconduct on the basis of scanty evidence[9] nor may he give unjustified warnings with a view to disheartening the employee.[10] This extended duty of co-operation is particularly important in the context of unfair dismissal, since an employee is entitled to resign and claim to have been 'constructively dismissed' if the employer breaches this duty.

    1. *E.g. Woods* v. *W. M. Car Services (Peterborough) Ltd.* [1982] ICR 693 (CA).
    2. *Post Office* v. *Roberts* [1980] IRLR 347 (EAT).
    3. *Courtaulds Northern Textiles Ltd* v. *Andrew* [1979] IRLR 84.
    4. *Woods* v. *W. M. Car Services (Peterborough) Ltd., supra.*
    5. *Wigan Borough Council* v. *Davies* [1979] IRLR 1278.
    6. *Courtaulds Northern Textiles Ltd* v. *Andrew, supra.*
    7. *British Aircraft Corporation* v. *Austin* [1978] IRLR 332.
    8. *Garner* v. *Grange Furnishing Ltd.* [1977]. IRLR 206; *Palmanor Ltd.* v. *Cedron* [1978] ICR 1008.
    9. *Robinson* v. *Crompton Parkinson Ltd.* [1978] ICR 401.
    10. *Walker* v. *Josiah Wedgwood & Sons Ltd.* [1978] ICR 744 at 754.

C. The provision of work

163. It is the duty of employer and employee to co-operate in fulfilling their obligations under the contract. From the employer's point of view however this generally means no more than a duty to pay remuneration. Failure to pay wages over a period of time is regarded as a breach of the employer's fundamental obligations, so entitling the employee to terminate the contract without notice. However, in general, the employer is under no obligation to provide work so long as he goes on providing remuneration.

164. There are *three* exceptional situations[1] in which the employer must provide work:
(1) in contracts in which the bargain is that the employer will provide a salary plus the opportunity of becoming better known, such as in the case of an actor or artist:
(2) in contracts with commission or piece-workers in which the employer promises to pay an agreed rate and impliedly promises to provide a reasonable amount of work;
(3) in contracts with skilled workers in which the employer promises to pay a salary and impliedly promises to provide a reasonable amount of work to maintain or develop skills.

1. *Langston v. AUEW (No. 2)* [1974] ICR 510, *per* Sir John Donaldson at p. 521.

165. It has been suggested by Lord Denning[1] that there is a general right to be provided with work, but this view is not generally accepted. In the exceptional situations mentioned where the employer is under a duty to provide work his failure to do so may entitle the employee to terminate the contract without notice. Occasionally the failure to provide work may be due to some supervening event, without the fault on either side, and so may be treated as a *frustration* of the contract bringing it to an end automatically (*e.g.* a fire burning down the place of work) (see para. 289, below).

1. *Langston v. AUEW* [1974] ICR 180 at p. 190.

§2. THE EMPLOYEE'S DUTY OF FAITHFUL SERVICE

166. The employee must serve his employer faithfully and honestly. This basic duty may be amplified by express terms but even if nothing is said it will be implied as a matter of law that the employee is not to misappropriate his employer's property or misuse his trade secrets or confidential information. (Restraints against competition by ex-employees are discussed in Ch. IX below.)

A. Misappropriation of property

167. The employee is obliged to keep proper accounts, and if he receives any secret profit or bribe this belongs to his employer and he can be made to account for it.[1] Misappropriation of property is a ground for summary dismissal at common law, even if the facts come to light only after the dismissal.[2] The dismissal will be lawful under the unfair dismissals legislation provided that the employer had reasonable grounds for his belief at the time of dismissal, and carried out as much investigation as was reasonable in the circumstances.[3] Where misappropriation is discovered only after the contract has been terminated with due notice, the employee is still entitled to the contractual remuneration for the period after the breach during which normal services were rendered.[4]

1. Goff and Jones, *The Law of Restitution*, 2nd ed., London, 1978, p. 508.
2. *Boston* v. *Ansell* (1888) 39 Ch. D. 339 (CA).
3. *British Home Stores Ltd.* v. *Burchell* [1980] ICR 303; approved in *Weddell & Co. Ltd.* v. *Tepper* [1980] ICR 286 (CA).
4. *Horcal* v. *Gatland* [1984] IRLR 291 (CA).

B. Spare-time work

168. Unless the parties have expressly agreed to the contrary, there is generally no restriction on a worker taking spare-time work. However, he cannot take a job which might inflict harm on his principal employer. So an injunction may be granted to restrain an employee from working for a rival employer during his spare-time, and competitive work would normally justify dismissal by the employer. It is probably not enough that the spare-time work is in the same field of activity as that of the principal employer. There must be substantial drain on the employee's time or energies or some clear danger causing loss to the employer.[1]

1. *Hivac Ltd.* v. *Park Royal Scientific Instruments Ltd.* [1946] Ch. 169; *Nova Plastics Ltd.* v. *Froggett* [1982] IRLR 146.

C. Trade secrets and confidential information

169. An employee must not disclose the employer's trade secrets to a third party, nor misuse confidential information acquired in the course of employment. In some situations, this obligation may continue even after the employment has ended (on which see para. 365, below). In the absence of an express term on these matters, the obligations of the employee are the subject of implied terms. While the employee remains in the employment of the employer, the extent of the duty of fidelity will vary according to the nature of the contract. The duty will be broken if an employee makes or copies a list of the customers of the employer for use after his employment ends or deliberately memorises such a list. The obligation not to use or disclose information clearly covers secret processes of manufacture, such as chemical formulae, or designs and other information which is of a sufficiently high degree of confidentiality to amount to a trade secret.[1] In *Thomas Marshall (Exports) Ltd.* v. *Guinle*[2] a general test of the class of protected information was suggested, namely if (i) the owner reasonably believed that its release would be injurious to him or her; (ii) the owner reasonably believed that it was not yet in the public domain, and (iii) the information could be judged confidential in the light of the usage and practices of the particular industry or trade.

1. *Faccenda (Chickens) Ltd.* v. *Fowler, The Times,* 11 December 1985, CA; *Herbert Morris Ltd.* v. *Saxelby* [1916] AC 688 at 704.
2. [1978] ICR 905.

170. It is not a breach of the employee's duty of confidentiality if he disclosed 'any misconduct of such a nature that it ought in the public interest to be disclosed to others'.[1] This category of 'misconduct' no doubt includes the commission of a crime or other unlawful act by the employer, but it is not clear what other matters must be disclosed 'in the public interest'. It was held in one case that an employee was entitled to reveal an arrangement by his former employers to maintain prices, allegedly in contravention of fair competition legislation, on the grounds that this affected the 'public interest'.[2] In such cases the person to whom the information is disclosed must have a 'proper interest' in receiving it. It would be rare for the misconduct to be of such a nature to justify disclosure to the press.

1. *Initial Services Ltd.* v. *Putterill* [1968] 1 QB 396.
2. *Initial Services Ltd.* v. *Putterill* [1968] 1 QB 396.

171. The employer who alleges that his trade secrets or confidences have been betrayed may seek remedies in the ordinary civil courts. An injunction may be granted restraining the employee or ex-employee from acting in breach of his duties, and he may be ordered to account for the profits made through their use, and also to pay damages for breach of contract. The employer may be able to dismiss the employee without notice provided proper procedures are followed (below, Ch. VII).

172. A consequence of the rules about confidential information is that individual employees are not at liberty to disclose information which may be relevant to collective bargaining to trade unions, and workers representatives on company organs are likewise bound by the ordinary rules as to breach of confidence. A trade union official who induces an employee to disclose information for collective bargaining purposes before a claim has been prepared may be restrained by injunction and ordered to pay damages.[1] However if a dispute with an employer exists or is in immediate contemplation, the trade union official inducing the employee to disclose information would be immune from civil proceedings by reason of the statutory protection given to any person inducing a breach of contract 'in contemplation or furtherance of a trade dispute'.[2] The employee who disclosed such confidential information to a trade union may nevertheless be in breach of contract even during a trade dispute.[3]

1. *Bent's Brewery Co. Ltd.* v. *Hogan* [1945] 2 All ER 570.
2. TULRA 1974, s. 13; see Part II, Ch. V.
3. *Norbrook Laboratories* v. *Sands* [1984] IRLR 201. (Northern Ireland CA).

173. An employer is under a *duty* to disclose information to trade unions for collective bargaining purposes in certain circumstances, which are discussed in Part II, Ch. IV.

174. The duty of fidelity does not, however, oblige the employee to disclose his or her own misconduct. In the leading case, Lord Atkin said: 'The servant owes a duty not to steal, but having stolen, is there a superadded duty to confess that he has stolen? I am satisfied that to imply such a duty would be a departure from the well-established usage of mankind and would be to create obligations entirely outside the normal contemplation of the parties'.[1] This decision of the House of Lords seems to rest upon the general idea of the right not to incriminate oneself, and serves to protect the right to retain wages already paid, before the misconduct is discovered.[2] However, the principle of fidelity dictates that the employee, particularly if he or she is in a managerial or supervisory position, may be obliged to disclose the misconduct of fellow employees.[3]

1. *Bell* v. *Lever Bros. Ltd.* [1932] AC 161 at p. 813.
2. Mark Freedland in (1984) 13 *Industrial Law Journal* 25 at p. 30.
3. *Sybron Corporation* v. *Rochem Ltd.* [1983] ICR 801 (CA); *Swain* v. *West (Butchers) Ltd.* [1936] 3 All ER 261.

§3. The Duty of Reasonable Care

A. The employee's duty

175. An employee is under a duty to exercise reasonable skill and care in the exercise of his or her duties. What is reasonable depends upon all the circumstances, and different standards may apply according to whether (1) the employer seeks damages or an indemnity from the employee for the financial loss to the employer resulting from the negligence, or (2) the employer seeks to dimiss the negligent employee.

I. The employer's claim for damages or an indemnity

176. There are two legal bases upon which an employer may seek damages or an indemnity. The first arises under the Civil Liability (Contribution) Act 1978, which allows a joint tortfeasor (*i.e.*, wrongdoer) who is liable to a third party in respect of any damage to recover a contribution (which may be a full indemnity) from any other tortfeasor who is, or would if sued have been liable in respect of that same damage. The usual situation in which this applies is where an employee in the course of his employment negligently injures a fellow-employee, who then claims damages from their common employer. The employer may then join the negligent employee as a third party to the proceedings, if he is not already a co-defendant, and seek a contribution. The second basis for an indemnity rests on a controversial decision of the House of Lords in the case *Lister* v. *Romford Ice and Cold Storage Co. Ltd.* (1957)[1] in which it was decided, as a matter of law, that there was an implied duty in a lorry-driver's employment contract to exercise reasonable care about his employer's business.

1. [1957] 1 All ER 125.

177. In practice, these rights are not often enforced against employees.[1] The reason is that usually the employer does not suffer any loss because he is insured in respect of liability to his own employees (such insurance has been compulsory since 1 January 1972),[2] and for liability to third parties suffering injuries in road accidents (such insurance is also compulsory). Only if the employer's insurance company chooses to exercise its rights of subrogation under the contract of insurance will an attempt be made to claim an indemnity from an employee. In fact, as a result of a threat of nationalization after *Lister*'s case (above), most insurance companies are now parties to a 'gentlemen's agreement' not to enforce their rights of subrogation against employees. Recently, the Court of Appeal has refused to allow the right of subrogation to be enforced in an industrial setting, because of the potential disruption to labour relations, in circumstances where the 'gentlemen's agreement' did not apply.[3]

1. An example of the (rare) use of the right of action is *Janata Bank* v. *Ahmed* [1981] ICR 791 (CA) where the damages exceeded £36,000.
2. Employers Liability (Compulsory Insurance) Act 1969.
3. *Morris* v. *Ford Motor Co. Ltd.* [1973] QB 792.

II. The power of dismissal

178. In general, a single act of negligence will not justify termination of the employment contract without notice.[1] Under the law of unfair dismissal it is only gross negligence which would justify dismissal without a warning and an opportunity to improve performance. It has been recognised, however, that there are certain occupations (such as the pilot of an aircraft and the driver of an express train) where a single act of negligence in a matter central to the employee's duties might render the dismissal fair although there has been no previous misconduct, and the employee has rendered long service (see Ch. VII, below).[2]

1. *Jupiter General Insurance Co. Ltd.* v. *Shroff* [1937] 3 All ER 67.
2. *Turner* v. *Pleasurama Casinos* [1976] IRLR 151.

B. The employer's duty

179. An employee who is injured at work may seek to hold his employer responsible on two possible grounds: (1) the breach of a common law duty to exercise reasonable care for the safety of employees in the course of their employment, or a statutory duty to take specified precautions for the employee's safety; or (2) the breach of a common law or statutory duty owed by a fellow-employee to the injured employee, the employer being vicariously liable for the torts (delicts) of his employees. The first of these duties may be classified either as an implied term of the contract of employment or as arising in tort (*ex delicto*). The second is normally classified as a duty in tort alone. (Before 1948,[1] an action against the employer on the second ground was barred by the doctrine of common employment.) This subject of compensation for work accidents, which in part rests on the employer's liability, and in part on Social Security law, lies beyond the scope of this monograph.[2] It must, however, be mentioned that, under section 2(1) of the Unfair Contract Terms Act 1977 (in force since 1 February 1978) any term of a contract or notice which excludes or restricts liability for death or personal injury resulting from negligence is void. Section 2(2) of the Act of 1977 prohibits exclusion or restriction of liability for negligence in the case of 'other loss or damage' (*e.g.* to property or economic interests) unless the term or notice satisfies a test of 'reasonableness'. These provisions extend to the contract of employment, but only in favour of the employee not the employer. These provisions do not appear to affect the kind of indemnity clause in *Lister*'s case (above para. 176).

1. Law Reform (Personal Injuries) Act 1948, s.1.
2. See J. L. Munkman, *Employer's Liability at Common Law*, 10th ed., London, 1985.

Chapter IV. Working Time and Holidays

§1. The Importance of Collective Agreements

180. It is a distinctive feature of British labour law that there is no general legislation laying down minimum standards for the length of the working day or the number of rest days and holidays. There is a regulation of hours and holidays in agriculture and in those industries covered by wages councils but this coverage is in the process of being substantially reduced by removing workers under 21 years of age from protection and eliminating a number of wages councils (see paras. 205–212, below). Indeed, the United Kingdom Government has declined to accept the obligations in ILO Recommendation No. 116 and article 2(1) of the European Social Charter, concerning reduction of hours of work, on the grounds that these are 'not consistent with the methods by which conditions of employment are normally determined in the United Kingdom'.[1] Instead, the substantial gains which have been achieved in most industries in this respect are largely the result of collective agreements. Where trade unions are recognised for collective bargaining purposes, both the length of the working week and holiday entitlement are subjects of negotiation.[2] Particularly important gains have been made since 1980, with a general reduction in the average basic hours per week from 40 in 1979 to 39 in 1984.[3] While this is in accordance with well-established trade union policies,[4] the economic recession is also an important contributing factor. Similarly, entitlements to paid holidays (in addition to public or customary holidays) have increased since 1979. By the end of 1984, 95 per cent of manual workers subject to national collective agreements had a minimum entitlement of four weeks or more and nearly a fifth had a minimum entitlement of five weeks or more. The average was about 22 days. In many cases, actual holiday entitlements are higher than minima because of additions for seniority, local arrangements etc.[5] It should nevertheless be stressed that the absence of statutory minimum standards means that it is always possible for individual employers and employees to override collectively agreed minima by expressly agreeing a longer working week or fewer holidays.

1. Cmnd. 1993, London, HMSO, 1963.
2. Daniel and Millward, *op. cit.*, p. 197.
3. *Employment Gazette*, April 1985, p. 154.
4. It has been TUC policy since 1972 to achieve a reduction in the working week with no loss of pay.
5. *Employment Gazette*, April 1985, vol. 93, p. 156.

181. Proof that a collective agreement has been incorporated into the individual contract is facilitated by the requirement in section 1 of the Employment Protection (Consolidation) Act 1978 that the employer must give the employee particulars relating to hours of work, and entitlement to holidays and holiday pay (above para. 133). The statement of particulars may refer to a collective agreement.

§2. STATUTORY RESTRICTIONS ON THE WORKING DAY

182. There are a number of Acts of Parliament, a legacy of 19th Century social reforms, which limit the working hours of children, young persons and women in particular industries and certain occupations. These are enforced by the Health and Safety Executive. The most important of these statutes relate to *women and young persons* (*i.e.* under 18 years of age) *in factories.* Part VI of the Factories Act 1961 provides that the total hours worked by a woman over 18 in a factory may not exceed 9 a day or 48 in any week; a woman may not begin work earlier than 7 a.m. and end later than 8 p.m., and periods of continuous employment are limited. These rules and various others laid down in the legislation are subject to complicated exceptions. The Secretary of State and, in some cases, the Health and Safety Executive have the power to grant exemptions from these provisions. The fact that an employer has (as required by law) introduced equal pay for men and women is not in itself a ground for exemption. This protection for women is kept under review by the Equal Opportunities Commission in consultation with the Health and Safety Executive.[1] Legislation is expected in 1986 to repeal those provisions relating to adult women (see para. 352, below).

1. SDA, s. 55.

183. Young persons are given similar protection under the Factories Act, and their overtime working is strictly limited to 50 hours a year and then only by special permission. There are also special restrictions on shift work and *continuous* employment by young persons in factories. The Employment of Women, Young Persons and Children Act 1920 and the Hours of Employment (Conventions) Act 1936, giving effect to ILO Conventions, severely restrict the employment of women and young persons in industrial undertakings between 10 p.m. and 5 a.m.

*184.*There is other legislation prescribing the meal times and hours of employment of young persons in shops,[1] and the hours of women and young persons on the surfaces of mines are also limited by statute.[2] The Young Persons (Employment) Acts 1938 and 1964 control the hours and holidays of young persons in specified jobs such as goods delivery, errands, hotels, public places, lifts, cinemas and laundries.

1. Shops Act 1950.
2. Mines & Quarries Act 1954, ss. 124–128, Sched. IV.

185. It is rare for there to be any statutory limits on the hours of work of adult men. Among the few instances are (1) Under Acts passed in 1908, 1919 and 1954, a miner may spend no more than 7 hours a day underground, with certain exceptions; (2) Under the Baking Industry (Hours of Work) Act 1954, night work in bakeries is limited; (3) The Hours of Employment (Conventions) Act 1936 restricts the hours of sheet glass-workers; (4) Part VI of the Transport Act 1968 limits the hours of work of drivers of certain classes of vehicles to 10 hours a day, or exceptionally 14, with a maximum of 60 hours per week, and lays down rest periods and limits continuous driving. EEC Regulation 543/69 on the harmonization of legislation on road transport applied to international transport operations from 1 April 1973 and Community rules in respect of national operations since 31 December 1980.[1]

1. Commission Decision 78/85 of 21 December 1977 (OJ 1978, L33/78 of 3 February 1978). For the detailed regulations see *Encyclopedia of Labour Relations Law* (eds. Hepple and O'Higgins) Part 11A.

§3. STATUTORY PROVISIONS RELATING TO HOLIDAYS

186. There is no general legislation on holidays.[1] Indeed, the only legislation which imposes a direct obligation on the employer is the Factories Act 1961 which requires a *factory* occupier to allow the whole of Christmas Day, Good Friday and every Bank (*i.e.* Public) Holiday to women and young persons employed in the factory. On giving 3 weeks' notice the occupier may substitute some other weekday for each of these holidays. Bank Holidays apply as of right only to those men and women working in financial institutions,[2] but they are not infrequently applied (by collective agreement or managerial discretion) to other employees, or alternative days off in lieu of these holidays are granted. However, for such employees these holidays are not enjoyed as of statutory right. The current Bank Holidays are – New Year's Day, Easter Monday, the first and last Mondays in May, the last Monday in August, 26 December (if not a Sunday), 27 December (in a year in which 25 or 26 December is a Sunday).

1. There is regulation of holidays by Wages Councils in agriculture and several other industries not effectively covered by collective bargaining (see paras. 205–212, below).
2. Banking and Financial Dealings Act 1971, which confers a power to suspend financial and other dealings on bank holidays. In Scotland 2 January is also a bank holiday.

§4. TIME OFF WORK

187. Employees have the statutory right to take time off during working hours in six situations.

A. Union officials

188. Employees who are officials of independent trade unions recognised by the employer for purposes of collective bargaining are entitled to reasonable time off with pay.[1] (An official includes a shop steward.) This time may be used for any duties concerned with industrial relations with the employer or an associated employer or for industrial relations training relevant to the official's duties, and approved by his union or the TUC. A Code of Practice, giving guidelines, on the amount of time off and circumstances in which it can be taken has been issued by ACAS.

1. EPCA 1978, s. 27.

B. Union members

189. Members of independent trade unions recognised by the employer are entitled to reasonable time off for activities of their union and in order to represent the union.[1] This does not include time off for industrial action. It is time off without pay. The ACAS Code of Practice gives guidelines.

1. EPCA 1978, s. 28

C. Public duties

190. An employee must be allowed reasonable time off for certain specified public duties (such as justice of the peace, member of a tribunal, or member of a local authority or the governing body of any educational establishment).[1] This time off may be used only for attending meetings and for executive functions. This is time off without pay. No Code of Practice is to be issued.

1. EPCA 1978, s. 29.

D. Redundant employees

191. An employee who has been given notice of dismissal by reason of redundancy has the right to reasonable time off during the notice period to seek new employment or to make arrangements for training.[1] The employee must have been continuously employed for 2 years or more.

1. EPCA 1978, s. 31.

E. Ante-natal care

192. An employee who is pregnant has the right not to be unreasonably refused time off with pay during her working hours to enable her to keep an appointment to attend at any place for the purpose of receiving ante-natal care.[1] This has to be on the advice of a medical practitioner, midwife or health visitor and a certificate or appointment card must be produced for a second or subsequent appointment.

1. EPCA 1978, s. 31A.

F. Safety representatives

193. The Safety Representatives and Safety Committees Regulations 1977[1] require employers to permit safety representatives[2] appointed by an independent trade union to take such time off with pay as is necessary for the purposes of performing his or her statutory safety functions and undergoing reasonable training in relation to those functions having regard to the Health and Safety Commission's Code in regard to training.

1. S.I. 177 No. 500, reg. 3(1).
2. See Part II, Ch. III below for the structure and functions of these committees and representatives.

G. Claims for breach of rights

194. In each of the above cases, the employees may complain to an industrial tribunal within 3 months of the failure to give time off. If the complaint is well-founded, the tribunal may make a declaration. In the case of trade union officials and safety representatives, the tribunal may award the remuneration due as well as compensation, having regard to the employer's default and the employee's loss. Union members and employees with public duties may be awarded compensation but no remuneration is due to them. A redundant employee may claim up to two-fifths of a week's pay and a pregnant woman may claim the remuneration due in respect of time off for ante-natal care.

H. Excluded classes of employees

195. The most important exclusion from the above rights concerns part-time workers. Those normally working less than 16 hours weekly (or 8 hours in some situations) are excluded from the first three rights set out above, and the requirement of two years' continuous service in the case of redundant employees makes it difficult for part-timers to qualify. Part-timers are, however, eligible for time off for ante-natal care, as are all other employees. Employees normally working outside Great Britain are excluded from all the remaining rights as are share fishermen. Merchant seamen may not claim time off for public duties or workseeking when redundant.

Chapter V. Remuneration and Benefits

§1. REGULATION OF REMUNERATION

196. Apart from periods of incomes policy (see Introduction, paras. 57–63, above), there has been little state intervention into levels of pay. The main examples of pay regulation are the minimum wage legislation, which only operates in small pockets of industry (see paras. 205–212, below) and the Equal Pay Act 1970, which obliges employers to pay men and women at the same rates for like work or work of equal value (see Part I, Ch. VIII, below). Pay determination is largely left to collective bargaining, individual negotiation or unilateral management decision-making. The pattern of wage differentials between industries has remained remarkably stable over time, with industries such as newspaper printing, oil refining and air transport consistently among the best paid industries and catering, agriculture and retail distribution among the worst paid.[1]

1. See generally D. Marsden, Ch. 11, *Industrial Relations in Britain* (ed. G. S. Bain), Oxford 1983, pp. 264–265.

§2. PAYMENT SYSTEMS

197. Methods of remuneration are a central feature of workplace industrial relations. They have an important influence on the opportunities available for bargaining and the extent of management control.[1] In addition, they reflect crucial distinctions within the workforce, particularly the differences between manual and non-manual workers. Manual workers are more likely to be subject to payment systems based on direct sanctions and incentives than non-manual workers. On the other hand, incentive-based payment systems tend to present more opportunities for bargaining than the fixed remuneration paid to most non-manual workers.[2]

1. W. Brown (ed.), *The Changing Contours of Industrial Relations*, p. 110.
2. W. W. Daniel and N. Millward, *Workplace Industrial Relations*, p. 200.

198. There is a wide variety of pay systems in Britain. One common form of payment is based on units of *Time* (monthly, weekly, daily or hourly). Monthly payment is an indication of high ('staff') status and is usually associated with non-manual workers. *Overtime*, which is generally remunerated at a higher (premium) rate (*e.g.* time-and-a-half) constitutes an important element in the pay of manual employees. In 1984, for example, employees in manufacturing industries worked an average of 8.9 hours per week overtime.[1] It remains true to say, as the Donovan Royal Commission did in 1968, that 'overtime is widely used in Britain to give adult males levels of pay which they and those who arrange the overtime regard as acceptable'.[2] The statutory definition of a 'week's pay' for the purposes of compensation in the event of redundancy, unfair dismissal and other statutory rights does not, however, include overtime pay unless overtime is obligatory on both the employer and the employee.[3] Problems arising out of uneven distribution of overtime have been a frequent source of shop floor conflict, and there are many informal and formal rules enforced by unions to ensure equality of overtime.

1. *Employment Gazette*, June 1985, vol. 93, p. 519.
2. Report of the Royal Commission on Trade Unions and Employers' Associations, Cmnd. 3623, para. 92.
3. EPCA 1978, Sch. 14. *Tarmac Roadstone Holdings Ltd.* v. *Peacock* [1973] 1 WLR 594 (CA); *c.f. Lotus Cars Ltd.* v. *Sutcliffe & Stratton* [1982] IRLR 381 (CA). See below, para. 214.

199. Also important is the payment system known as *Payment By Results* (PBR), whereby pay is related to effort and output. Although the traditional aim of PBR is to encourage workers to raise their output, it has increasingly become an instrument of management control designed to ensure consistency of output. There is a wide variety of PBR systems, ranging from long established pieceworking to complex systems of commission and bonus payments. In 1982, as many as 44.5 per cent of full-time men aged 21 or over were in receipt of PBR. PBR is most common among male manual workers in the private sector and is relatively rare among non-manual workers.[1]

1. Daniel and Millward, *op. cit.*, p. 20; for an earlier view see Donovan Commission, paras. 87–89.

200. Payment by results systems have been a fertile source of dispute over such matters as price fixing, inequality of earnings of different members of a work group and shortage of work. This gives many opportunities for informal plant level bargaining and the establishment of customary arrangements. For example, workers themselves may set limits on earnings to equalise benefits, or institute various forms of 'fiddling the system' to help members of a group over fluctuations in output. Recently, however, there has been a tendency to base schemes on relatively rigorous work study techniques rather than the traditional intuitive methods of rate fixing, decreasing the scope for informal and fragmented pay bargaining.[1] Moreover, some bonus schemes, such as that operated by the National Coal Board, are assessed on a plant to plant basis, rather than considering individual output, leading, as in the coal-mining industry, to conflicts of interest between workers at pits with more productive potential and those at less productive pits. Unlike overtime, PBR is included in the statutory calculation of a week's pay.[2]

1. K. Sisson and W. Brown, Ch. 6 in Bain (ed.), *op. cit.*, p. 141.
2. EPCA 1978, Sch. 14 Part II, paras. 3(3), (4), (6).

201. One system which enjoyed a brief period of popularity was called *Measured Day Work*, according to which workers were paid at time rates higher than those usual in the industry in return for maintaining a specified level of work performance. Measured day work schemes spread rapidly in the late 1960s in response to the pay policy of 1965–1969 (above, paras. 57–63), under which improved productivity was a justification for exceptional pay increases. With the demise of incomes policies, this system has been of declining significance.

202. Great emphasis is placed in pay bargaining on comparisons between different grades of workers, and disagreements over differentials are a common cause of dispute. One way of rationalizing grading systems is to use a *Job Evaluation Scheme*, defined by the Trades Union Congress as a method to 'determine the relationship between jobs and to establish a systematic structure of wage rates for them'.[1] Several methods of job evaluation are in use. Some are based on a simple ranking of jobs, while others use a more complex system whereby jobs are awarded points according to characteristics such as skill, responsibility and physical effort. Job evaluation is used in relation both to time payments and payments by results. In 1980, about 23 per cent of establishments reported that some employees at the establishment were covered by job evaluation schemes, and such schemes were particularly prevalent in larger establishments, in the private sector and in manufacturing industry.[2] In many cases, employee representatives sit on review bodies. Job evaluation is also significant in relation to claims for equal pay under the Equal Pay Act 1970 (see para. 357, below).

1. TUC, *An Outline of Job Evaluation and Merit Rating*, London 1964, p. 1.
2. Daniel and Millward, *op. cit.*, pp. 203–205.

§3. Fringe Benefits

203. Fringe benefits, which may be defined as payments in cash or kind additional to salary, bonus and commission, are an increasingly significant form of remuneration, particularly among high-income earners and high-status occupations. Examples of such benefits among higher-paid employees are company cars, subsidised lunches, medical insurance and share acquisition schemes (interest free or at a reduced rate). In order to prevent tax avoidance on non-cash benefits, the Finance Act 1976 (ss. 60–72), as amended, provides a complex system of taxation, the broad effect being to tax as many benefits as possible. The Act provides that directors (with some exceptions) and higher paid employees, currently those earning £8,500 per year or more, are to be charged tax at the 'cash equivalent' of all benefits (normally the cost to the employer of providing the benefit). Special rules apply to provision of cars, petrol, beneficial loan arrangements and share purchase schemes. Although employees who are not directors or who earn less than £8,500 per annum are generally in a more favourable position, special rules apply to living accommodation, credit cards and vouchers.

§4. Occupational Pensions

204. Membership of occupational pension schemes has risen although the level of employment has fallen. Before the Second World War there were about 2.5 million members of such schemes; by 1983 there were 18 million members, of whom 11 million were current employees, 2 million with a right to a preserved pension relating to an earlier period of employment and about 5 million pensioners. In the private sector about 5.8 million, or 48 per cent of employees, are members; in the public sector there are about 5.3 million, or 95 per cent of employees.[1] Encouragement to occupational pensions was given by the Social Security Pensions Act 1975. Men aged 65 and over and women aged 60 and over who have retired from regular employment are entitled to the basic state pension, depending on their record of national insurance contributions over their working life, and also an additional earnings-related pension, depending on earnings since April 1978 on which contributions have been paid. The 1975 Act permits partial contracting-out from the full earnings-related contributions and benefits, where an occupational pension scheme provides the pensions required by the Act. The effect of contracting-out is that members of occupational schemes pay a reduced contribution to the state scheme and receive less benefit from it. The occupational scheme has to satisfy certain minimum standards and must secure a 'guaranteed minimum pension' (GMP) which broadly matches the state additional pension. An employer wishing to contract-out has to give notice to employees and any independent trade union recognised to any extent for the purpose of collective bargaining. The employer must also give information to and consult with such a trade union.[2] There must be equal access for men and women to the scheme, and breach of this requirement may also give rise to a complaint to an industrial tribunal.[3] The Government announced radical proposals, at the end of 1985, to reduce considerably the benefits under the state earnings-related scheme for those retiring after the year 2000; to make it easier for employers to set up contracted-out schemes, and to give employees the right to opt out of both the state earnings-related scheme and their employer's scheme by making their own personal pension arrangements instead. The result of these measures will be to reduce sharply the responsibility of both the state and employers for providing pensions. However pensions are likely to remain an important issue in pay negotiations for higher-status employees. They can also assume import- ance in the context of labour discipline, as evidenced by the controversy between the National Coal Board and the National Union of Mineworkers as to whether the Board is obliged to pay contributions to the Mineworkers' Pension Fund for miners who were on strike for the year 1984–1985.[4]

1. *Financial Times*, 2 January 1986.
2. Social Security Pensions Act 1975, s. 31(5), and the Occupational Pension Schemes (Contracting-out) Regulations 1984, SI 1984 No. 380, regs. 4, 10, 12, which provide for questions as to the independence of the trade union and compliance with the consultation requirements to be referred to an industrial tribunal.
3. Social Security Pensions Act 1975, s. 53 and the Occupational Pensions Scheme (Equal Access to Membership) Regulations 1976, SI 1976 No. 142, which modifies the Equal Pay Act 1970 (see Part I, Ch. VIII, below).
4. *The Guardian*, 9 January 1986.

§5. Minimum Wage Legislation

205. There is no general minimum wage legislation in Britain. In the words of Kahn-Freund:

> 'Ever since its inception in the [Trade Boards] Act of 1909, British minimum wage law (as distinct for example from French and American legislation) has had the characteristic of being selective. Minimum remuneration is not fixed for the whole of the economy, but for carefully chosen categories of workers. It is one example of the *ad hoc* nature of much of British labour legislation. Minimum remuneration is fixed only for workers in need of a statutory "floor" of wages and this was subsequently extended first to holidays and holiday remuneration and then to all other terms and conditions of employment. Criteria for selecting these workers have changed as one minimum wage statute followed another, and this has enabled the legislation to be adjusted to changing social conditions.'[1]
>
> 1. O. Kahn-Freund, *Labour and the Law*, 3rd ed., London 1983, pp. 46–47.

206. This approach is best understood in the context of two parallel policy objectives, namely, the prevention of low pay and the encouragement of collective bargaining. The earliest minimum wage legislation, instituted in 1909, concentrated on combating low pay, particularly in relation to 'sweated labour', employment characterised by starvation wages and inhuman working conditions. Later legislation also embodied the policy of encouraging collective bargaining, in the belief that low pay was closely associated with the absence of adequate collective bargaining machinery and correspondingly, that the development of such machinery was the best way of counteracting low pay. Thus, minimum wage fixing machinery may be established for a category of workers if the Secretary of State considers that no adequate machinery exists for the effective regulation of the remuneration of those workers or that such machinery as does exist is likely to cease to operate effectively.[1]

> 1. The current legislation is the Wages Councils Act 1979, but this is likely to be severely modified by legislation in 1986, see below, para. 212.

207. The policy of encouraging collective bargaining also helps to explain the structure of the wage-fixing machinery. Minimum wages are not determined centrally, but by wages councils, which set wages and other terms and conditions of employment for particular categories of workers. Wages councils consist of equal numbers of representatives of employers and employees (usually nominated by relevant employers' associations and trade unions), together with up to three independent persons (usually lawyers, university teachers or social workers) nominated by the Secretary of State, one of whom acts as chairman. The function of the independent members is to conciliate between the two sides, but if no agreement can be reached, the independent members may vote with either side. Ministers have no power to veto or amend decisions of wages councils. Interested persons are entitled to make representations. Agricultural Wages Boards regulate the wages of agricultural workers.[1]

1. Agricultural Wages Act 1948 and Agricultural Wages (Scotland) Act 1949.

208. Orders laying down minimum levels of pay and other terms of employment made by Wages Councils and the Agricultural Wages Boards are legally binding. Hence, unlike collective agreements, wages councils orders operate as compulsory minimum standards replacing any less favourable terms in the express or implied contracts of employees to whom they apply. Thus workers who are under-paid have a claim for breach of contract, subject to the usual limitation period of six years. In addition to the civil remedy, criminal sanctions apply. An employer who fails to comply with an order commits a criminal offence, triable before magistrates, and is liable on conviction to a fine of up to £200. There is provision for the magistrates to order a guilty employer to pay up to two years' arrears of remuneration to the relevant employees. The function of policing these provisions is entrusted to the Wages Inspectorate (and Agricultural Wages Inspectorate). The inspectors have powers to obtain information from employers and to bring legal proceedings in the name of and for the benefit of underpaid employees. But these powers are little used in practice (see below para. 210).

209. The system of wages councils has undergone several waves of expansion and contraction. It grew rapidly at the outset, and by 1921 there were 42 trade boards (as wages councils were then called) covering about 3 million workers mainly in manufacturing industry.[1] A peak of 66 wages councils concerned with 3.5 million workers was reached in 1953. Since then, abolitions and mergers have proceeded apace, so that in 1985 there were 26 wages councils covering about 2.75 million workers. Whereas the earlier wages councils were concentrated in manufacturing, the present system is largely concerned with service trades, with 86 per cent of all wages council workers in retailing and catering (1 million each) and hair-dressing (136,000). The most important manufacturing wages council is in clothing manufacture (0.25 million). The remaining wages councils are concerned with a patchwork of occupations, ranging from button manufacture to ostrich and fancy feather and artificial flowers to coffin furniture and cement making. As many as four-fifths of wages council employees are women.

1. See generally on the background, F. J. Bayliss, *British Wages Councils*, Oxford 1962. All figures are from the Department of Employment's Consultative Paper on Wages Councils, 1985.

210. The system of wages councils has been the object of much controversy. Neither of its dual aims has been wholly achieved. Low pay is an increasing problem in the economic recession of the 1980s, and few wages councils have been successfully substituted by collective bargaining machinery. There are several reasons for the lack of success in counteracting low pay. First, wages councils tend to set low minimum rates. In March 1985, most minimum full-time rates set by wages councils ranged from £63 to £72 per week, less than half the average weekly pay of adults. About1 million wages council workers are paid little or no more than the statutory minimum. Secondly, the Wages Inspectorate lacks the resources for effective enforcement. In 1984, there were only 120 inspectors and they were able to check about 11 per cent of establishments on the register, relying in the majority of cases on postal questionnaires rather than personal visits. The inspectors' policy is to secure compliance by advice and persuasion, rather than by prosecutions. Hence only two prosecutions reached the courts in 1984, leading to fines of about £107. A total of £1.87 million in arrears was paid to 18,000 employees. In addition, wages council orders have become inordinately complex, and the Wages Inspectorate attributes much of the underpayment to employers' misunderstanding of the orders. Finally, substantial pockets of low paid employees are found within high paying sectors,such as the civil service, where wages councils do not operate. Similarly, the lack of success in establishing adequate collective bargaining machinery has several explanations. In particular, wages councils industries have certain characteristics which make unionization difficult. Most establishments tend to be small, with the result that it is difficult to achieve a collective identity and to shield employees from direct employer pressure, whether patronizing or oppressive. Furthermore, almost two-thirds of wages council employees are part-timers (compared with about one-fifth in the economy generally) who are particularly difficult to recruit into unions.[1]

1. C. Pond, Ch. 8 in Bain (ed.), *op. cit.*, p. 196; D.E. Consultative Paper on Wages Councils, 1985; *Employment Gazette*, September 1985, vol. 93, p. 355.

211. The economic crisis of the 1980s has brought about a marked change in the flavour of the debate about wages councils. In the years of full employment of the 1950s and 1960s, it was argued that wages councils were no longer necessary, since a reasonable level of wages was maintained by market conditions. Indeed, it was thought that wages councils merely inhibited the establishment of effective bargaining. Councils could only be abolished on a joint application by employees and employers and the latter tended to oppose abolition in order to avoid direct bargaining.[1] Consequently, measures were enacted with the aim of making abolition easier, for example by allowing an application by either side. Similarly, provision was made for the Secretary of State to convert wages councils into Statutory Joint Industrial Councils (SJIC) which have similar powers to wages councils without independent members. These were intended to function as a half-way stage to full collective bargaining but none have been established.

1. *E.g.* Report of the Royal Commission on Trade Unions and Employers' Associations, Cmnd. 3623.

212. Present Government policies towards wages councils favour abolition for very different reasons, the argument being that wages councils restrict job opportunities and thus aggravate high unemployment, particularly among young people. According to a Department of Employment Consultative Paper in 1985, 'wages councils interfere with the freedom of employers to offer and job seekers to accept jobs at wages that would otherwise be acceptable'.[1] The

Government therefore proposes to introduce legislation in 1986 which would remove all employees under 21 from wages council regulation, and confine the functions of wages councils to that of setting a single minimum hourly rate and a single overtime rate for those over 21. In addition, procedures for abolishing wages councils are likely to be significantly simplified.[2] Such reforms would conflict with the UK's obligations under ILO Convention No. 26, which requires the creation and maintenance of wage-fixing machinery. To facilitate the new legislation, the Government notified the ILO of its intention to withdraw from the Convention with effect from July 1986.

1. DE Consultative Paper 1985, para. 7.
2. Statement in the House of Commons by Tom King, Employment Secretary, 17 July 1985.

§6. PAYMENT AND CALCULATION OF WAGES

A. A question of contract

213. Outside the Wages Councils industries, pay rates are fixed entirely as a matter of contract. As has been indicated above, pay is central to collective bargaining, with 9.5 million manual workers covered by national collective agreements in 1984. In such cases, the relevant collective agreements will usually be incorporated into the individual's contract of employment, either expressly or impliedly (see above, para. 149). In a few isolated cases (*e.g.* where an employer has failed to comply with an operative order to disclose information to a trade union), there may be a binding arbitration award of the CAC which is incorporated into the contract. The determination of wages is therefore a matter of agreement, and this may involve questions of interpretation. As explained earlier (above, para. 44) these questions of interpretation are often themselves resolved through a dynamic ongoing bargaining process and are generally not seen as disputes of rights. Only rarely will such questions reach the courts, for interpretation. The CAC has power to interpret its own awards.

B. The concept of a 'week's pay'

214. Special rules exist for the calculation of a 'week's pay' for statutory purposes. This precise calculation needs to be made, for example, to determine the amount of redundancy payment, and guaranteed payments during periods of lay-off and during the minimum periods of notice to determine the contract. These rules are set out in Schedule 14 to the Employment Protection (Consolidation) Act 1978. This makes it necessary to determine whether there are 'normal working hours' (these exclude overtime unless the employee is required to work overtime and the employer is required to provide it). If there are, the amount of a 'week's pay' depends on whether or not the amount of pay varies with the amount of work done. If it does not, a 'week's pay' is the amount payable under the contract on the 'calculation date' (this date differs according to the statutory rights in question). If it does vary, the amount of the 'week's pay' is then usually the amount of pay for the number of normal working hours in a week calculated at an hourly rate of remuneration payable in respect of a 12-week period. In cases where there are no 'normal working hours' a week's pay is the amount of the employee's average weekly remuneration over a 12-week period. In calculating pay for these purposes, benefits in kind (such as travelling allowances) are disregarded. The maximum amount of a week's pay for various statutory purposes is varied from time to time.[1]

1. From 1 April 1986, this has been raised from £152 to £155.

C. No agreement as to amount

215. If there is no express or implied provision in the contract of employment regarding the rate of rumeration the employee may claim a reasonable remuneration. So long as it can be shown that the work was agreed to be done on the basis that some payment was to be made, the common law implies a promise to pay what the services are worth (*quantum meruit*). However, if the circumstances show that the employer and employee did not intend an agreement to come into effect until the rate of remuneration was agreed then such a term cannot be implied. For example, a promise to pay an employee 'such remuneration as the directors may determine' will prevent the employee from claiming any remuneration unless and until the directors make a determination.[1] Similarly an arrangement that the parties will agree a future rise in salary does not oblige the employer to reach such an agreement.

1. *Re Richmond Gate Property Co. Ltd.* [1965] 1 WLR 335.

D. Payment for incomplete periods

216. Remuneration is payable only in arrears at the end of each period for which it is due, in the absence of an agreement between the parties to make advances on pay. The period of the employment for which payment is due depends on the express or implied agreement of the parties; for example it may be hourly, weekly, monthly or quarterly. At common law, the rule appears to have been that an employee could not recover any remuneration at all for a period which he did not complete, for any reason other than a breach of contract by the employer.[1] However, the Apportionment Act 1870, s. 2, provides that 'salaries' shall 'be considered as accruing from day to day and shall be apportioned in respect of time accordingly'. It is usually assumed that 'salaries' includes 'wages' (*i.e.* all remuneration) but this has not been authoritatively decided by the courts.[2] Nor is it entirely clear whether an employee who fails to complete a period because he is summarily dismissed on grounds of his own misconduct can claim wages for that part of the period for which he has worked, although the weight of academic opinion believes that he is so entitled.[3] Where the contract has come to an end by reason of 'frustration' (*i.e.* supervening impossibility of performance) without the fault of either party, the Law Reform (Frustrated Contracts) Act 1943 allows the court to order payment of a 'just' amount in respect of services to which the employer has had the benefit before the frustrating event (*e.g.* a fire burning down the workplace). In practice, employers nearly always pay for services actually performed even though the period of payment has not been completed.

1. *Cutter* v. *Powell* (1795) 6 TR 320.
2. *Moriarty* v. *Regent's Garage Co. Ltd.* [1921] 1 KB 423.
3. Glanville Williams, *Law Quarterly Review* 57 (1941) at p. 383; but cf. Paul Matthews *Legal Studies* 2 (1982), p. 302.

E. Manner of payment and deductions

217. As a general rule, employer and employees are free to agree as to the manner of payment, that is whether it is to be in cash or by cheque or otherwise. Similarly, the place of payment and the periods at which payment is to be made are left to the parties' determination. Only manual workers (other than domestic or menial employees)[1] and in some cases shop assistants are afforded legislative protection against employers' attempts to deprive them of the full value of their wages. Such protection is provided by the Truck Acts 1831 to 1940, which, as their vintage suggests, have become anachronistic and are expected to be repealed and replaced by new legislation in 1986.

1. See above, para. 120.

218. The Truck Acts regulated both the manner of payment and deductions from pay. With respect to the former, section 1 of the Truck Act 1831 rendered 'illegal, null and void' any contract for the payment of wages to a manual worker 'otherwise than in the current coin of the Realm'. The expression 'current coin' included banknotes. This was initially intended to prevent abuse of workers by enforced trading and payment in kind, but with the decline of payment in kind, such protection has become obsolete. Indeed, this legislation arguably obstructs the development of safer and easier methods of cashless pay. Some reform was instituted by the Payment of Wages Act 1960, which permits payment into a bank account, by money order, postal order or cheque, provided the consent of the manual worker is obtained and a number of other conditions are satisfied. The Wages Bill 1986 proposes to repeal the sections of the Truck Acts and related legislation dealing with manner of payment, on the grounds that 'the method of wage payment to manual workers need no longer be constrained by statute and can be left to be determined by employers, their employees and, where appropriate, their representatives. The methods of payment for non-manual employees has always been established in this way without statutory restriction or protection and, certainly in modern circumstances, without giving rise to serious practical problems'.[1]

1. Consultative Document issued by the Secretary of State for Employment, *Employment Gazette*, November 1984, p. 504.

219. The question of deductions from pay is more controversial. It is not uncommon for employers to deduct sums of money from employees' remuneration for negligent work, disciplinary offences, or cash and stock shortages, in some cases leading to a substantial reduction in wages.[1] The Truck Act 1896, which applies to shop assistants as well as manual employees, authorised deductions for fines, damaged goods and damaged materials provided certain criteria were satisfied. The Wages Bill 1986 proposes new procedures on deductions. These proposals, which would cover both manual and non-manual workers, would permit deductions only if they were authorised by statute (*e.g.* income tax and national insurance) or provided for in the individual's contract of employment, or if the employee has previously consented in writing. Where a worker's employment involves selling directly to the public any deduction from his or her wages on account of a cash shortage or stock deficiency may not exceed one-tenth of the gross amount of wages payable to him or her. A remedy would lie to an industrial tribunal for breach of these provisions. The emphasis in these proposals on the contract of employment has been criticised for providing inadequate protection for unorganised workers.[2]

1. See Tamara Goriely, 'Arbitrary Deductions from Pay and the Proposed Repeal of the Truck Acts' *Industrial Law Journal* 12 (1983), p. 236.
2. *Ibid.*

220. The courts interpreted the Truck Acts in such a way as to permit deductions from the wages of a manual worker at his or her request to be paid to a third person independent of the employer.[1] It is this interpretation which has permited trade union subscriptions to be deducted at the worker's request from wages (the check-off).[2] This will remain lawful under the proposed new legislation. There is, however, statutory regulation of the check-off in respect of any deduction from wages of the political levy which some unions collect from mebers to support their political funds[3] (see Part II, Ch. II, below).

1. *Hewlett* v. *Allen* [1894] AC 383.
2. *Williams* v. *Butlers Ltd.* [1975] ICR 308.
3. Trade Union Act 1984, s. 18.

221. The Wages Bill proposes to repeal a number of the old Acts relating to deductions from wages of special groups of workers. The new legislation will cover all workers, including not only these under contracts of service or apprenticeship but also any contract under which a person undertakes to do or perform personally any work or services for another party to the contract whose status is not that of a client or customer of any profession, or business undertaking carried on by the individual (see para. 116, above).

F. Payment by weight or value of materials

221. The method of calculation of wages is specially regulated in industries where employees are paid according to the weight or measure of the material produced. For example, in mining there have been statutory provisions since 1887. Miners may, at their own cost, and by a majority vote, appoint a checkweigher to determine correctly the weight of the mineral and the deductions to be made.[1] (A deduction may be made from miners' wages to pay the checkweigher.) This principle was extended to certain other industries by the Check Weighing in Various Industries Act 1919. Under the Factories Act 1961 wages inspectors may check the accuracy of weighing and measuring instruments used in factories in the ascertainment of wages. These statutes illustrate the fragmented patchwork of legislation concerning wage payment.

1. Stannaries Act 1887, s. 15; Coal Mines Regulation Act 1887, s. 13; Coal Mines (Weighing of Minerals) Act 1905; Coal Mines (Check Weigher) Act 1894 as amended by Mines & Quarries Act 1954, ss. 188, 189, Scheds. IV and V

G. Itemized pay statements

223. The Employment Protection (Consolidation) Act 1978, s. 8, gives every employee the right to be given, every time payment of wages or salary is made, a written pay statement, itemizing (1) the gross amount of wages or salary; (2) variable and fixed deductions; (3) the net amount of wages or salary payable; (4) where different parts of the net amount are paid in different ways, the amount and method of each part payment. A remedy for non-compliance with this provision may be obtained in an industrial tribunal.

§7. RIGHTS TO REMUNERATION ON EMPLOYERS' INSOLVENCY

224. Unpaid wages or salary owed to an employee by an employer are treated as preferential debts on the insolvency of the employer. The priority over other creditors extends only to 'wages' accrued during the four months before the date of insolvency and is limited to an amount of £800. 'Wages' is defined to include remuneration in respect of holidays, sick pay, and accrued holiday remuneration, and commission payments.[1] Preference is also accorded to certain statutory payments.[2]

1. Bankruptcy Act 1914 s. 33; Bankruptcy (Scotland) Act 1913, s. 118; Companies Act 1947, s. 115; Companies Act 1948, s. 319, as amended by Insolvency Act 1976, s. 1 and Sched. 1.
2. EPCA 1978, s. 121(2).

225. The Employment Protection (Consolidation) Act 1978[1] gives an employee the right to recover certain amounts owing to him by the insolvent employer from the Redundancy Fund (see below, para. 323). This includes up to 8 weeks' arrears of pay, pay for the minimum legal notice period, up to 6 weeks' holiday pay; any basic award of compensation for unfair dismissal, and reimbursement of premiums paid for apprenticeship or articles of clerkship, subject to certain maximum amounts which may be varied from time to time. The trustees of an occupational pension fund may also obtain payment of unpaid contributions owing to the fund. The Secretary of State, upon making a payment from the Fund, is subrogated to the rights and remedies of the employee against the insolvent employer. Disputes are dealt with by industrial tribunals.

1. EPCA 1978, s.122

§8. Remuneration during Lay-off and Short-time

226. Workers may be 'laid-off' or put on short-time for a variety of reasons, such as temporary fluctuations in production, closure of a plant due to causes beyond the employer's control (*e.g.* a failure of power supplies), or recession. The term 'lay-off' does not have a legal definition apart from the context of redundancy payments (below, para. 239) where it means that workers are not provided with work and, under their contracts, they are not entitled to pay. This, however, is not the meaning adopted in everyday industrial practice where the notion of 'lay-off' is taken to include any situation where the worker is not provided with work, and 'short-time' is a situation where the worker is provided with work for less than his or her normal working hours.

227. The legal rules regarding the maintenance of income during lay-offs and short-time are extremely complicated. It is necessary, first of all, to appreciate that a lay-off may take one of four different legal forms depending on the circumstances. These are discussed in turn.

A. Frustration of the contract

228. 'Frustration' means supervening impossibility of performance as by some event making the performance of the contract a physical impossibility or unlawful (*e.g.* the burning down of the factory). It is rare for a lay-off to occur in these circumstances, and if there is a possibility of the worker being re-employed within a short period there will be no frustration. If there is, then the worker loses any right to remuneration from the moment the event occurs.

B. The employee is dismissed

229. This is rare because lay-offs are generally of short duration. However, in a few exceptional cases (above, para. 164) failure to provide work to an employee (such as an actor) may constitute a dismissal by the employer. In that event the employee has no right to continue to receive his contractual remuneration but he may have claims in respect of unfair dismissal or for a redundancy payment (below Ch. VII).

C. The employee is dismissed but re-engaged when work resumes

230. This is frequent in certain industries such as shipbuilding and construction. Since he is dismissed he is not entitled to any contractual remuneration during the period of lay-off, but he may be able to claim a redundancy payment (below, para. 239) or if he has been unfairly selected for dismissal on grounds of redundancy he may be able to claim a remedy for unfair dismissal (below, Ch. VII). If he does not claim redundancy payment and is subsequently re-engaged, the 'temporary cessation of work' due to the lay-off will not affect his continuity of employment (*i.e.* seniority rights) (below, para. 282).

D. The employee is suspended from work

I. At common law

231. We have seen that although, at common law, an employer is under no general obligation to provide work, he must pay the employee. He cannot suspend an employee without pay, unless there is an express agreement to that effect. This means that whether the worker is paid according to time, or according to results (piece-work) he is entitled to his contractual remuneration even though there is no work for him to do.

232. There are, however, two exceptions to this general rule. First, the right to be paid may be excluded by express or implied agreement or by custom. An example of an express term was a case in 1936 where the contract provided that musicians would not be paid when they did not play, but the court interpreted this narrowly holding that the employers could refuse to pay only for those performances which it was reasonable for them to cancel.[1] Only one reported case is known to the authors in which an implied term or custom allowing the employer to refuse payment has been proved. This was where a boiler-scaler was employed whenever there was a job to be done. In between jobs he was laid-off. There was held to be an implied term, because of the casual nature of his employment, to lay him off without pay.[2] (In those circumstances he was then entitled to a redundancy payment, see below, para. 239.) Where, however, the employer does have a contractual right to lay a worker off indefinitely without pay, there is no implied term that the duration of the lay-off should be reasonable. Thus an employee cannot claim that the employer has repudiated the contract and thus that he or she has been constructively dismissed.[3]

1. *Minnevitch* v. *Café de Paris (Londres) Ltd.* [1936] 1 All ER 884.
2. *Puttick* v. *John Wright & Sons (Blackwall) Ltd.* [1972] ICR 457. Such a term is even less likely to be implied in the case of a white-collar employee: *Namyslo* v. *Secretary of State for Employment* [1979] IRLR 450 (Industrial Tribunal). A custom would have to be reasonable, certain and notorious: *Bond* v. *C.A.V. Ltd.* [1983] IRLR 360.
3. *Kenneth MacRae & Co. Ltd.* v. *Dawson* [1984] IRLR 5.

233. A second exception is where the employer's failure to provide work is due to circumstances beyond his control. For example, in a case in 1926 a colliery had to be closed to allow a dangerous state of affairs underground to be remedied. This had occurred through no fault of the employers. The court held that it was the implied intention of the parties that the risk of untoward events such as unsafe conditions or breakage of machinery should be shared.[1] It is not clear exactly how far this principle goes. What circumstances are 'outside the employer's control'? It seems likely that lay-offs caused by strikes at premises of suppliers of the employer fall within this concept. On the other hand, the court in an earlier case regarded a lay-off due to a trade recession as being within the employer's control, and so the employees laid-off remained entitled to remuneration.[2] This means that English law draws a curious distinction between lay-offs due to the fluctuations in trade, when remuneration must continue to be paid, and lay-offs due to circumstances such as mechanical failure or lack of materials, when a principle of risk-sharing is applied. Recent cases have tended to limit the scope of this exception.[3]

1. *Browning* v. *Crumlin Valley Collieries Ltd.* [1926] 1 KB 572.
2. *Devonald* v. *Rosser & Sons* [1906] 2 KB 728.
3. *Johnson* v. *Cross* [1977] ICR 872; *Bond* v.*C.A.V. Ltd.* [1983] IRLR 360.

II. Guaranteed week collective agreements

234. The insecurity of workers' income during periods of lay-off has led to the negotiation of many different types of collective agreement to maintain income during the first few days or weeks or lay-off or short-time working. Most of these agreements require the employee to be willing to accept an offer of suitable alternative employment, and the amount guaranteed is normally less than a full week's pay. These agreements generally take effect as express or implied terms of the individual contract (above, para. 149). In general the employer cannot unilaterally 'suspend' the guaranteed agreement without the consent of the employees concerned. If the standards laid down in the agreement are less favourable than the statutory guarantee payments they are superseded by the latter (below, para. 237). Conversely, it is possible to obtain exemption from the statutory scheme where alternative collective arrangements have been made. By 1985, 22 such exemptions had been granted.

III. Guarantee payments under the Employment Protection (Consolidation) Act 1978[1]

235. Collective bargaining has not provided adequate protection for earnings during lay-offs, and since 1 February 1977 every employee (with minor exceptions) is entitled to a guarantee payment for certain days when he is not provided with work. The maximum amount payable is currently £10.50 per day and in any period of 3 months an employee cannot receive guarantee payments for more than 5 days. The Secretary of State has power to raise these limits.

1. EPCA 1978, ss. 12–18.

236. In order to be eligible the employee must have been continuously employed by the same employer for 4 weeks. He can claim only in respect of a day on which he is normally required to work and he must have had no work throughout the whole of the day because of a dimunition in the requirements of the employer's business for work of the kind he was employed to do, or because of any other occurrence affecting the normal working of the employer's business in relation to work of the kind which the employee was employed to do. Guarantee payments may not be claimed if the failure to provide work is the result of a trade dispute (*i.e.* industrial action); or if the employee unreasonably refuses an offer of suitable alternative employment for the workless day; or if the employee fails to comply with reasonable requirements imposed by his employer to ensure that his services are available.

237. Although the rights to guarantee payments under statute are separate from rights to such payments under contract (including as we have seen collective agreements), a rule of mutual set-off applies. Any contractual remuneration received by an employee in respect of a workless day goes towards discharging the employer's liability to make the statutory payment. Conversely the statutory payment is set-off against the contractual remuneration. Disputes regarding statutory guarantee payments may be referred to industrial tribunals.

IV. Social Security benefits

238. State provision for employees affected by shortages of work has been available for much of the century. Unlike those countries which have special schemes for 'partial employment', in Britain this is dealt with by the general system of unemployment benefit, even if the employee has not been dismissed.[1] Employees are eligible provided they have made sufficient National Insurance contributions, but, as in other areas of social security, no benefit is payable for the first three ('waiting') days. More recently, as we have seen, some of the burden has been transferred to employers, via the system of statutory guarantee payments. Unemployment benefit is not payable for days in respect of which a guarantee payment, whether statutory or collectively agreed, is payable, and the waiting days only begin to run after the period of eligibility for statutory guarantee payments has ended. This complex inter-relationship may lead to difficulty where there is dispute as to whether or not an employee is eligible for statutory payments. The employer may take the view that the guarantee payment is not payable, but the social security adjudication officer may disagree, and refuse unemployment benefit. The employee's remedy as against the employer lies to an industrial tribunal, and an appeal is available within the social security system against the adjudications officer's decision, but both entail substantial delays and may lead to conflicting decisions.[2]

1. Other State subsidies have been available under a variety of schemes, the most recent being the Temporary Short-time Working Compensation Scheme, under which employers were re-imbursed for the costs of short-time working if they could show that this was an alternative to redundancy. This has been closed for further applications since March 1984. See further below, para. 277.
2. *Clemens* v. *Peter Richards* [1977] IRLR 332.

V. Redundancy payments

239. The Employment Protection (Consolidation) Act 1978 allows an employee to claim compensation for redundancy based on age and length of service for lay-offs and short-time in two situations: (1) where the employee is dismissed for redundancy, and (2) where the employee is laid-off or put on short-time within the definition of those terms in section 87 of the Act. The first situation is like any other redundancy dismissal and will be discussed in Chapter VII below. In both situations the employee must have been continuously employed for two years or more to qualify. In the second situation, to claim a redundancy payment the lay-off or short-time (or combination of the two) must have continued for 4 consecutive weeks or have occurred during 6 out of 13 weeks (weeks affected by strikes or lock-outs do not count). The employee must give notice of intention to claim a payment and give the minimum notice needed to terminate the contract. The employer must then contest liability by serving a counter-notice within 7 days of the employee's notice to claim, and by proving that there is reasonable expectation of work being provided. In order to fall under these provisions the 'lay-off' must be one in which the employee's pay depends upon being given work by the employer and the employee must not be being given this work and he must not be entitled to pay. The 'short-time' provisions apply where the dimunition of work causes the employee's earnings to drop to less than half a week's pay. These provisions are little used in practice.

Chapter VI. Incapacity for Work

§1. STATISTICS OF WORK ABSENCE

240. About 8 per cent of workers (including both employees and the self-employed) are absent from work in any one week, a figure which has remained constant for some years. The main reason for absence is illness or injury, with about 5 per cent of workers off sick in a random week. Generally, manual workers have higher levels of sickness than non-manual workers. Until 1980, there was no significant difference between sickness rates for men and for women but in 1980 and 1982, fewer men were found to be off sick than women, especially in the case of full-time workers. Women with dependent children under the age of 5 are the most likely to be absent for personal and other reasons.[1] Absence rates vary significantly between socio-economic groups and between industries.

    1. *General Household Survey*, 1982.

241. Research into the reasons for absence[1] indicates that many factors contribute to absences. Among these are: (1) age structure, with 'old' labour forces having greater amounts of absence than 'young' labour forces; (2) size of firm, with smaller firms having lower absence rates; (3) length of journey to work with long journeys being associated with higher absence rates; (4) lack of supervision in the firm, this often resulting in high absence rates; (5) sick-pay schemes in firms with those providing leave with pay having higher absence rates than those which do not.

    1. A review of the literature will be found in Incomes Data Services, *Absence*, Study No. 111, London, December 1975.

§2. INCOME MAINTENANCE DURING ABSENCE FROM WORK DUE TO SICKNESS OR INJURY

242. The maintenance of income of an employee who is absent from work because of sickness or injury depends on the interaction of three distinct sources. (1) The terms of the employee's contract of employment, express or implied or as a matter of custom and practice. (2) Social security benefits and statutory sick pay. (3) Lump-sum damages awarded by a court (or paid in settlement of a claim) where the sickness or injury is due to the fault of the employer or of those for whom he is responsible.

A. Remuneration under the contract of employment

243. Sick pay schemes set up either as a result of collective bargaining or unilaterally provided by management, have become widespread in the past 30 years. According to official statistics, by 1974 about 80 per cent of full-time employees were in occupational sick pay schemes.[1] However, recently published survey evidence indicates that these statistics are not an accurate guide to the actual receipt of sick pay.[2] In the survey, of those who had held their employment for less than 6 months, only 25 per cent obtained some sick pay; for those with 6 months' but less than 2 years' service, 49 per cent obtained some; and for those with more than 5 years' service, 62 per cent obtained some. A typical recipient (in 1976 and 1977) was someone absent for up to 26 weeks being paid £26 to £30 per week. Where there is a sick pay scheme this will usually be incorporated into the contract of employment either expressly or by implication. Proof of the employee's rights is aided by the employer's statutory obligation to give written particulars of any terms and conditions relating to incapacity for work due to sickness or injury, including any provisions for sick pay.[3] However, there remain significant numbers of employees without contractual provision particularly among female manual and part-time workers.

1. Department of Health and Social Security, *Report on a Survey of Occupational Health Schemes*, 1977.
2. Donald Harris *et al.*, *Compensation and Support for Illness and Injury*, Oxford Socio-Legal Studies, Oxford 1984, pp. 321–323.
3. EPCA 1978, s. 1(3) (*d*)(ii).

244. If there is no sick pay scheme, there may be a custom relating to sick pay or a term may be implied. In some older cases, it was held that if the contract was silent as to the employee's right to sick pay, there was a presumption that the employer's obligation to pay wages continued until the contract was determined by notice.[1] However, the existence of such a presumption has been rejected in more recent cases.[2] Instead, the Court of Appeal has said that the evidence in each case should be approached with 'an open mind, unprejudiced by any precondition, presumption or assumption',[3] the aim being to discover what the agreement was. In seeking evidence of the agreement, the court is entitled to look at the subsequent conduct of the parties. Thus if an employee has never received sick pay, the Court is likely to imply that he or she has no right to it.[4] Moreover, if there is a contractual right to sick pay, but the duration is not specified, there is no presumption that sick pay lasts until the contract is determined. Instead the court will imply a reasonable term as to duration, and in an industry where the normal practice is to apply sick pay for a limited period only, the reasonable term to imply is the term normally applicable in that industry.[5] The only statutory requirement is that the employee should be paid in full during the compulsory minimum period of notice.[6]

1. *Marrison* v. *Bell* [1939] 2 KB 187; *Orman* v. *Sasville Sportswear Ltd.* [1960] 1 WLR 1055.
2. *Mears* v. *Safecar Security Ltd.* [1982] ICR 626 (CA); *Howman* v. *Blyth* [1983] ICR 416 (EAT).
3. [1982] ICR 626 at p. 649.
4. [1982] ICR 626.
5. *Howman* v. *Blyth* [1983] ICR 416.
6. EPCA 1978, s. 50 and Sched. 3.

B. Social security benefits and statutory sick pay

245. The principle of compulsory insurance was adopted (following the example of Germany) in the National Insurance Act 1911. In return for contributions, manual employees and certain low-earning non-manual employees were entitled to free medical treatment from doctors who agreed to participate, and the contributor also received sickness benefit which lasted for 26 weeks but could be extended for disablement. The scheme was administered by Approved Societies, including friendly societies and trade unions. The number of persons covered gradually increased between 1911 and 1946. In 1942, in his famous report on Social Insurance and Allied Services,[1] Sir William Beveridge criticised the provision for sickness and invalidism on the grounds that it was insufficiently concerned with improving health, provided too low a level of benefits, and was inadequately administered by the Approved Societies. The scheme initiated in 1946 under the inspiration of the Beveridge report retained the basic principle of social insurance conferring benefits at a flat-rate subsistence level in respect of major causes of income loss. Social insurance was made comprehensive, covering previously excluded groups and administration was unified under a Department of State. At the same time, a free and comprehensive National Health Service was established. The Beveridge scheme failed to meet its basic objective of establishing a national minimum of income support for 'normal needs' while leaving 'room and encouragement for voluntary action by each individual to provide more than that minimum for himself and his family'.[2] Successive governments kept the level of flat-rate insurance benefits below the subsistence level, so that the number of those relying on means-tested supplementary benefits (formerly called national assistance) has steadily increased. The means-tested benefit, rather than contributory social insurance, provides the minimum level of income for the poorest section of injured and disabled persons. Moreover, the Beveridge scheme failed to make adequate provision for the long-term disabled. This has led governments, in response to pressure groups, to make *ad hoc* provision for specific sections of the disabled such as workers suffering from certain dust-related diseases whose former employers are no longer in business.[3] There was a departure from the flat-rate principle when earnings-related sickness benefits were introduced in 1966 and this was extended to certain other benefits such as invalidity pensions, so bringing the British social security system closer to that on the Continent of Europe. However, there was a radical reversal in 1982 when earnings-related supplements were abolished in respect of short-term sickness benefit. This was designed to save public expenditure and to facilitate bringing the relevant benefits into taxation. The Beveridge principle of flat-rate contributions failed to generate an adequate level of benefits, and as a result there was a shift to a system of earnings-related contributions.

1. Cmnd. 6404 (1942).
2. *Ibid.*, para. 9.
3. Pneumoconiosis etc. (Workers' Compensation) Act 1979.

246. The Beveridge scheme, as implemented in post-war legislation, improved sickness benefit and made provision for dependants' allowances. Benefit was payable for an unlimited period but the distinction between short-term and long-term benefits was retained after a year's entitlement to benefit. In 1971, an invalidity benefit was introduced for those incapable of work for more than 6 months. This supplemented the standard flat-rate benefit by an allowance graded according to the age at which the claimant became incapable of work. The invalidity benefit is available (from 6 April 1986, after 28 weeks of incapacity) with fewer contribution conditions than the standard benefit, and dependants are treated more generously. A number of other specific needs of the disabled are met with non-contributory benefits such as attendance allowance for the severely disabled who require frequent attention, an invalid care allowance for those who are unable to work because they have to care for a severely disabled relative, and a severe disablement allowance for those continuously incapable of work and disabled to the extent of 80 per cent for more than 28 weeks. There is also a disablement benefit and associated allowances, at higher rates than other benefits, for those who suffer injury due to a work-related accident or precribed industrial disease. This is a weekly pension or lump sum for loss of mental or physical faculty according to a fixed tariff depending on the degree of disablement.

247. The major source of income support for those incapable of work for short periods owing to illness or injury since April 1983 has been statutory sick pay (SSP). Before that date a short-term industrial injury benefit was payable for work-related accidents and prescribed industrial diseases, and state sickness benefit for other illnesses. The value of these state benefits to high-earners was considerably reduced by the withdrawal of earnings-related supplements in 1982. Employers are now obliged to pay SSP to employees. From 6 April 1986, this is for a maximum of 28 weeks for any one period of incapacity for work.[1] During this period the employee has no entitlement to state sickness benefit. (The unemployed and self-employed who have paid the requisite contributions continue to be eligible for state sickness benefit.) The main justification put forward for the introduction of SSP was the reduction of administrative expenditure by placing responsibility in the employer's hands. However, it is doubtful whether the savings will be substantial because during the legislative process the government abandoned the original objective of off-loading costs on to employers without compensating them in full. The State retains ultimate financial responsibility because employers can recoup the SSP they pay by deducting it from their social security contributions.

1. Social Security Act 1985 which amends the Social Security and Housing Benefits Act 1982 which made the employer responsible only for the first 8 weeks in any tax year.

247bis. As with unemployment benefit, SSP is not payable for the first three days of sickness, but unlike unemployment benefit, there is no requirement that the employee fulfil contribution conditions. Thus an employee may become eligible for SSP as soon as he or she begins working. Formerly, an employee was entitled to state sickness benefit even if the employer paid sick pay under the contract of employment. The new scheme, however, allows the employer to discharge contractual liability for sick pay by paying SSP (and vice versa), thus preventing double recovery and relieving the employer of some contractual obligations. SSP is not designed to replace earnings, but provides flat rate recovery on three earnings bands.[1] Many occupational sick pay schemes therefore operate by topping up the state entitlement to the level of the employee's earnings. The Government is at present considering allowing employers to substitute private payments for SSP This would allow an employer to opt out of SSP provided that he or she pays wages at least as good as the appropriate SSP rate. Although such an employer would forego the right to recoup payments of SSP from national insurance contributions, there would be a saving on administrative costs.

1. Currently, £44.35 per week where normal weekly earnings are greater than £70; £37.20 where normal weekly earnings lie between £53 and £70; and £30 in any other case.

C. Lump sum damages

248. If the employee is able to establish that the employer was in breach of his common law duty to take reasonable care for the employee's safety, or in breach of a statutory safety duty, or that the employer is vicariously responsible for the negligence or breach of duty by a fellow-employee, then he may receive damages in the form of a lump sum payment. In assessing the amount of damages deductions will be made for remuneration received from the employer (or likely to be paid in future) since the basic principles of the damages award is compensatory. In addition, when assessing the damages for loss of earnings, one half of the value of social security benefits for five years from the time the cause of the action accrued will be deducted.[1] The law relating to the employers' liability for damages falls outside the scope of this monograph.

1. Law Reform (Personal Injuries) Act 1948, s. 2(1).

§3. MATERNITY PAY

249. An employee absent from work because of pregnancy or confinement may be able to receive three types of maternity benefit: (1) From her employer, under her contract of employment; (2) From the state, under the social security scheme; and (3) From her employer, under the provisions of the Employment Protection (Consolidation) Act 1978. Any amounts received under (1) and (2) must be deducted from the maternity pay received under (3). Moreover, every employer liable to pay who pays a maternity payment under (3) is entitled to claim a 100 per cent rebate from a Maternity Pay Fund to which all employers (whether or not they employ women) paying employers' social security contributions must contribute. At the end of 1985, the government announced proposals to place the responsibility for payment of maternity allowances under (2) on the employer, on lines similar to SSP (above).[1]

1. Department of Health and Social Security, Statutory Maternity Allowance, Consultation
   paper, December 1985.

A. Under the contract of employment

250. Some employers have schemes granting women paid leave for
maternity, not infrequently on the same terms as sick leave. Prior to the
introduction of statutory provisions, only 15–20 per cent of employers operated
such schemes.[1] In other cases there are agreements to provide maternity leave
for defined periods without pay. For example at industry level there are
collective agreements for the biscuit industry, the cocoa and chocolate confec-
tionery industry and food manufacture, allowing 26 weeks' unpaid maternity
leave. Such schemes may be expressly or impliedly incorporated into individual
employment contracts. A few employers have introduced paid or unpaid
paternity leave for limited periods.

1. N. Fonda, 'Statutory Maternity Leave in the UK' in P. Muss and N. Fonda, *Work and the
   Family*, London 1980, p. 121.

B. Social security benefits[1]

251. There are two forms of benefit: (1) a lump sum payment (maternity
grant), and (2) a maternity allowance. The first can be claimed if a woman has
been confined in Great Britain or her pregnancy has advanced to within nine
weeks of expected confinement. Either the woman or her husband must satisfy
the contribution conditions. The second is payable for 18 weeks from the
eleventh week before the anticipated confinement but this may be extended in
cases of late confinement. The woman must satisfy contribution requirements,
and there are disqualifications which have the effect of excluding a substantial
number of women.[2]

1. Social Security Act 1975, ss. 21–23.
2. In 1984, 350,000 women received the allowance at a cost of £160 million (figures supplied by
   Department of Health and Social Security).

C. Employment Protection (Consolidation) Act maternity pay[1]

252. This is payable for six weeks. It does not matter that the woman does
not intend to return to work after her confinement. The main conditions which
she must satisfy are these: (1) She must have continued to be employed until
immediately before the beginning of the eleventh week before the expected
week of her confinement. (2) She must, at the beginning of the eleventh week,
have been continuously employed for more than 16 hours each week for a
period of not less than two years (five years if she works 8 to 16 hours a week).
(3) She must inform her employer (in writing if he so requests) at least 21 days
before her absence begins (or otherwise as soon as reasonably practicable) that

she will be absent because of pregnancy or confinement. (4) She must produce, on request, for the employer's inspection, a medical or midwife's certificate stating the expected week of her confinement. The woman remains entitled to a maternity payment, even though her contract has come to an end during her period of absence. If she is unfairly dismissed because of her pregnancy or confinement or not re-engaged, the amount of the maternity pay she should have received will be included in the assessment of her compensation for unfair dismissal. If she resigns before the eleventh week she loses her right to maternity pay. If she resigns after the eleventh week she does not.

    1. EPCA 1978, ss. 33–44.

253. The amount of maternity pay is nine-tenths of a week's pay for the first six week's absence starting on or after the eleventh week before the expected week of confinement. As mentioned above (para. 249) certain deductions have to be made from this payment. In effect, employers are required to 'top up' state social security benefits to a level not exceeding nine-tenths of basic wages and employers have the right to reimbursement from a common fund.

§4. SUSPENSION FROM WORK ON MEDICAL GROUNDS[1]

254. Under health and safety legislation an employer may be required to suspend an employee from work on medical grounds, because of unsafe conditions etc. During the period of suspension under these statutory requirements the employee is entitled to be paid by his employer for not more than 26 weeks, subject to certain qualifications.

    1. EPCA 1978, ss. 19–22.

§5. RIGHT TO RETURN TO WORK

A. Sickness or injury

255. A long absence may bring the contract to an end automatically through 'frustration' (supervening impossibility of performance). The test, applied by the courts, is 'was the employee's incapacity of such a nature, or did it appear likely to continue for such a period, that further performance of [the employee's] obligations in the future would either be impossible or would be a thing radically different from that undertaken by him and accepted by the employer under the agreed terms of his employment?'.[1] Among the relevant factors will be the sick pay provisions in the contract, whether the employee is in a key position, the nature of the illness and the employee's length of service. Recent cases have tended to limit the doctrine to long-term contracts with no notice provisions.[2]

    1. *Marshall* v. *Harland & Wolff Ltd.* [1972] 1 WLR 899 at pp. 902–904.
    2. *Harman* v. *Flexible Lamp Ltd.* [1980] IRLR 418.

256. If the contract has not been frustrated, then the employer who dismisses the employee by reason of sickness or injury ('incapability') will have to satisfy an industrial tribunal, under the unfair dismissals law, that in all the circumstances (having regard to equity and the substantial merits of the case) he acted reasonably in treating the incapability as a sufficient reason for dismissal. This applies only to those who satisfy the eligibility requirements for unfair dismissal (see Ch. VII, below). The employer who acts slowly and is generous to the sick or injured employee is likely to satisfy the tribunal. There are no set rules, the only test being fairness in all the circumstances. In general it will be necessary for the employer to show that he has investigated the facts, warned the employee and heard the employee's side of the story. It will usually be found unfair to dismiss where the period of sick pay under the contract has not yet expired. The employer is not obliged to create a special job for a sick employee, suitable to his capacities, however long his service; but there may be cases, where other lighter jobs are available, that these should be offered to an employee not in good health. In some enterprises there are collective agreements which provide for sick employees to be transferred to a 'holding department' or 'inactive register' with clearly defined rights, normally after an agreed period of absence. This type of agreement does not give an automatic right to be put back in the old job but it preserves the employee's continuity of employment although he is not actually working. If the employee has not been dismissed, and the contract has not been frustrated, the employee has no automatic right to the identical job he was doing before absence from work. His right will depend on the terms of the job description in his contract of employment, which may allow flexibility. If the job has disappeared the employee may be entitled to a redundancy payment (below, Ch. VII).

B. Pregnancy and confinement

257. An employee is automatically treated as unfairly dismissed if the principal reason for her dismissal is that she is pregnant, or is 'any other reason connected with her pregnancy'.[1] The employer may, however, show that the dismissal was fair, for one of the following reasons. (1) The woman is, because of her pregnancy, incapable of adequately doing her job. (2) Some enactment prohibits her employment because of her pregnancy. In either case, the employer must offer a suitable alternative vacancy if one exists.

1. EPCA 1978, s. 60. This applies only to those employees who satisfy the eligibility requirements (see Ch. VII, below).

258. An important part of the package of maternity rights is the right to return to work at any time up to 29 weeks from the week in which the date of confinement falls. The employee who has been absent wholly or partly due to pregnancy or confinement is entitled to return to work with her original employer or successor, at her old job and on terms and conditions not less favourable than those which would have been applicable to her had she not been absent, provided she fulfils the eligibility criteria.These are similar to

those required for maternity pay, namely that she must have continued to be employed until immediately before the eleventh week before the beginning of the expected week of confinement, and that at that date she has been continuously employed for at least 2 years (or 5 years if she works 8 to 16 hours per week) with the same employer. The notification provisions were made stricter and more complex in 1980. The main notification requirements are the following: (1) At least 21 days before she begins her maternity absence (or as soon as reasonably practicable), she must inform the employer in writing that she will be absent from work wholly or partly because of pregnancy or confinement, that she intends to return to work for her employer and the date of the expected week of confinement. (2) If requested by her employer, she must produce for inspection a certificate of the expected week of confinement signed by a doctor or midwife. (3) If the employer sends a written request (not earlier than 49 days after the expected week of confinement) asking her to confirm in writing that she intends to return, she must give written notification of her intention within 14 days of receiving the request. (4) She must inform the employer in writing of the date she proposes to return at least 21 days before that date. The employee can postpone this day of return but on one occasion only, for up to 4 weeks, even if this means extending the 29 week period. The woman may do this for medical reasons only. The employer can put off the day of return, on more than one occasion, for up to 4 weeks in all, but must state his reasons. A woman not complying with all these formalities will lose the right to return to work.

259. If the employer fails to permit the employee to return she may then complain that she has been unfairly dismissed. There are, however, three important restrictions on the right to return: (1) *Redundancy.* Where her former job is no longer available because of redundancy, the employee's rights depend on whether there is a suitable alternative vacancy. If there is a vacancy the employer is obliged to offer this to her, failing which the dismissal will be unfair. If there is no alternative vacancy, she is entitled to redundancy pay. The right to redundancy pay is forfeited if she unreasonably refuses a suitable offer. (2) *Small employers.* If the total number of employees employed by her employer and any associated employer immediately before the beginning of her maternity absence was 5 or fewer, the employer may refuse to take her back if he or she can show that it is not reasonably practicable to re-employ her in the same job or in suitable alternative work. In this case, the failure to permit her return will not be treated as a dismissal and she will therefore have no claim. (3) *Offer of alternative work.* In a non-redundancy situation, if any employer (irrespective of size) shows that it was not reasonably practicable to offer the employee her original job, but that she has been offered available suitable alternative work, which she has either accepted or unreasonably rejected, she will not be treated as dismissed for the purposes of an unfair dismissal claim. In all three circumstances, the alternative work must fulfil certain criteria, in particular that the terms, conditions and location are not substantially less favourable than those of her employment before her maternity absence.

260. In practice, the right of return is not used as extensively as might be expected. A survey published in 1980 found that only 10 per cent of all women employed during pregnancy gave notice of return and subsequently returned to the same employer. This low rate of return is partly attributale to the fact that many pregnant women do not qualify for the right to return. The same study found that 46 per cent of all women who worked during pregnancy did not meet the statutory conditions for reinstatement.[1] Moreover an important contributing factor to the low rate of return is the shortage of childcare facilities. The UK Government has opposed the introducton of an EEC Directive on Parental Leave (which could include rights for fathers, as is already the case in a number of other EEC Member States) on the grounds that this would impose unjustified burdens on employers and public funds.[2]

1. W. W. Daniel, *Maternity Rights: The Experience of Women*, London, Policy Studies Institute, 1980; see too *Maternity Rights: The Experience of Employers*, 1981.
2. Draft Directive on Parental Leave (COM (84) 63 FINAL) November 1984.

§6. PROTECTION OF SENIORITY RIGHTS[1]

261. An employee will be credited with certain weeks of absence from work for purposes of calculating his continuity of employment, and his continuity will not be broken by those absences. These are weeks of absence: (1) during all or part of which the employee is incapable of work in consequence of sickness or injury, up to a maximum of 26 weeks; and (2) during which the employee is absent from work wholly or partly because of pregnancy or confinement.

1. EPCA 1978, Sched. 13, para. 10.

Chapter VII. Job Security

§1. DEVELOPMENT OF THE CONCEPT OF JOB SECURITY

262. Since 1963 there has been a spate of legislation intended to give employees a measure of security against abrupt or unfair dismissal and to provide compensation when jobs disappear for economic reasons. A variety of imprecise concepts has been applied by commentators. One is the idea of 'property in the job' or the right to undisturbed possession of a job which cannot be taken away without due process of law.[1] This, as Professor H. A. Turner has remarked, 'is the employee's compensation for his relative lack of property in the capital that employs him'.[2] Another concept is the 'right to work' which in Britain means 'not only access to a new job after having quit or lost an old one, but also a right to continue at the old'.[3] It has, however, been argued that so far from increasing job security or job-property rights, the effect of the legislation has been to encourage British workers to abandon their 'protective' attitudes to jobs and to accept dismissals in return for cash payments.[4] It has also been suggested that the emphasis on individual rights in respect of disciplinary action by management has weakened the collective control of jobs by workers and, to some extent, strengthened managerial control.[5]

1. The classic exposition is by F. Meyers, *Ownership of Jobs: A Comparative Study*, Los Angeles, 1964, p. 1; see generally B. Hepple, 'A Right to Work?', *Industrial Law Journal* 10 (1981) p. 65.
2. H. A. Turner *et al.*, *Labour Relations in the Motor Industry*, London, 1967, p. 337.
3. Meyers, *op. cit.*, p. 18.
4. R. H. Fryer, 'The Myths of the Redundancy Payments Act', *Industrial Law Journal* 2 (1973) p. 1.
5. M. Mellish and N. Collis-Squires, 'Legal and Social Norms in Discipline and Dismissal', *Industrial Law Journal* 5 (1976) p. 164.

263. Before 1875 the employee was, in fact, bound to his employer because desertion (breach of contract) was punishable as a criminal offence and employees could also be imprisoned for debts (such as wage advances) owed to the employer. The criminal liability for desertion was modified in 1867 and abolished in 1875. 'This fundamental revolution in the law' (as Sidney and Beatrice Webb called it)[1] meant that from then on employer and employee became equal parties to a civil contract. The contractual classification of the relationship means that the employer cannot compel the employee to continue in service – that would 'turn contracts of service into contracts of slavery'[2] – and, on the principles of reciprocity and mutual confidence, the employee cannot compel the employer to keep him in service. Reinstatement of a wrongfully dismissed employee is not possible.

1. S. & B. Webb, *History of Trade Unionism*, Rev. ed., London 1919, p. 291.
2. *Per* Fry L. J. in *De Francesco* v. *Barnum* (1890) 45 Ch.D. 430 at p. 438.

264. The presumption at common law was that a general hiring was for a year. This gave the employee some security during the seasons of the year, but at the same time it meant that the employee was not free to quit before the end of the period. This rule was suited to an agricultural society, but by the mid-19th century it had been replaced *de facto* by a general rule that industrial hirings for an indefinite period could be terminated by notice. The period of notice was determined by custom or, if there was no custom, was to be 'reasonable'. Before the abolition of criminal liability for desertion in 1875, trade unions pressed employers to grant 'minute contracts' (terminable at will) because this protected the right of workers to leave their employment either individually or by way of strike action. This pressure evaporated after 1875 and the rule from then until 1963 was that the contract could be terminated on either side by notice, and that the employer could summarily (*i.e.* abruptly) dismiss the employee for misconduct.

265. Before 1963 relatively few collective agreements contained notice periods and where they did the periods were short (*e.g.* in the construction industry 2 hours' notice terminating on a Friday was sufficient). Appeals against dismissal by the use of agreed procedures were rare. At the same time, unofficial ('wildcat') strikes, not authorised by a trade union, were frequent. In the words of Frederick Meyers, 'British workers are quite willing to invoke their solidarity and economic strength to protect themselves . . . and . . . their object is to secure reinstatement and not merely pay in lieu of notice.'[1]

    1. Meyers, *op. cit.*, p. 29.

266. There were, however, collective agreements relating to dismissals for reasons connected with the operating requirements of the enterprise, such as market fluctuations, structural reorganisation or closure of establishments. These dismissals are loosely referred to as *redundancies* in Britain, although the term 'redundancy' now has a special meaning in legislation (see below, para. 320). Some agreements provided for alternatives to redundancy, such as a redistribution of overtime or voluntary transfers between establishments; some laid down selection procedures to be followed when redundancies occurred, such as 'last in first out'; and some provided for severance pay, that is lump-sum cash payments to redundant workers.

267. Proposals for improving job security in the early 1960s generally took the form of a requirement that employers should give longer formal notice of dismissal. The original Contracts of Employment Bill 1963 (the first general legislation in Britain on terms of employment since 1875) placed a reciprocal obligation on employers and employees to give one another the same minimum periods of notice. The trade unions were concerned that this would restrict the right to strike after giving notice to terminate contracts, and, under pressure, the Conservative Government modified the original proposals so as to make the minimum period of notice to be given by an employee to terminate his contract the period of one week. The minimum period to be given by the employer, on the other hand, varied from one week (in respect of employees

with between 26 weeks' and 2 years' service) to four weeks (for those with 5 years' or more service). These periods of notice by the employer have been extended in later Acts. The current legislation is the Employment Protection (Consolidation) Act 1978 (below, para. 292).

268. The Redundancy Payments Act 1965 (now included in the Employment Protection (Consolidation) Act 1978, Part VI) made employers liable to pay lump-sum compensation based on age and length of service, to redundant employees. The employer was at first able to recover two-thirds of the payment from a Redundancy Fund made up of contributions from all employers. This rebate was later limited to one-half and then 41 per cent and later 35 per cent. From 1986, the rebates will be paid only to employers with fewer than 10 employees. Between 1974 and 1984, an annual average of 468,000 statutory redundancy payments was made, with a peak of 810,000 in 1981.[1] It has been estimated that only about one-quarter to one-fifth of employees dismissed for economic reasons has been eligible for payments under the Act, and the average lump sum payment is only about one-fifth of the median adult average wage.[2] Part of the reason for this is that there is a two-year qualifying period, and the definition of 'redundancy' is far more restrictive than the circumstances in which a worker in France can obtain severance pay or a worker in Belgium or Italy can receive payments supplementary to unemployment insurance following work-force reductions. The stated purposes of the Act included the mitigation of the economic consequences of redundancy, compensation for the loss of job property rights, and the encouragement of mobility. A survey of the main groups actually or potentially involved in redundancy[3] found that the Act has had some impact on attitudes and behaviour, increasing mobility and flexibility of labour and reducing the level of dispute activity over redundancies. One of the most important demonstrated consequences of the Act has been to increase the significance of age as a criterion for redundancy because the larger payments to older workers with long service acts as a mechanism to induce them to leave employment.[4] In this sense, the Act has facilitated movement out of the labour force.

1. *Employment Gazette*, May 1985, p. 203.
2. R. H. Fryer, 'Redundancy, Values and Public Policy', *Industrial Relations Journal* 4 (1973) no. 2, p. 12; see too *Industrial Law Journal* 2 (1973), p. 1.
3. S. R. Parker *et al., Effects of the Redundancy Payments Act*, London, HMSO, 1971.
4. Department of Employment, 'Age and Redundancy', *Employment Gazette* 86 (1978) 1038.

269. In 1971, as part of the Industrial Relations Act, the Conservative Government introduced unfair dismissals legislation, in large measure based on and owing its main inspiration to the ILO Recommendation No. 119 (1963) concerning termination of employment. With a number of improvements, the 1971 legislation was re-enacted in the Trade Union and Labour Relations Act 1974, Schedue 1, and this was further amended by the Employment Protection Act 1975. This legislation was consolidated in the Employment Protection (Consolidation) Act 1978, Part V. The coverage of the legislation was significantly reduced by the introduction of a one-year qualifying period of service in

1979[1] (in place of the former 6-month period), a two-year period for those employed by small employers in 1980,[2] and a two-year period for all employees in 1985.[3] The standard of proof of fairness was also weakened in 1980,[4] and important changes were made in the nature and type of remedies in 1982, discriminating in favour of those dismissed in closed shop situations.[5] The present British legislation is less extensive than that found elsewhere in Europe, and law and practice is in some respects below the standards in the ILO Termination of Employment Convention 1982, which the UK government has not ratified.

1. Unfair Dismissal (Variation of Qualifying Period) Order 1979, SI 1979 No. 959.
2. Employment Act 1980 s. 8(1) (2 year period for firms with 20 or less employees).
3. Unfair Dismissal (Variation of Qualifying Period) Order 1985, SI 1985, No. 782. There is no qualifying period for dismissal on grounds of race, sex or trade union membership or activities.
4. Employment Act 1980, s. 6 substituting a so-called 'neutral' burden or proof in place of the former burden on the employer, and requiring the industrial tribunal to pay specific regard to the size and resources of the employer's undertaking.
5. Employment Act 1982, s. 5. See below, para. 384.

270. The right to complain of unfair dismissal marked a major departure from the common law. The employer's power to terminate employment without any reason by lawful notice or payment in lieu of notice, has been restricted. The employer has to prove the reason of dismissal (or, if more than one, the principal reason) and that this was one of a number of potentially fair reasons, namely the capability or conduct of the worker, or that he was redundant, or that he could not be employed without breach of some statutory requirement, or that there was some other substantial reason of a kind such as to justify the dismissal of an employee holding the position in question.[1] Certain reasons are automatically unfair, such as trade union membership, or activities or non-membership of a trade union. In other cases, the tribunal has to determine whether the dismissal was fair or unfair in the circumstances, having regard to the reason shown by the employer, in 'accordance with equity and the substantial merits of the case'.[2] Control over jobs has been depersonalised in the sense that the employer can take them away from certain employees only after due process of law.[3] Moreover, there is a relatively cheap, informal and expeditious remedy for an aggrieved employee by way of complaint to an industrial tribunal (see Introduction, para. 80, above) within 3 months of the effective date of termination. Unlike the common law, the legislation (since 1976) provides that the successful employee may be granted an order of reinstatement or re-engagement (previously only a recommendation to this effect could be made).

1. EPCA 1978, s. 58(1).
2. EPCA 1978, s. 57(3) as amended. See below, para. 309.
3. It was in this sense that Frederic Meyers, op. *cit.*, p. 1 spoke of the 'ownership of jobs'.

271. In reality, however, the right to be continuously employed, unless in the words of article 4 of the ILO Termination of Employment Convention 1982, 'there is a valid reason connected with the capacity or conduct of the worker or based on the operational requirements of the undertaking, establishment or service', has been far less effective than might have been expected. First, the proportion of dismissed workers utilizing the statutory remedy has been extremely modest. Although the number of unfair dismissal applications to industrial tribunals increased from 5,197 in 1972 (the first year of the legislation) to 37,000 in 1984,[1] with some fluctuations due to variations in the length of the qualifying period, the number of applications has been declining since 1982, a process likely to be accelerated when the two-year qualifying period takes effect in mid-1986. The hidden nine-tenths of dismissed employees who make no claim is indicated by a survey of manufacturing establishments employing over 50 workers by the Industrial Relations Research Unit at Warwick University who found that just under 2 per cent of the workforce had been dismissed for various reasons other than redundancy in the previous 2 years but less than 10 per cent of them had sought to challenge the unfairness of their dismissal in an industrial tribunal.[2] As Linda Dickens and her colleagues remark in their major study of unfair dismissals and the industrial tribunal system, 'claiming unfair dismissal via the industrial tribunal system is an atypical minority response'.[3] They found that 'applicants are typically male, non-union manual workers dismissed after relatively short service. Respondent employers are generally small companies, often single-establishment employers. Those industries characterised by small employment units and below average unionisation produce the most unfair dismissal claims'.[4]

1. ACAS Annual Report for 1984, London, 1985.
2. W. Brown (ed.), *The Changing Contours of British Industrial Relations*, Oxford 1981, pp. 35–37, 115–116.
3. L. Dickens *et al.*, *Dismissed: A Study of Unfair Dismissal and the Industrial Tribunal System*, Oxford, 1985, p. 31.
4. *Ibid.*, p. 51.

272. Secondly, employees who bring claims have found themselves at a relative disadvantage vis-à-vis the employer. The percentage of complaints upheld by tribunals has been less than one-third.[1] One reason which has been suggested for this is the unequal representation of employees and employers before tribunals, with employers more likely than employees to have skilled lay or legal advocates.[2] However, a more important reason is the judicial interpretation which has been given to the standard of fairness in the legislation. As will be seen (below, paras. 305–312), the courts and tribunals have interpreted the statutory concept of unfair dismissal as resting upon the foundation of the common law contract of employment. The underlying assumption is the natural authority of management emanating from the property rights of the owners of the business. This has led to a wide interpretation of the potentially fair reasons for dismissal (in particular the residual category of 'other substantial reason'), it being sufficient for the employer to show a subjective belief in the existence of that reason, and the adoption of the view that it is not for tribunals to impose their own opinion as to whether they would have dismissed in the same circumstances but rather to decide whether the dismissal was within the range of responses which reasonable employers *might* adopt. Moreover, procedural requirements have been weakened by the adoption of the 'futility' argument, namely that a dismissal is not unfair because of a defect of procedure where, on the balance of probabilities, the employer could reasonably have dismissed even if a fair procedure had been adopted. This non-interventionist approach has reinforced traditional contractual notions that the employee's interest in job security must take second place to the employer's right to manage. The assumption has been that there are certain enlightened management styles, such as a corrective rather than a punishment-centred view of discipline. By considering how a reasonable body of employers might behave the tribunals have become, in Patrick Elias's words,[3] norm-reflecting rather than norm-setting. Not surprisingly tribunal decisions reflect conceptions of common practice rather than more radical notions of worker control of jobs.

1. Dickens, *op. cit.*, p. 86.
2. *Ibid.*, pp. 85–93.
3. P. Elias, *Industrial Law Journal* 10 (1981) p. 201.

273. Thirdly, the legislation has failed to secure re-employment of unfairly dismissed employees. This remedy is rarely awarded by tribunals, although on paper it has been the primary remedy, with compensation an alternative, since 1976. The proportion of *all* claims awarded this remedy has been less than 2 per cent since 1977.[1] The remedy in nearly all other cases was compensation, the median award in 1983 being £1,345;[2] or roughly nine times the average weekly earnings in that year. Cases which are compromised without a hearing are settled at an average of 40 per cent of the compensation awarded by tribunals. This level of compensation cannot be said to meet the point made by the ILO Committee of Experts in 1974 that compensation is most effective as a remedy where it can act as a deterrent against unjustified termination. A number of reasons have been suggested for the small number of unfairly dismissed employees who are ordered to be re-employed. ACAS suggested in its annual report for 1983,[3] that 're-employment is neither sought by nor acceptable to many applicants'. This assumption has been strongly questioned by the Warwick study[4] which showed that a quarter of all claimants expressed a preference for re-employment when lodging their complaints. Another reason for the low level of reinstatement is employer resistance. Where the employer objects, the tribunals has to decide whether it would be 'practicable' for the employer to comply with the order. The tribunals have adopted a criterion of 'practicability' that is the employer's, 'namely, upon return the employee will cause no managerial problems, rather than the employee's criterion, namely that he or she will benefit from re-employment if only for a short period' (below, para. 313). There is little incentive for management to re-employ because the sanction is only a relatively small additional award of compensation.[5] The Conservative Government implicitly acknowledged that the levels of additional compensation were too low to deter employers from dismissing employees unfairly when they came in 1982 to reform the law relating to the closed shop. The Employment Act 1982 introduced a new 'special award' of £15,750 (£16,500 from April 1986) or 156 weeks' pay (whichever is the greater) where an order of re-employment is made but not complied with in those relatively few cases where the dismissal is for non-membership of a union or for participation in trade union activities (below, paras. 376 and 384). For the vast majority of those unfairly dismissed, however, the sanction of the small additional award remains unchanged.

1. See generally L. Dickens *et al.*, 'Re-employment of unfairly dismissed workers: the lost remedy' *Industrial Law Journal* 10 (1981) 160.
2. *Employment Gazette* 92 (1984) p. 487, Tables 2a and 2b.
3. ACAS Annual Report 1983, London, 1984, para. 5.11.
4. Dickens, *op. cit.*, note 1 above; see too K. Williams and D. Lewis, *The Aftermath of Tribunal Reinstatement and Re-engagement*, Department of Employment Research Paper No. 23, London, 1981.
5. L. Dickens *et al.*, *Industrial and Labor Relations Review* 37 (1984) p. 507.

274. Fourthly, the legislation appears to have had relatively little success in providing a 'floor of rights' upon which collective bargaining may improve. The design of the legislation was to allow collective agreements to replace the statutory provisions with ministerial approval where the standards in the agreement were at least as high as those in the legislation. In fact, these exemption arrangements have rarely been used: only 3 exempted agreements for redundancy payments in 20 years and one for unfair dismissal in 13 years. The reasons are complex.[1] In the case of redundancy payments, it is difficult to spread the burden evenly across industry where only one or two employees agree to an exempted scheme and it is difficult to maintain flexibility because of the practical limitations in an enterprise offering suitable alternative employment instead of a payment. In the case of unfair dismissal, the legislation has had a major impact in encouraging the growth of formal disciplinary procedures: in 1969 only about 8 per cent of private sector establishments had such procedures; in 1980 this figure was 80 per cent.[2] However, most of these procedures are drawn up and imposed by management[3] and very few of them make provision for independent third party intervention, whether by ACAS or an arbitrator. As a result they have not qualified for exemption. Collective agreements play only a supplementary role to legislation, for example providing for 'add-on' voluntary payments over and above the statutory minima or prescribing voluntary procedures but not replacing the legislation. Such agreements show a great deal of variety.

1. C. Bourn, 'Statutory exemptions for collective agreements' *Industrial Law Journal* 8 (1974) 85.
2. W. W. Daniel and N. Milward, *Workplace Industrial Relations in Britain*, pp. 163–170; see too W. Brown (ed.), *op. cit.*, pp. 35–37, 43–48; Dickens, *Dismissal: A Study of Unfair Dismissal and the Industrial Tribunal System*, pp. 232–234, 252–255.
3. S. Evans, J. Goodman, L. Hargreaves, *Unfair Dismissal Law and Employment Practice in the 1980s* Department of Employment Research Paper No. 53, London, 1985, p. 31, found that in 80 per cent of cases in their sample in the private sector, disciplinary procedures had been introduced without consultation or negotiation with employees or unions.

275. In summary, then, it can be said that the attempts to give 'job property' or 'job security' rights to employees have proved no match for the property rights of employers. The legislation has given a boost to procedural rules made unilaterally by managers. It has supported the power of managers to buy out jobs. At the same time, however, it has given protection to individual workers against arbitrary action, where trade union organisation is ineffective or non-existent. It has also enabled trade unions to offer better services to members in small and dispersed groups on whose behalf it is difficult to negotiate collectively, but in general British trade unions have shown relatively little willingness to use a combination of individual rights and collective procedures. Underlying trade union ambivalence about these individual rights is the feeling that individuals do not get through the tribunal procedure 'a sort of legal substitute for collective bargaining'.[1] In the future, trade union pressure is likely to be for greater recognition of the collective interest in respect of dismissals and workforce reductions. The EEC Directives on collective redundancies[2] and transfer of undertakings[3] have led to some limited statutory rights for recognised unions to information and consultation (below, paras. 287 and 325) but the general trend of government policy and legislation since 1979 has been to remove the traditional legal supports from collective bargaining.

1. M. Mellish and N. Collis-Squires, *Industrial Law Journal* 5 (1976) at p. 167.
2. Directive 75/129 of 17 February 1975, OJ 1975, L48/29; EPA 1975, Part IV.
3. Directive 77/187 of 14 February 1977, OJ 1977 L61/26; Transfer of Undertakings (Protection of Employment) Regulations 1981, SI 1981, No. 1794.

276. Those who favour deregulation argue that the legislation imposes additional costs of employment (including administrative costs of screening and supervising workers) and deters recuitment by reducing the flexibility of undertakings to respond to market changes by dismissals. It is also argued that the legislation induces inefficient use of labour because of the fear of claims for unfair dismissal. These costs are said to fall disproportionately on small firms and on those establishing new or expanded operations. Surveys of management attitudes and responses[1] have shown that in practice the legislation has had only a minor impact in these respects. Few employers expressed reluctance to recruit additional labour because of the legislation. What the legislation has done is to induce greater care in the selection of recruits so as to improve quality rather than to restrict quantity.[2] This tends to support the view of those who argue that the legislation aids efficiency by achieving labour forces closer to the needs of the undertaking. There is evidence that the use of temporary contracts and casual labour is increasing, but this seems to have been prompted more by economic than legal considerations.[3] Another argument for deregulation is that the legislation has introduced greater formalism into labour relations which undermines flexible management control of the workforce. Against this, it has been strongly argued that the widespread adoption of fair procedures has made the administration of discipline more open and acceptable and has removed legitimacy from collective industrial action against dismissals.[4] A recent survey[5] indicates that the vast majority of employers now take more care in preparing for a dismissal so as to ensure that it is legally 'safe', although many small firms continue to act informally. About two-thirds of the sample of employees and trade union representatives felt that generally management dealt fairly with disciplinary matters, but some concern was expressed that procedures and unfair dismissal legislation were undermining the scope for unions to negotiate over disciplinary cases.[6]

1. W. W. Daniel and E. Stilgoe, *The Impact of Employment Protection Laws* London, Policy Studies Institute, 1978; R. Clifton and C. Tatton Brown, *Impact of Employment Legislation on Small Firms*, Department of Employment Research Paper No. 6, London, 1979; S. Evans, J. Goodman, L. Hargreaves, *Unfair Dismissal Law and Employment Practice in the 1980s*, Department of Employment Research Paper No. 53, London, 1985; L. Dickens, *op. cit.*, Chap. 8.
2. This is a conclusion from all the above surveys.
3. S. Evans *et al.*, *op. cit.*, pp. 15–18.
4. S. Henry, *Private Justice*, London, 1983; K. Williams, 'Unfair dismissal, myths and statistics' *Industrial Law Journal* 12 (1983) 157. The available evidence indicates that the introduction of statutory protection has not, in fact, reduced the level of strikes over dismissal: see Dickens, *op. cit.*, pp. 224–232.
5. S. Evans *et al.*, *op. cit.*, pp. 33–35.
6. *Ibid.*, pp. 35–40.

§2. JOB CREATION MEASURES

277. To complete the overall picture in relation to job security, one must note that in the period of large-scale redundancies and high unemployment since 1974, there have been a number of Government measures designed first to preserve jobs and secondly to create new job opportunities. These schemes have been dubbed 'leaflet law'[1] since they are not contained in legislation, but in a series of administrative circulars from the Department of Employment. Measures designed to preserve jobs have chiefly consisted of subsidies paid by the Government to employers who were prepared to defer proposed redundancies. Some of these have been relatively successful. Thus the temporary employment subsidy scheme, introduced in 1975 and ended in March 1980, supported some 540,300 jobs in the first $3\frac{1}{2}$ years. The most recent such scheme, the temporary short-time working compensation scheme, appears to have averted a substantial proportion of notified redundancies in 1980 and 1981.[2] This was closed for applications from March 1984.

1. P. Davies and M. Freedland, *Labour Law: Text and Materials*, 2nd ed., p. 29.
2. *Employment Gazette*, May 1985, vol. 93, p. 203.

278. In the category of schemes designed to create new job opportunities, most attention has recently been paid to encouraging the employment of young people on low wages. The most important current scheme, begun in 1983, is the Youth Training Scheme (YTS), a year-long training programme designed to help school leavers who remain or become unemployed in the post-school year. There are two modes of funding: Under Mode A, the Manpower Services Commission contracts with the employer (the 'managing agent') to train the young person, providing a block grant of £1,850 per person plus £100 for administration. This enables the trainee to be paid an allowance of £26.25 per week and covers costs of training. Under Mode B, the MSC runs its own training programmes through colleges, community projects etc. and provides the whole cost. (For employment status of trainees, see para. 123, above.) In its

147

first two and half years' operation, there were 960,000 YTS entrants, and the estimated total cost of the first three years is £2.465 million.[1] The training period is due to be extended to two years from 1 April 1986. A similar scheme is the Young Workers' Scheme, which allows employers to claim £15 per week from the Department of Employment for a maximum of 52 weeks for each employee who is under 18 when his or her employment begins and whose gross average earnings are £50 per week or less for a minimum 35-hour week. This scheme is to be wound up in March 1986, to coincide with the extension of YTS. Other schemes, not confined to young people, include the Job Release Scheme which provides new job opportunities by helping older workers to withdraw from the employment field, creating vacancies for workers who are unemployed. Under this scheme, an employee who agrees to leave work a year before retiring is paid an allowance by the Department of Employment if certain conditions are fulfilled, the chief one being that the employer recruits an unemployed person as the replacement for the Job Release applicant. Under the Community Programme, 159,000 long-term unemployed adults are provided with a year's work on projects of benefit to the community. Under another scheme, introduced in January 1986, on a pilot basis, long-term unemployed people accepting jobs paying less than £80 per week receive an additional £20 'job-start' payment from the state each week for 6 months.

1. Department of Employment statistics.

§3. CONTINUITY OF EMPLOYMENT

279. In order to qualify for statutory job security rights an employee must have a requisite period of 'continuous employment'. For example, unless the employee has been continuously employed for two years there is no right to a statutory redundancy payment, and the amount of the payment depends upon age and length of continuous employment. He or she does not get the rights to statutory minimum periods of notice prescribed by the Employment Protection (Consolidation) Act 1978 unless he or she has been continuously employed for the requisite period. The employee cannot complain of unfair dismissal unless he or she has been continuously employed for 2 years, in most cases. The length of continuous employment also affects other job rights, such as maternity pay, guarantee payments and so on.

280. The method of determining whether a person has been continuously employed is set out in Schedule 13 to the Employment Protection (Consolidation) Act 1978 as amended. These provisions are extremely complex and only the main principles are set out here. Essentially there are two elements in the concept of 'continuous employment'. The first is *continuity*, that is the existence of an employment relationship based on a contract of employment or a series of contracts with the same employer or, in some cases, successors to that employer. The second is that the employee must have continuity for a requisite *period of employment*, that is he must have been credited with the requisite period of weeks. For a week (which always ends on Saturday) to count it must be a week in which the employee has worked for 16 hours or more, or it must be a week for part or all of which the employment relationship is governed by a contract 'which normally involves employment for 16 or more hours weekly'. Special rules exist to protect the continuity of employment (for up to 26 weeks) of an employee whose normal hours are reduced from 16 to 8 or more a week. An employee with 5 years or more can count weeks normally involving 8 hours or more.

281. The general rule is that if a week occurs which cannot be credited to an employee then not only does that week not count as a period of employment, but also it destroys continuity of employment. If continuity is broken then any weeks credited to the employee are cancelled and the employee has to start from week one again when he resumes work. There is a presumption that employment is continuous and it is for the employer to produce evidence to rebut this presumption. It is necessary for the written statement of employment terms (above, para. 132) to include particulars of any period of continuity of employment with a previous employer which counts as a period of employment with the present employer. The effect of such a statement may be to prevent an employer contending that a change of employer had broken continuity.

282. There are two main exceptions to the general rule. First, there are certain weeks which do not count as a period of employment but which do not break continuity. These are weeks during any part of which the employee took part in a strike or was absent from work because of a lock-out. Secondly, there are weeks during which there was no contract in existence but the employee is still entitled to have such weeks counted as periods of employment and treated as not breaking continuity. These are weeks during all or part of which the employee is absent because of sickness or injury, or a temporary cessation of work,[1] or by arrangement or custom he or she is regarded as continuing in the employment, or because of pregnancy or confinement.

1. *E.g.* where a teacher was engaged on a series of fixed-term contracts for the academic session (October to June), it was held that the interval between contracts was a 'temporary cessation of work': *Ford* v. *Warwickshire CC* [1983] 2 AC 71, House of Lords.

§4. Acquired Rights on Transfer of Undertakings

283. Changes in the control of an undertaking may have a significant effect on the job security of employees. The most common form of takeover in Britain is by transfer of share capital: shares in the company which is the formal employer become vested in an acquiring company of which it becomes a subsidiary; or the shares may be taken over by the shareholders of the acquiring company; or the undertaking may be managed by the acquiring company while the undertaking remains nominally the property of the company taken over. In these cases the identity of the employer, for purposes of the collective agreement and the contract of employment, remains the same. But the repercussions for trade unions and employees may be considerable. At present, labour law provides no protection in these circumstances. However, if the takeover, merger or amalgamation takes the less usual form of acquisition of the ownership of the undertaking in a way that there is a change of the identity of the employer, then legislation provides some protection for the acquired rights of employees. The statutory rules aim to overcome the inadequacy of the common law according to which a change of employer terminates the contract of employment and the new employer does not automatically succeed to the old employer's rights and obligations.[1]

1. *Nokes* v. *Doncaster Amalgamated Collieries Ltd.* [1940] AC 1014, House of Lords.

284. The statutory rules are extremely complex and their interpretation is controversial. Transfers of undertakings (or parts of undertakings) before 1 May 1982 are governed by rules set out in the Employment Protection (Consolidation) Act 1978. Broadly speaking, these rules enable an employee who was re-engaged by the new employer within a week of the termination of his employment with the old employer to preserve his continuity of employment for most statutory purposes but not for contractual ones (*e.g.* arrears of wages or damages for breach). This includes cases where there has been a transfer to an associated employer, or a transfer of the trade, business or undertaking in which he was employed at the time of transfer. Obligations are also imposed on the successor of an employer in the case of re-engagement of an unfairly dismissed employee and of a woman who has exercised her statutory right to return to work after pregnancy or confinement.

285. In the case of transfers of undertakings on or after 1 May 1982, the Transfer of Undertakings (Protection of Employment) Regulations 1981[1] (a response to the EEC Council Directive 187 of 14 February 1977[2]) provides for the automatic transfer of contracts of employment and of 'all the transferor's rights, powers, duties or liabilities under or in connection with any such contract'.[3] Unfortunately the wording of the regulations makes it debatable whether or not *statutory* 'rights, powers, duties and liabilities' are included (this was clearly the intention of the EEC Directive) and there have been conflicting decisions of different divisions of the Employment Appeal Tribunal on the question whether it is the old or the new employer who is responsible for such statutory obligations as redundancy payments and unfair dismissal compensation where the employee was dismissed before the transfer.[4] The regulations apply only to transfers in the nature of a 'commercial venture', so apparently excluding bodies such as social clubs.[5] Borderline cases have arisen in the public sector with the growing privatisation of public services. Only if the privatised service was a 'commercial venture' at the time of transfer will the employees' rights be protected under the regulations. Another important exception applies to the practice of 'hiving down'. In the case of insolvency the receiver or liquidator may 'hive down' to a subsidiary that part of the business which he considers to be a commercial package for sale, leaving the employees in the employment of the insolvent parent company which provides their services to the potentially profitable subsidiary until it is sold. It appeared to those who drafted the regulations that their effect might be to hamper this kind of 'rescue' operation and so harm the interest of creditors including possibly the employees themselves. Accordingly the regulations provide[6] that the transfer is deemed to be suspended until immediately before either (i) the transferee company ceases to be a wholly owned subsidiary of the transferor company, or (ii) the business is sold to another person, whichever first occurs. At this point in time there is deemed to be a transfer from the insolvent company to the subsidiary company. The effect is that if the hiving-down operation is successful the employees still left in the employment of the parent company immediately before the transfer to the purchaser are automatically transferred to the subsidiary and so are acquired by the purchaser. Although this limits some of the freedom previously given by hiving-down, the purchaser can still avoid liability by insisting that the parent company dismisses those employees whom he does not wish to retain before he acquires control of the subsidiary or the business is transferred to him. This, of course, means that the employees who are not transferred are left only with their claims against the asset-stripped parent company. It is questionable whether this is compatible with article 3(1) of EEC Directive 77/187.

1. SI 1981 No. 1794; see generally, B. Hepple, *Industrial Law Journal* 11 (1982) p. 29, and for the background, *ibid.*, 5 (1976) p. 197; 6 (1977) 106; and *Common Market Law Review* 14 (1977) 489.
2. 77/187/EEC OJ L61/26, 5 March 1977.
3. Reg. 5(2)(a).
4. Compare *Premier Motors (Medway) Ltd.* v. *Total Oil Great Britain Ltd.* [1984] ICR 58 with *Apex Leisure Hire* v. *Barratt* [1984] ICR 452 and *Lister* v. *Forth Dry Dock & Engineering Co. Ltd.* IDS Brief 313, November 1985, pp. 2, 16.
5. Reg. 2(1).
6. Reg. 4.

286. The regulations provide that a dismissal before or after a relevant transfer is automatically unfair 'if the transfer or a reason connected with it is the reason or principal reason' for dismissal.[1] There is, however, an important exception where there is 'an economic, technical or organisational reason entailing changes in the workforce of either the transferor or the transferee'. This applies both to transferred employees and those not transferred. Where such a reason is shown, then the tribunal has to decide whether the employer acted reasonably in treating it as a sufficient reason for dismissal, for example was there unfair selection, or a failure of consultation or a failure to seek suitable alternative employment?

1. Reg. 8.

287. The regulations provide that collective agreements existing at the time of transfer shall continue in force after the transfer as if made with the transferee,[1] and also that trade union recognition is transferred provided that the undertaking retains a distinct identity under the new employer. These provisions, modelled on the EEC Directive, do not provide any *legal* safeguard in the British context because of the general presumption that collective

agreements are not intended by the parties to be legally enforceable contracts (see para. 465, below). More important are the duties imposed by the regulations to inform and consult with recognised trade unions.[2] The duty to inform trade union representatives of the fact and timing of the transfer, the 'legal, economic and social implications' and the measures envisaged rests on both the transferor and the transferee in relation to any employee who may be affected by the transfer, whether or not a union member, and whether or not employed in the undertaking or the part to be transferred. The duty to consult also rests upon both the transferor and the transferee. The remedies for a breach of these obligations is by way of complaint to an industrial tribunal. Where the union's complaint is well-founded the tribunal must make a declaration and may award 'just and equitable compensation' to affected employees. If this is not paid the employee, not the union, must present a further complaint and the tribunal may then order the employer to pay the amount. The maximum award is 2 weeks' pay in respect of any employee and there is a set-off of any amounts received as damages for breach of contract. The failure to provide an effective sanction for breach of the duty to consult may mean that the UK has not fully complied with the requirements of the EEC Directive.

1. Regs. 6 and 9.
2. Regs. 10 and 11.

§5. DISCIPLINARY SUSPENSION FROM WORK

288. A common sanction for misconduct of an employee is suspension from work. Since this may infringe the employee's right to be paid (above, para. 213) this sanction may be imposed only with the express or implied consent of the employee. The consent may be given in advance, and is therefore frequently found in disciplinary rules issued to employees. One of the curious consequences of the Employment Protection Act 1975 was to make it easier for employers to impose disciplinary sanctions of this kind on employees because the Act, now consolidated in the Employment Protection (Consolidation) Act 1978, s. 1(4) requires an employer to include a note of grievance and disciplinary procedures with the written statement of employment terms (above, para. 134). This facilitates proof that the disciplinary rules form part of the contract of employment. These rules are frequently not the product of collective bargaining, and so the Act may have widened the unilateral rule-making powers of the employer to impose disciplinary sanctions short of dismissal. Apart from suspension without pay, fines are sometimes imposed, although there are certain statutory restrictions on these in the case of manual workers, hosiery workers and shop assistants (see paras. 219–221, above). Legislation in 1986 is expected to introduce new controls over deductions to all employees.

§6. Methods of Termination of Employment

A. Frustration

289. The contract of employment is regarded as essentially personal in nature and so some events lead automatically to its termination, for example the death of the employer, the dissolution of a partnership, or an order for the compulsory winding up of a company. There is also a broad general principle of frustration (supervening impossibility of performance). Under this principle, if a change of circumstances makes performance of the contract unlawful, or physically impossible, or its objects incapable of achievement, the contract will be automatically brought to an end, without the need for dismissal by the employer or resignation by the employee. Illustrations are prolonged absence of the employee due to illness (above, para. 255), compulsory military service of the employee, or the physical destruction of the workplace. A sentence of imprisonment is not an automatically frustrating event.[1] Recent case law has limited the application of the doctrine of frustration.[2] In particular, there is a crucial distinction between frustration and the case where one party by his own conduct makes it impossible to perform the contract (repudiatory breach), which entitles the other party to terminate the contract. Examples of the latter are where a person deliberately absents himself or commits an offence which results in his or her imprisonment.[3]

1. *Chakki* v. *United Yeast Co. Ltd.* [1982] ICR 140 (EAT).
2. *Tarnesby* v. *Kensington and Chelsea and Westminster AHA* [1981] ICR 615 (HL) (suspension of medical consultant from register for 12 months not frustration).
3. *Norris* v. *Southampton City Council* [1982] ICR 177 (EAT).

B. By agreement

290. The parties may agree that the contract is to last (i) for a limited period of time; or (ii) until the happening of an uncertain event (*e.g.* until war is declared); or (iii) until the happening of a certain event, the time of which is uncertain (*e.g.* for the life of the Sovereign); or (iv) to perform a specific task (*e.g.* deliver a course of lectures, or chop down a tree). Certain statutory rights (*e.g.* to guarantee and medical suspension payments, paras. 235 and 254 above) do not apply to employment under a contract for a fixed term of 12 weeks or less, and an employee whose contract is for a fixed term of two years or more may agree in writing to exclude any right to a redundancy payment[1] or of one year or more to complain of unfair dismissal.[2] The Court of Appeal has held that a contract for a fixed term covers only category (i) above, that is for a specified stated time; this is the case even if the contract is determinable by notice within that term.[3] The statutory definition of dismissal[4] includes, where the contract is for a fixed term, the expiry of the term without it being renewed under the same contract. Since this does not cover contracts in categories (ii), (iii) and (iv) above, persons in those categories have no grounds to complain of unfair dismissal or to claim redundancy payments when the event occurs or the task is completed.[5] Some difficulty has arisen where employer and employee agree that the employment will end automatically if the employee fails to fulfil a condition (*e.g.* that the employee return from extended leave by a given date). This may be an agreed termination rather than a termination by the employer if the condition was clear and the employee can be shown to have genuinely agreed. But the presumption is that an employee would not intend to give up his or her rights to claim that there has been a dismissal by the employer.[6]

1. EPCA 1978, s. 142(2) as amended.
2. EPCA 1978, s. 142(1) as amended.
3. *Dixon* v. *BBC* [1979] ICR 282, CA.
4. EPCA 1978, ss. 55(2)(b), 83(2)(b).
5. *Wiltshire County Council* v. *NATFHE [1980] ICR 455, CA.*
6. *British Leyland UK Ltd.* v. *Ashraf* [1978] ICR 979 (EAT); *Midland Electrical Engineering* v. *Kanji* [1980] IRLR 185 (EAT); *Tracey* v. *Zest Equipment Co. Ltd.* [1982] ICR 481 (EAT).

C. Dismissal by employer with notice

291. An employee is treated as 'dismissed' for the purposes of unfair dismissal and redundancy law, if the contract under which he is employed by the employer is terminated by the employer, whether it is so terminated by notice or without notice. At common law, the employer is entitled to terminate a contract for an indefinite period by giving a reasonable period of notice. The parties may expressly limit the right of either side to terminate by notice except for specified reasons. For example, the contract may be stated to be one 'until reaching the retirement age' or 'for life' or 'permanent and pensionable'. In such cases it may not be terminated by notice.

292. Where the length of notice is not specified by the contract expressly or by custom, then the length of a reasonable period of notice depends upon all the circumstances. Among relevant factors are the employee's status, the nature of the job and the general character of the services to be rendered. The frequency of payment (*e.g.* weekly or monthly) may be a convenient guide but this is not conclusive. These common law rules are now subject to the provisions of section 49 of the Employment Protection (Consolidation) Act 1978 which lays down the following minimum periods of notice:

1 week to a person continuously employed for between 4 weeks and 2 years
1 week for each year of continuous employment, to a person continuously employed for 2 years or more but less than 12 years.
12 weeks to a person continuously employed for 12 years or more.

The employee may accept payment of wages in lieu of notice, but the provision in a contract of employment for shorter periods of notice than those laid down in the Act is ineffective.

293. The Act of 1978 also guarantees the employee's income during the statutory minimum notice period. The detailed rules are set out in Schedule 3 to the Act.

D. Dismissal by employer without notice

294. At common law, an employer is entitled to dismiss an employee summarily, that is without notice, if the employee has disregarded an essential term of the contract. This is an area of law in which old cases are of little assistance because of changing judicial attitudes. Early decisions were often not concerned with the rights of 'master' and 'servant' but with the question which arose under the Poor Laws as to whether a particular community was legally obliged to provide aid to a destitute person because he had acquired a settlement by virtue of having been employed there for a certain period. Other decisions, before 1867, arose under the criminal law of desertion. Modern cases have moved towards the general principles of contract law, by stressing factors such as whether an important term of the contract has been broken, whether the employee's actions have undermined mutual confidence, and whether the employee has a reasonable excuse for his conduct. Each case depends on its own circumstances. The contract is terminated not by the employee's repudiatory conduct, but by the employer's act in accepting that repudiation.[1]

1. *London Transport Executive* v. *Clarke* [1981] ICR 334 (CA).

E. Variation of contract distinguished from dismissal

295. In some situations the employer may introduce changes in working conditions, either with or without notice, which affect the employee adversely. If the employee consents either expressly or impliedly to such a change in terms this is called a 'consensual variation' and the employee may not then complain that he has been 'dismissed'. However, the courts have more than once made it clear that they dislike an attempt by an employer to make 'use of the employee's willingness to work, and to work for a lower wage' as a means of avoiding 'dismissal' and resultant liability for a redundancy payment or unfair dismissal. The courts will 'be slow to find that there has been a consensual variation where the employee has been faced with the alternative of dismissal and where the variation has been adverse to his interest'.[1] Sometimes, however, an employee will be held to have agreed to a change unless he works under clear protest against the new terms.

1. *Sheet Metal Components Ltd.* v. *Plumridge* [1974] ICR 373. Unilateral withdrawal by the employer from a collective agreement is not a variation unless the employee consents: see para. 153, above).

296. Because of this difficulty, employees have been given a statutory right in respect of claims for redundancy payments to a month's trial period in any changed terms of employment. But in unfair dismissal cases (and in redundancy cases where the employee has stayed in the changed job for more than one month) the old rules apply and the employee may lose his right to claim that he was 'dismissed' if he does not make it clear that he is working under protest, or if he continues for a long time in the changed job.

F. Termination by the employee

297. At common law the employee may terminate the contract by giving the agreed notice, or where no period is specified by giving reasonable notice, depending on the circumstances. Under the Employment Protection (Consolidation) Act 1978, the statutory minimum period of notice which an employee must give is *one week*. In some employments the period required by contract is much longer.

298. At common law, the employee is entitled to terminate the contract without notice if the employer breaks a fundamental term of the contract. This is the reverse of the situation in which the employer is entitled to dismiss the employee summarily. Unilateral changes in the contract by the employer will amount to a repudiation of the employer's fundamental obligations only if they go to the basis of the contract; for example by reducing the employee's pay, suspending the employee without pay where the contract does not provide for this, making drastic changes in the working hours, forcing an employee to join a trade union, requiring an employee to work under unsafe conditions or forcing him to hand in his resignation. Generally speaking, changes made as a result of collective agreements will not amount to a repudiation of contract by the employer unless the terms of that agreement cannot be said to have been incorporated into the individual employment contract (above, para. 149). For example, where employees have resigned from a union and have made it clear that they will not accept terms of employment negotiated after their resignation, it may be that freshly negotiated terms are not binding on them.[1]

1. *Singh* v. *British Steel Corporation* [1974] IRLR 131; cf. *Land* v. *West Yorkshire CC* [1979] ICR 452.

299. The main importance of these common law rules is that the employee may claim that he has been dismissed for the purposes of unfair dismissal and redundancy law if he terminates his contract, with or without notice, in circumstances such that he is entitled to terminate it at common law without notice. This is popularly known as 'constructive dismissal'. The test is whether the employer has repudiated the contract.[1] Strictly speaking, it is only where the employee accepts the employer's repudiation by resigning and leaving that one can speak of a 'constructive dismissal'.

1. *Western Excavating (ECC) Ltd.* v. *Sharp* [1978] ICR 221 (CA).

§7. Reasons for Dismissal and References

300. At common law, an employer is not required to give any reason for dismissal. Moreover, if the employee brings an action for damages for wrongful dismissal the employer is entitled to justify the dismissal by proving reasons which were not known to him at the time of the original dismissal.[1]

1. *Boston Deep Sea Fishing Co.* v. *Ansell* (1888) 39 Ch. D. 339.

301. Both these common law rules have now been modified by legislation. An employee who has 6 months' continuous employment is entitled, under section 53 of the Employment Protection (Consolidation) Act 1978, to be provided by his employer within 14 days of his so requesting 'a written statement giving the particulars of the reasons for his dismissal'. If the employer 'unreasonably refuses' an industrial tribunal may award the employee a penalty equivalent to two weeks' pay. The written statement is admissible in unfair dismissal and other proceedings. The common law rule regarding subsequently discovered misconduct does not apply to proceedings for unfair dismissal, in which the employer may rely only on those facts which were known to him at the time of dismissal.[1] In the case of termination by notice this may include events up to the time of expiry of the notice.[2]

1. *W. Devis & Sons* v. *Atkins* [1977] ICR 662 (House of Lords).
2. *Stacey* v. *Babcock Power Ltd.* IDS Brief 315, December 1985, p. 5 (EAT).

302. There is, however, no obligation on an employer to provide an employee with a character reference. If the employer does provide a reference he must take care not to say anything defamatory, deceitful or without reasonable care as to its accuracy. An employer may not refer to certain spent convictions of a rehabilitated offender or to any circumstances ancillary to those convictions.[1]

1. Rehabilitation of Offenders Act 1974, s. 4(4). There are detailed rules as to when a conviction becomes 'spent'.

§8. DAMAGES FOR WRONGFUL DISMISSAL

303. The concept of *'wrongful dismissal'* is applied to any dismissal where the employer, not being entitled at common law to terminate the contract summarily, failed to give the period of notice required by law. The employee's sole remedy will usually be a claim for damages in the county court (if the claim is less than £5,000) or the High Court. For reasons mentioned earlier (para. 263), the courts will not grant injunctions which in effect require specific performance of contracts of employment. An exception to this is where mutual confidence remains between employer and employee and it is clear that the employment will continue peaceably.[1] The courts are prepared to grant *declarations* determining the rights of the parties without any order of court to their fulfilment, where the employee enjoys a special statutory status, for example as a registered dockworker under a statutory scheme. Recently, there has been a greater willingness to grant injunctions and declarations to protect procedural rights even of employees in the private sector.[2]

1. *Hill* v. *C. A. Parsons & Co. Ltd.* [1972] 1 Ch. 305, as explained in *Chappell* v. *Times Newspapers Ltd.* [1975] ICR 145 at pp. 173, 176, 178; *Irani* v. *Southampton and South West Hampshire AHA* [1985] IRLR 203.
2. *R.* v. *BBC, Ex parte Lavelle* [1983] ICR 99.

304. The measure of damages for wrongful dismissal will normally be the remuneration which the employee has lost by not being given the requisite period of notice. Damages are not awarded for hurt feelings, or for the manner in which the dismissal took place[1] or for the fact that dismissal made it more difficult to find alternative employment. But damages have been awarded for loss of an opportunity envisaged by the contract (such as an actor losing the chance to enhance his reputation) and for depression, anxiety and illness caused by the dismissal.[2] The damages are awarded net of tax and social security contributions and subject to deduction of certain other benefits received, such as wages earned in an alternative employment, unemployment benefit[3] and supplementary benefit.[4] The employee is under a duty to mitigate his or her loss by taking reasonable steps to find alternative employment.

1. *Addis* v. *Gramophone Co.* [1909] AC 488 (House of Lords); *Bliss* v. *South East Thames RHA* [1985] IRLR 308 (CA).
2. *Cox* v. *Phillips Industries Ltd.* [1974] IRLR 344.
3. *Westwood* v. *Secretary of State for Employment* [1984] IRLR 209 (House of Lords).
4. *Lincoln* v. *Hayman* [1984] 2 All ER 819.

§9. UNFAIR DISMISSAL

305. Every employee, with certain exceptions set out below, has the right not to be unfairly dismissed by his employer. The employee must prove that he was 'dismissed'. This means either (1) termination of the contract by the employer (paras. 284 and 291 above); or (2) expiry without renewal of a fixed term contract (para. 290 above); or (3) 'constructive dismissal' (paras. 297–299 above). The burden of proof is then on the employer to show the reason (or if there was more than one, the principal reason) for the dismissal. In contrast to the I.L.O Termination of Employment Convention 1982, there are only four reasons which render a dismissal automatically unfair: trade union membership and activities, refusal to belong to a trade union, selection for redundancy in breach of an agreed procedure or customary arrangement, and pregnancy and confinement. All other reasons may justify dismissal, but only if the tribunal is satisfied that the employer acted reasonably in treating the nominated reason as a sufficient reason for dismissal.

A. Reasons allowed for dismissal

306. The employer must show a set of facts known to him, or it may be beliefs held by him, at the time of dismissal which caused him to dismiss the employee. These facts must fall within one of the following categories:[1] (1) 'The capability or qualifications of the employee for performing work of the kind that he was employed by the employer to do' ('capability' is assessed by reference to skill, aptitude, health or any other physical or mental quality). (2) 'The conduct of the employee'. (3) The employee was 'redundant'. This concept is defined by reference to the redundancy payments legislation (see below, para. 320). (4) 'The employee could not continue to work in the position which he held without contravention (either on his part or on the part of his employer) of a duty or restriction imposed by or under any enactment' (*e.g.* safety legislation, or a driving disqualification imposed on a lorry driver). (5) 'Some other substantial reason of a kind such as to justify the dismissal of an employee holding the position which the employee held'. Among reasons which have been found to fall within this category are unreasonable refusal to agree to changes in employment terms, pressure from an important customer to dismiss the employee, the temporary nature of the employment, and an irreconcilable conflict of personalities. By statute[2] dismissal of a temporary replacement for an employee who is absent from work because of a pregnancy or confinement or medical suspension is treated as a 'substantial reason', provided fair warning of the temporary nature of the job was given to the replacement. Moreover, dismissal for an 'economic, technical or organisational reason entailing changes in the workforce of either the transferor or transferee' on the transfer of an undertaking is deemed to be a 'substantial reason'.[3] In all these cases the tribunal still has to determine whether the employer acted reasonably in all the circumstances[4] (see para. 309, below).

1. EPCA 1978, ss. 57(1), 57(2).
2. EPCA 1978, s. 61.
3. Transfer of Undertakings (Protection of Employment) Regulations 1981, SI 1981 No.1394 (para. 286 above).
4. *Kent County Council* v. *Gilham* [1985] IRLR 18 (CA).

307. A dismissal is not capable of giving rise to a complaint of unfairness if a certificate is produced signed by a Minister of the Crown that the dismissal was taken 'for the purpose of safeguarding national security'.[1] Nor may an industrial tribunal entertain a complaint where at the time of dismissal the employer was instituting or conducting a lock-out, or the employee was taking part in a strike or other industrial action, subject to an exception in the case of certain selective dismissals. (This is discussed in Part II, Ch. V.)

1. EPCA 1978, Sched. 9, para. 2. See para. 375, below.

308. It has already been indicated that certain reasons are automatically unfair. The dismissal of a pregnant employee and the right to return to work after confinement were discussed in Ch. VI above. Selection for redundancy is discussed in para. 312, below. The other automatically unfair reasons (the burden of proving which rests upon the employee) are that the employee –

'(a) was, or proposed to become a member of an independent trade union; (b) had taken, or proposed to take, part in at any appropriate time the activities of an independent trade union; or (c) was not a member of any trade union, or of a particular trade union, or one of a number of particular trade unions or had refused, or proposed to refuse, to become or remain a member of a trade union.'[1]

The definition of an 'appropriate time' envisages that an employee may participate outside working hours off the employer's premises, or on the premises while there with the express or implied permission of the employer (*e.g.* during meal breaks) but while not actually at work. The right to participate during working hours depends on the employer's consent, which may be gathered from the circumstances. ACAS has issued a Code of Practice containing guidelines. There is an exception to the right not to be dismissed in respect of trade union membership and activities where there is a 'union membership agreement' (*i.e.* a closed shop). These rights will be discussed, in connection with trade union freedom, in Part II, Ch. I.

1. EPCA 1978, s. 58(1), as amended by the EA 1982, s. 3.

B. Reasonableness

309. Unless the dismissal was for a reason which was automatically unfair, the tribunal is required to decide whether the employer acted reasonably. Section 57(3) of the Employment Protection (Consolidation) Act 1978 states: 'The determination of the question whether, having regard to the reason shown by the employer, the dismissal was fair or unfair, shall depend on whether, in the circumstances (including the size and administrative resources of the employer's undertaking), the employer acted reasonably or unreasonably in treating it as a sufficient reason for dismissing the employee, and that question shall be determined in accordance with equity and the substantial merits of the case'. Since 1980, there has been no formal burden of proof in the determination of this question. The tribunal, with its tripartite composition, is expected to act as an 'industrial jury', drawing on the industrial experience of its lay members to reach a conclusion based on common sense and common fairness. The statute has, however, been interpreted to mean that the tribunal members should not substitute their own opinion for that of management. Lord Denning said that 'It must be remembered that in all these cases there is a band of reasonableness, within which one employer may reasonably take one view: another quite reasonably take a different view'.[1] Thus, the function of the industrial tribunal, 'as an industrial jury, is to determine whether in the particular circumstances of each case, the decision to dismiss the employee fell within the band of reasonable responses which a reasonable employer might have adopted'.[2]

1. *British Leyland UK Ltd* v. *Swift* [1981] IRLR 91 (CA) at p. 93.
2. *Iceland Frozen Foods* v. *Jones* [1983] ICR 17 (EAT).

310. The 'band of reasonable responses' test clearly gives the employer considerable latitude in decision-making, particularly if the concept of the reasonable employer simply reflects actual practices of most employers. One way of circumscribing this managerial perogative without interfering too much with the ultimate substance of the decision has been to require the employer to follow certain procedures in order to ensure that a dismissal is fair. Thus earlier cases stressed the importance of warning the employee and giving him or her the opportunity to be heard before being dismissed.[1] However, these requirements have been considerably diluted in cases in which the tribunal considers that the employee suffered no injustice by the lack of procedure. Thus tribunals have either decreased the compensation to nil or held the dismissal to be fair on the basis that the decision would probably have been no different if the correct procedure had been followed. 'The right approach', it has been held, 'is to ask two questions. In the first place, have the employers shown on the balance of probabilities that they would have taken the same course had they held an inquiry, and had they received the information that the inquiry would have produced? Secondly, have the employers shown, and the burden is on them, that in the light of the information they would have had had they gone through the proper procedure, they would have been behaving reasonably in still deciding to dismiss?'[2] There may be circumstances in which this principle is difficult to reconcile with the earlier principle established by the House of Lords in *Devis* v. *Atkins*[3] that the employer is not entitled to adduce information which came to light after the employee was dismissed.

1. *Earl* v. *Slater & Wheeler (Airline) Ltd.* [1972] ICR 365 (NIRC).
2. *British Labour Pump* v. *Byrne* [1979] ICR 347 at 353–354 (*per* Slynn J.), approved in *W. & J. Wass* v. *Binns* [1982] ICR 486 (CA).
3. [1977] ICR 662 (House of Lords); and see *Sillifant* v. *Powell Duffryn Timber Ltd.* [1983] IRLR 91 (EAT).

311. The question of reasonableness is one of fact for the tribunal, appeals being limited to points of law. Thus an appeal is only available where either the tribunal misdirected themselves in law in that they misconstrued their function in considering the question of reasonableness, or they reached a conclusion which no reasonable tribunal, properly directed in law, could have reached.[1] This approach has been critizised for leading to inconsistent decisions as between tribunals. However, in the words of a recent Appeal Court decision:

'Whether or not an employer has behaved reasonably in dismissing an employee is a question of fact, and it is a question upon which different people, looking at the same set of circumstances, may reasonably come to different conclusions. It is therefore endemic in a system where there is no appeal on fact that from time to time different industrial tribunals will give different answers to broadly similar situations, and neither decision can be challenged. It is therefore important that this court should resist the temptation to seek to overturn a factual decision with which it may not agree, by searching for some shadowy point of law on which to hang its hat for the purpose of bringing uniformity to the differing decisions. If we were to take this course, it would have the very undesirable effect of encouraging innumerable appeals which raised no point of law, but depended upon comparative findings of fact.'[2]

1. *Gilham* v. *Kent County Council (No. 2)* [1985] ICR 233 (CA) at 243–244.
2. *Ibid., per* Griffiths L. J. at p. 240.

312. There are two special situations in which selection for redundancy must be treated as unfair. These are where the employee shows that the principal reason for selection was trade union membership or activities or refusal to join a trade union, or that he was selected in contravention of a 'customary arrangement' or 'agreed procedure relating to redundancy'.[1] It is not possible for an employee to rely on a general 'custom' such as 'last in first out'; he must show that the custom is well-known, certain and reasonable in respect of the establishment in which he worked. In other redundancy cases, normal criteria of reasonableness apply such as whether attempts were made to find suitable alternative employment for the redundant employee and whether his or her union was consulted.

1. EPCA 1978, s. 59.

C. Remedies for unfair dismissal

313. The primary remedies available under the Employment Protection (Consolidation) Act 1978 are (1) *Reinstatement,* which means that the employer must treat the employee in all respects as if he or she had not been dismissed, restoring pay, pension and other benefits; and (2) *Re-engagement,* which differs from reinstatement in that the employee may be re-engaged in a different job from that which he or she formerly held, provided that the new job is comparable to the old or is otherwise suitable. Re-engagement may be by a successor or associated employer. In exercising its discretion whether to grant reinstatement or re-engagement the tribunal must consider the complainant's wishes, whether he or she caused or contributed to the dismissal, and whether it is practicable for the employer to comply with an order for reinstatement or re-engagement.[1] The mere fact that the employer has engaged a permanent replacement does not automatically make these remedies 'impracticable'. If the employee is reinstated, but the terms of the order are not fully complied with, the tribunal must award compensation to the extent that partial non-compliance has caused the employee's loss, with a maximum award, currently fixed at £8,000. If the order for reinstatement or re-engagement is not complied with at all, then the tribunal must award a basic and compensatory award (see para. 315, below) and an *additional* award of compensation. In an ordinary case, the additional award is between 13 and 26 weeks' pay; and in the case of discrimination on the grounds of race or sex, it is 26–52 weeks' pay.

1. EPCA 1978, ss. 69–71.

314. Since the Employment Act 1982, the tribunal must make a *special* award where the employer refuses to reinstate an employee who has been dismissed for being a member of a trade union, engaging in trade union activities, or refusing to be a member of a trade union.[1] The special award is 156 weeks' pay, subject to a minimum, currently fixed at £15,750, (£16,500 from 1 April 1986) and no maximum, but where an employer shows it is impracticable to comply, this is reduced to 104 weeks' pay, with a minimum, currently fixed at £10,500 and a maximum of £21,000 (£11,000 and £22,000 respectively from 1

April 1986). Similarly, where an employee who has been dismissed for trade union membership or non-membership or trade union activities requests reinstatement or re-engagement, but the tribunal refuses this request, the additional award of 104 weeks' pay should be ordered, with a minimum of £10,500 and a maximum of £21,000 (£11,000 and £22,000 respectively from 1 April 1986). The special award may be reduced if the employee was partly at fault in causing the dismissal, or unreasonably prevented the order for reinstatement or re-engagement being complied with, or unreasonably refused an offer of reinstatement. (For figures on the use of reinstatement as a remedy, see above, para. 273.)

1. EPCA 1978, ss. 72, 72A, 75A, inserted by Employment Act 1982, s. 5.

315. If orders for reinstatement or re-engagement are not made, the tribunal must award compensation under two heads. (1) *A basic award:* This is calculated similarly to a redundancy payment (below, para. 323), on the basis of age and years of service. The employee receives one and a half week's pay for each year in employment at the age of 41 or over; one week's pay for each year from 22 to 40; and half a week's pay for each year under 22. This is reduced by one-twelfth for each calendar month over the age of 64 for men and 59 for women. The maximum week's pay is (from 1 April 1986) £155, and the award is subject to a maximum of 20 years' employment. This means that the maximum basic award is £4,650. (For figures on actual awards see above, para. 273.) There is no minimum basic award, except in two cases. First, where the dismissal is unfair on the grounds of redundancy, but no redundancy payment is payable because the employee accepted or unreasonably refused alternative employment, a minimum award of two weeks' pay must be ordered. Secondly, where the dismissal is automatically unfair because of trade union membership or activities or non-membership of a trade union, or an automatically unfair redundancy selection, the minimum award is £2,100 (£2,200 from 1 April 1986), before deductions. The basic award may be reduced, to nil if necessary, in the following circumstances: (a) the employee has contributed to his or her dismissal; (b) the employee has received a redundancy payment made pursuant to legislation or otherwise; (c) the employee has received any other amount expressly or impliedly referable to the basic award; (d) the employee has unreasonably refused an offer of reinstatement; (e) the employee's conduct prior to dismissal warrants a reduction.[1] (2) *A compensatory award:* This is such amount as the tribunal 'considers just and equitable in all the circumstances having regard to the loss sustained by the complainant in consequence of the dismissal insofar as that loss is attributable to action taken by the employer'.[2] This is calculated according to principles laid down by the courts, and includes loss of earnings and benefits up to the date of hearing and subsequently, and loss of pension rights, expenses and statutory employment protection rights. It excludes injury to feelings, inconvenience or other non-pecuniary loss (compare Sex and Race Discrimination and wrongful dismissal). Deductions are made in respect of the employee's failure to mitigate his or her loss, the employee's contribution to the dismissal and any other payment received from the employer or earnings elsewhere. The maximum is currently fixed at £8,000.

    1. EPCA 1978, s. 73.
    2. EPCA 1978, s. 74(1).

316. A special procedure, called interim relief, is available for those who claim that they have been dismissed for trade union membership or activities, or refusal to join a trade union. This procedure enables the tribunal to order that the employee be reinstated, or if both parties agree, re-engaged in another job, or if the employer refuses to do either, suspended on full pay ('an order for the continuation of the contract of employment') until final determination of the complaint.[1] The claim has to be presented within seven days of dismissal, there must be a likelihood of the employee succeeding at the final hearing and, in the case of a trade union member, it must be supported by a certificate from an authorised official of an independent trade union. This is the only situation in which a dismissal may be suspended pending the determination of the question.

    1. EPCA 1978, ss. 77–79.

D. Relationship with other claims

317. Few employees bring claims in the ordinary courts in respect of wrongful dismissal at common law (above, para. 303). It must be noted, however, that it is not relevant to the question of unfair dismissal (in respect of which proceedings may be brought only in an industrial tribunal) whether or not the dismissal was wrongful at common law. If damages are awarded in a court in respect of loss of earnings then these would be deducted from the compensatory award for unfair dismissal. Tribunal hearings will usually be completed long before an action before the ordinary courts comes to trial. If the tribunal has awarded compensation for unfair dismissal this will include loss of pay in lieu of notice and so there is unlikely to be any loss left to compensate by an award of damages. In other words, it is only if the dismissal was fair, but wages have not been paid in lieu of notice that actions are likely to be brought in the ordinary courts.

318. A statutory redundancy payment (see below, para. 320) or a payment voluntarily made by the employer, will be deducted from the award of compensation for unfair dismissal. Double awards may not be made in respect of an act which is both an unfair dismissal and compensatable as sex or race discrimination under other legislation (see para. 354, below).

E. Exclusions from unfair dismissals legislation

319. The following is a summary of those classes of employee who may not bring a complaint of unfair dismissal. (1) Employees who have been continuously employed for less than 2 years, unless the dismissal was for trade union membership or activities or non-membership of a trade union. (This qualifying period applies to those engaged on or after 1 June 1985; previously the period was one year, or 2 years in the case of firms with 20 or fewer employees.) (2) Employees who have reached the age of 65 in the case of a man and 60 in the case of a woman, or who have reached the normal retiring age (below 65 or 60) for the particular job. (3) Registered dockworkers (who have their own scheme). (4) Share fishermen. (5) Persons ordinarily working outside Great Britain. (6) Persons employed on United Kingdom registered ships wholly outside Great Britain, or not ordinarily resident in Great Britain. (7) Persons employed under fixed-term contracts made before 28 February 1972, or fixed-term contracts for one year or more made after that date if they have waived their rights in writing. (8) Persons who do not present claims within 3 months of the date of termination, or such further period as the tribunal considers reasonable in a case where it is satisfied that it was not reasonably practicable for the complaint to be presented before the end of 3 months.

§10. REDUNDANCY

A. Meaning

320. With the enormous increase in unemployment since 1979, redundancies have been a central feature of labour relations. Advance notifications of pending redundancies reached a peak of 1.5 million in 1980, from which it has declined to 405,000 in 1984. Employees have a statutory right to a redundancy payment under the provisions of the Employment Protection (Consolidation) Act 1978, Part IV. Subject to the exclusions in para. 324 below, there are two main criteria for a redundancy payment. The first is that the employee has been dismissed, and dismissal for these purposes is defined in the same way as for unfair dismissal (above, para. 305). Secondly, the dismissal must be by reason of 'redundancy'. This concept has a special meaning in the 1978 Act, s. 81, namely that the employee's dismissal is attributable wholly or mainly to:

> '(a) the fact that his employer has ceased or intends to cease to carry on that business in the place where the employee was so employed, or (b) the fact that the requirements of that business for employees to carry out work of a particular kind in the place where he was so employed have ceased or diminished or are expected to cease or diminish'.

There is a statutory presumption that the dismissal is by reason of redundancy. The burden therefore rests on the employer to prove otherwise.

321. The statutory definition, stressing as it does the necessity for diminished requirements for employees to do work of a particular kind, is a narrower concept than that to be found in the ILO Termination of Employment Convention 1982 – 'the operational requirements of the enterprise' – and the EEC Collective Redundancies Directive[1] which refers to 'reasons not related to the individual workers concerned' and the West German Protection Against Dismissal Act which speaks of 'urgent operating requirements'. As interpreted by the courts, the definition does not include all cases in which, in order to diminish labour costs or increase productivity, the employer has changed the terms and conditions of work or re-organised the workforce. Even if the employer's actions amount to a repudiatory breach of contract, or if the dismissal is wholly a result of the employer's operational requirements rather than the employee's conduct, this will not entitle the employee to redundancy compensation unless the employer's requirements for employees to do work of the particular kind the employee was employed to do has ceased or diminished. Thus, an employer was not required to pay redundancy payments to employees who could not make their own transport arrangements to and from work after the employer withdrew a free bus service. This was despite the fact that the employer was in breach of contract.[2] Similarly, a change in working arrangements and shift systems is not necessarily a redundancy situation, even if the change is a response to a fall-off in sales and leads to a substantial drop in earnings,[3] provided the employer still requires employees to do work of the particular kind. Nor will the courts question the employer's reasons for declaring employees to be redundant,[4] and conversely, if the employer honestly believes that the dismissal is justified by a reason other than redundancy, the employee is not 'redundant'.[5] As a result of the limited definition of redundancy, only straightforward cases are covered. The reference in section 81(2)(b) to the 'place where [the employee] was so employed' has been judicially interpreted to mean the place where the employee could be required by his or her contract of employment to work. Thus an employee who had worked at one place for seven years was not redundant when his employer moved his work to another establishment, since his contract required him to work at any of the employer's establishments.[6] It has been suggested that where an employee can be required by contract to do a wide range of types of work, no redundancy compensation is payable provided the employer requires employees to do any of the work within the contractual range. Thus an employee whose contract requires him to do any work within his capabilities may not be entitled to a redundancy payment so long as the employer requires employees to do work within that range.[7]

1. OJ 1975, L.48/29.
2. *Chapman* v. *Goonvean and Rostowrack China Clay Co. Ltd.* [1973] ICR 50 (CA).
3. *Johnson* v. *Nottinghamshire Combined Police Authority* [1974] ICR 170 (CA); *Lesney Products & Co. Ltd.* v. *Nolan* [1977] ICR 235 (CA).
4. *Moon* v. *Homeworthy Furniture* [1977] ICR 117 (EAT).
5. *Hindle* v. *Percival Boats Ltd.* [1969] ITR 86 (CA).
6. *UK Atomic Energy Authority* v. *Claydon* [1974] ICR 128 (NIRC), following *Sutcliffe* v. *Hawker Siddeley Aviation Ltd.* [1973] ICR 560 (NIRC).
7. *Cowen* v. *Haden* [1983] ICR 1 (EAT). The case was decided on different grounds by the Appeal Court.

322. The statute provides a limited incentive to employers to attempt to redeploy redundant workers, in that an employee is not entitled to a redundancy payment if he or she unreasonably refuses an offer of suitable alternative employment, or an offer to renew the contract on the same terms immediately or within four weeks of the dismissal.[1] The employee is entitled to a trial period of four weeks before deciding to accept the new job. An employee who does not remain on beyond the end of the trial period may be entitled to a redundancy payment in the same way as if no trial period had been embarked upon.[2]

1. EPCA 1978, s. 82.
2. EPCA 1978, s. 84.

B. Calculation of compensation and rebates

323. Schedule 4 to the Employment Protection (Consolidation) Act 1978 provides that for each year of employment between the ages of 18 and 21 the employee is to receive a half-week's pay; for each year of employment between 22 and 40 one week's pay; and for each year of employment between 41 and 64, one and a half week's pay. There is a scaling down for women in their sixtieth year and men in their sixty-fifth year, of one-twelfth for every month by which a woman is over 59 and by which a man is over 64. Remuneration over £155 per week, and employment for longer than 20 years are ignored. A week's pay is calculated in accordance with Schedule 14 to the 1978 Act. In effect the maximum award for a person with 20 years' service over the age of 41 is £4,650. The employer is entitled to claim a rebate for 35 per cent of the statutory payment from the Redundancy Fund, but the Government has announced that from a date in 1986 (still to be fixed) this will be limited to employers with 10 or fewer employees.

C. Exclusions

324. The following is a summary of the main classes of employee not entitled to receive a redundancy payment. (1) Employees who have not been continuously employed for two years or more. (2) Men who have reached the age of 65 and women who have reached the age of 60. (3) Employees unreasonably refusing an offer of suitable alternative employment from the employer, or from his successor in the case of a change of ownership. (4) Employees accepting a renewal of contract or re-engagement from the employer, or from his successor in the case of a change of ownership. (5) Employees who leave their employment during the period of their notice, unless they comply with certain formal requirements to give the employer counter-notice. (6) In some cases where the employee is guilty of misconduct or where he or she takes part in a strike during the period of notice.[1]

1. See para. 477, below, and for other exclusions see Hepple and O'Higgins, *Encyclopedia of Labour Relations Law*, para. 1–168.

§11. Collective Redundancies

325. Part IV of the Employment Protection Act 1975 is intended to give effect to the EEC Directive on Collective Redundancies.[1] The Act requires an employer contemplating the dismissal of one or more employees by reason of redundancy to consult the recognised trade union and also to notify the Department of Employment. The words 'collective redundancies' hardly seem appropriate because the obligation to consult arises even if a single employee is to be dismissed, and even though that employee is not a member of the recognised trade union or of any union. The obligation is to consult the union recognised by the employer for bargaining purposes in respect of the grade or category of employees from whose number the employer intends to select for redundancy. The obligation is to consult 'at the earliest opportunity'. If the employer is proposing to dismiss 100 or more employees at one establishment over a 90 day period, he must consult not less than 90 days before the first dismissal. If he is proposing to dismiss 10 or more employees at one establishment over a 30 day period, he must consult not less than 30 days before the first dismissal. There is no minimum period where the employer proposes to dismiss less than 10 employees.

1. OJ 1975, L.48/29 of 22 February 1975.

326. The duty to consult is more narrowly drawn than the corresponding provisions of Article 2 of the EEC Directive, which requires the employer to consult workers' representatives 'with a view to reaching agreement'. Under the British Act it is sufficient if the employer considers the trade union representations and states why he chooses to reject them. Nor is there any provision in the British Act like the requirement in Article 2 of the EEC Directive that the consultations should cover 'ways and means of avoiding collective redundancies or reducing the numbers of workers affected' although this is plainly the intention of the Act. The EEC Directive left Member States to determine who the 'workers representatives' are to be: the British position is that only where the employer recognises an independent trade union does he have to consult anyone. The British Act does specify the information to be given to the trade union, including the detailed reasons for the proposed dismissals, the number and class of employees to be dismissed, and the total number of employees in the grade or class from whom the redundant employees are to be selected, the method of selection to be used, and the method of dismissal including the timing.

327. If the employer fails to carry out his duty to consult, the trade union concerned may complain to an industrial tribunal which may make a *protective award*. The effect of the award is that the employees are to be kept on the payroll for the period of the award. This means that in addition to any other claims arising out of the dismissal (such as redundancy payments) the employees are entitled to be paid their wages for this period. The length of the period is within the discretion of the tribunal subject to certain limits. Where 100 or more employees are to be dismissed, then the award can be for up to 90 days; where 10 to 99 are to be dismissed, it can be for up to 30 days; and where less than 10 workers are involved it can be for up to 28 days. An employee not paid the amount of an award due to him may present a complaint to an industrial tribunal.

328. The employer must notify the Department of Employment of the proposed redundancies within the same time periods as are set out in para. 325, above. In his notice the employer must state the date on which he began consultation with any recognised union. He must also provide the Department with such other information as it may require. The penalty for failure to notify is either a fine of up to £400 on conviction or loss of up to 10 per cent of any redundancy rebate to which the employer might otherwise have been entitled. Where the employer is a limited liability company, a director or manager who fails to notify the Department may incur personal liability if he is guilty of fault or neglect.

Chapter VIII. Discrimination

§1. THE DEVELOPMENT OF LEGISLATION

329. The United Kingdom has not ratified ILO Convention No. 111 concerning discrimination in respect of occupation and employment, but it has signed the UN International Covenant on social and cultural rights, which requires action against a large number of pretexts for discrimination. It has also ratified the European Social Charter and the European Convention for the Protection of Human Rights which list a number of rights to be secured without discrimination. The most important influence has been that of EEC law protecting Community workers from discrimination on grounds of nationality (see above, para. 143) and article 119 of the Treaty of Rome on equal remuneration for men and women, which is directly applicable as is EEC Directive 75/117 which facilitates the practical application of that article. EEC Directive 76/207 on equal treatment for men and women has been held not to be sufficiently precise to be directly applicable in the absence of national implementing measures. The British Equal Pay Act and Sex Discrimination Act are construed subject to the overriding effect of Community law as interpreted by the European Court of Justice (see above, para. 18 for further discussion of the effect of EEC law).

330. The conscious model for domestic legal measures against racial and sex discrimination has been anti-discrimination legislation in the United States and Canada. The Race Relations Act 1968, which prohibited discrimination on grounds of colour, race, ethnic or national origins, was enforced by a Race Relations Board along the lines of a North American Human Rights Commission. In the employment field, a concession was made to TUC demands for autonomous enforcement by trade unions and employers by allowing voluntary industrial disputes procedures to be used as the primary means of enforcement in some 40 industries covering about one-third of the labour force. There was an appeal to the Race Relations Board from a finding of the voluntary machinery (in practice nearly all appeals were unsuccessful) and, where no voluntary machinery had received approval by the Secretary of State, it was the Race Relations Board and its local conciliation committees which had the responsibility of investigating complaints of racial discrimination and, where a settlement and assurance against future discrimination could not be obtained from the respondent, the Board alone had the power to institute legal proceedings before a specially constituted county court. The proportion of cases in which discrimination was found, between 1968 and June 1976, never exceeded 20.9 per cent. This, however, was a much higher proportion than the proportion of findings of discrimination by voluntary industry machinery. Between 1968 and June 1976, industry machinery received 1,006 complaints and disposed of 752. Only 20 opinions of unlawful discrimination were formed and in most of these cases no settlements were obtained. The Race Relations Board concluded that 'there can be no doubt that the experiment of using industry panels to deal with complaints of racial discrimination has failed and ought not to be repeated'.[1]

1. Report of the Race Relations Board January 1975 to June 1976, Home Office, 1976, para. 60.

331. The legislative action against racial discrimination had been prompted by a remarkable campaign to improve the social position and employment opportunities of Britain's immigrants from the New Commonwealth and the British-born black children (see above, para. 12). This campaign was not based on the trade unions, but rather on organisations of ethnic minorities and sympathetic liberals and the Labour Party and other left-wing political organisations.[1] The TUC had, however, for one hundred years been conducting a campaign for equal pay for women workers. In 1963 the TUC published a Charter for Women Workers, which has subsequently been revised, including demands for equal educational opportunities for girls with boys, equality of job opportunity for women with men, paid maternity leave and adequate child care facilities, and, for the first time, asked for legislation to secure equal pay. Equality of pay in the civil service had already been achieved by collective agreement.

1. The background is fully described in B. Hepple, *Race, Jobs and the Law in Britain*, 2nd ed., Harmondsworth, 1970.

332. The first legislative fruits of the TUC's equal pay campaign came with the enactment of the Equal Pay Act 1970, which requires equal terms of employment for men and women workers.[1] This Act came into force only on 29 December 1975, so as to give employers five years to meet its requirements. Both the Conservative and Labour Parties were committed to equal opportunity legislation and in 1975 the Sex Discrimination Act was passed, prohibiting discrimination on grounds of sex or marital status in the employment field in respect of matters not covered by the Equal Pay Act.

1. See B. Hepple, *Equal Pay and the Industrial Tribunals*, London, 1984.

333. The Sex Discrimination Act did not, however, follow the exact model of the Race Relations Act. Instead it allows aggrieved individuals a right of direct access to the industrial tribunals (or, in cases outside the employment field to county courts), while, at the same time entrusting strategic enforcement in the public interest to an Equal Opportunities Commission (EOC). The EOC deals with discriminatory practices by industries, firms and institutions and encourages positive action against discrimination (see above, para. 75).

334. The Sex Discrimination Act came into force at the same time as the Equal Pay Act. It was used as the model for a new Race Relations Act, enacted in 1976, which came into force in 1977. The new Act does away with enforcement through voluntary industry machinery and replaces this with individual enforcement through industrial tribunals and strategic enforcement by a Commission for Racial Equality (CRE) which has similar powers to the EOC (see above, para. 75). The EOC and CRE run along parallel lines, although the terms of the two pieces of legislation are, in many respects, identical. The Acts are supplemented by Codes of Practice, issued by the Commissions, which give practical guidance on the implementation of policies to eliminate discrimination.

§2. The Impact of the Legislation

335. Despite the Equal Pay Act 1970 and the Sex Discrimination Act 1975, women remain disadvantaged in British society. Although they form an important part of the workforce, women are still concentrated in lower-paid and less prestigious occupations. In 1984, there were an estimated 9.25 million women in the labour force in Great Britain, approximately 40 per cent of the total (see para. 29, above), and women are expected to take two-thirds of the net increase in jobs by 1990. However, women as a group earn markedly less than men. Although the initial effect of the Equal Pay Act 1970 was to increase women's average gross hourly earnings from 63.1 per cent of those of men in 1970 to 75.1 per cent in 1976, progress towards equal pay has come to a halt. For full-time workers, the ratio of women's average gross hourly earnings has settled in the range of 73–75 per cent since 1976, and the gap between male and female weekly pay is even wider, reflecting the longer hours and particularly the greater overtime worked by men. In 1983, the gross weekly earnings of full-time women workers averaged 66.6 per cent of men's.[1]

1. The statistics are taken from *Men and Women*, a Statistical Digest, EOC, July 1984.

336. The continuing differential between men's and women's pay is partly accounted for by the concentration of women in lower-paid occupations ('horizontal segregation'), and in the lower-paid grades of mixed occupations ('vertical segregation'). Thus, women workers are largely concentrated in relatively few occupations and industries, frequently those with a high demand for part-time labour. In fact, in manual employment, this concentration has increased in recent years. In 1983, 60 per cent of women manual workers were employed in catering, cleaning, hairdressing or other personal service occupations, as against 47 per cent in 1975. Among non-manual workers, who are concentrated in clerical and related occupations, the degree of concentration has reduced somewhat, from 58 per cent in 1975 to 52 per cent in 1983. Even where women work in mixed professions, there are far higher proportions of men than women in the better-paid grades. A central factor accounting for the continuing disadvantage of women is that the primary responsibility for child-care remains with women. As a result, women form the bulk of part-time workers, who earn substantially less than full-time workers (see above, para. 127). Indeed, the employment growth of the 1970s was almost entirely due to the increase in female part-time employment. Women are seriously under-represented in senior positions despite the Sex Discrimination Act. Moreover, although women comprise a growing proportion of trade union members (31 per cent in 1981 compared with 25 per cent in 1971), they form only a tiny proportion of trade union leadership even in unions with a predominantly female membership.

337. Ethnic minorities also continue to suffer serious discrimination and disadvantage in the labour market.[1] Male unemployment rates in 1984 were 34 per cent for Pakistanis/Bangladeshis and 29 per cent for West Indians compared to 11.5 per cent for white workers. In the 16 to 24 age group around 40 per cent of West Indian males and 25 per cent of Asian males were unemployed compared to about 20 per cent of white males. About 25 per cent of West Indian females and 35 per cent of Asian females were unemployed compared to about 15 per cent of white females. Ethnic minority unemployment rates in most regions are roughly double those for whites nearly everywhere. In almost all industries and occupations the unemployment rates for members of ethnic minorities are higher than those for whites. This is despite the fact that ethnic minority men are *more* likely to be qualified at certain levels than white men and black workers are as likely, if not more likely, to join trade unions than white workers.[2] The ethnic minorities are concentrated in low-paid industries and services (such as distribution, hotels and catering) and in jobs lower down the occupational ladder than whites. There has been very little change over the period 1974–1982 in the types of jobs in which blacks are found.[3] A recent study has concluded that racial discrimination has continued to have a great impact on the employment opportunities of black people, and says that 'even a conservative estimate would put the figure at tens of thousands of acts of racial discrimination in job recruitment every year'.[4]

1. The statistical information is derived from the *Employment Gazette*, December 1985, pp. 467–477.
2. CRE, *Trade Union Structures and Black Workers' Participation*, London, 1985.
3. Colin Brown, *Black and White in Britain: the third PSI Survey*, London, Policy Studies Institute, 1984; and compare Neil McIntosh and David J. Smith, *The Extent of Racial Discrimination*, PEP Broadsheet No. 547, London, 1974.
4. Colin Brown and Pat Gray, *Racial Discrimination: 17 years after the Act*, London, Policy Studies Institute, 1985.

338. In view of the persistence of discrimination against women and blacks, it seems surprising that little use has been made of the legislation. In 1976, the first year of operation of the Equal Pay Act there were 1,742 applications to industrial tribunals; in 1984 there were only 33 applications. The number of applications under the Sex Discrimination Act was 229 in 1977 and 225 in 1984. Under the Race Relations Act only 538 applications were registered in 1984. There are many reasons for this low take-up rate of legal rights, including lack of perception of the issues as legal ones, ignorance of the rights and how to go about enforcing them, lack of adequate representation, cost, delay, inconvenience, and unwillingness to relive a humiliating experience. To these must be added the cultural and linguistic barriers faced by some members of ethnic minorities and, in the words of Lord Scarman's report on the Brixton disorders, the 'signs among black youths, despairing of an end to white discrimination, of a disturbing trend towards a rejection of white society and the development of black separatist philosophies'.[1] Even those women and blacks who are inclined to use the law may be deterred by the derisory remedies available through the legal process (see para. 354, below), and by the relative lack of success of those who have used the legal procedures. Only about one in every 10 applicants who go to a tribunal hearing on a complaint of racial discrimination win their cases, and 2 in every 10 win their sex discrimination cases after a tribunal hearing.[2] The lack of use of the law has made it very difficult for tribunals to develop their expertise in this highly complex and unfamiliar field – discrimination cases make up less than 3 per cent of the tribunals' case load, and there is an absence of specialisation within the tribunals.

1. Report of an Inquiry by the Rt. Hon. Lord Scarman, November 1981, para. 6.35.
2. This is based on statistics published annually in the *Employment Gazette*.

§3. Grounds of Unlawful Discrimination

339. The Sex Discrimination Act and the Equal Pay Act prohibit discrimination on the grounds of sex against men and women of any age. The Sex Discrimination Act also covers discrimination against married persons in the employment field, but it is not unlawful to discriminate against a single person on grounds of being single. Like must always be compared with like. For example the treatment of a married woman must be compared with the treatment of a married man, and not with a single person of the opposite sex.

340. The Race Relations Act 1976 applies to discrimination on the grounds of colour, race, nationality, and ethnic or national origins. Discrimination on grounds of religion is not covered in Britain, although separate legislation passed by the Westminster Parliament covers this in Northern Ireland. Nor is there legislation preventing discrimination on grounds of language, social origin or political opinion. However, 'ethnic origin' has been interpreted broadly, to mean a segment of the population distinguished from others by a sufficient number of shared customs, beliefs, traditions and characteristics derived from a common or presumed common past so as to give them an historically determined social identity, so covering groups like Jews and Sikhs.[1] There are a number of important exceptions, particularly in respect of discrimination on grounds of nationality so as to preserve immigration control (see below, para. 349).

1. *Mandla* v. *Dowell Lee* [1983] ICR 385 (House of Lords).

§4. The Concept of Discrimination

341. The Sex Discrimination and Race Relations Acts recognise two main types of discrimination, direct and indirect. *Direct* discrimination occurs when someone treats a person less favourably than he treats or would treat other persons. It is a concept, as old as Aristotle, that likes must be treated alike.[1] Hostile intent is not essential[2] and it is discriminatory to treat one group less favourably than another on the basis of stereotypes, such as the belief that women are not breadwinners[3] or that married women are unreliable employees.[4] Contrary to earlier authority, it has now been held that it may be discriminatory to dismiss a woman on grounds of pregnancy where a man seeking compassionate leave of absence for a comparable period would have been treated more favourably.[5]

1. SDA s. 1(1)(a), s. 3(1)(a), RRA s. 1(1)(a).
2. *Minister of Defence* v. *Jeremiah* [1980] ICR 13 (CA).
3. *Coleman* v. *Skyrail Oceanic Ltd.* [1981] ICR 864 (CA).
4. *Hurley* v. *Mustoe* [1981] ICR 490 (EAT).
5. *Hayes* v. *Malleable Working Men's Club and Institute* [1985] IRLR 367 (EAT); *cf. Turley* v. *Allders Stores* [1980] IRLR 4 (EAT).

342. Indirect discrimination[1] is aimed at more complex forms of discrimination, sometimes called 'institutionalised' discrimination, which results from the effects of past and present disadvantage. Fewer women or blacks may be selected for a job or for promotion, not because the employer treats them less favourably, but because other factors make it more difficult for them to comply with the criteria for selection or promotion. Sexually or racially neutral rules may have a disproportionate impact on women or blacks. For example, since women have greater child care obligations than men, fewer women than men are able to comply with job specifications which include substantial overtime or mobility requirements. Similarly, educational disadvantage may make it more difficult for deprived ethnic minorities to comply with selection tests. The concept of indirect discrimination aims to make such requirements unlawful unless the employer can justify their use. The underlying theory is that in a society in which inequalities in the distribution of benefits are regarded as justifiable, the opportunities for attaining those benefits ought to be determined on a proportional basis of group entitlements. The concept was first developed in the United States. It has been translated[2] into the specific, complex and restrictive language of 'indirect' discrimination. The elements of the statutory definition are that: (i) the employer imposes a requirement or condition which is such that (ii) the proportion of persons of the complainant's group (*e.g.* women or blacks) who can comply is considerably smaller than the proportion of persons in the comparable group (*e.g.* men or whites) who can comply; (iii) the person suffers detriment because he or she cannot comply; and (iv) the condition is not justifiable irrespective of the sex, race etc. of the applicant. These elements will be examined in turn.

1. SDA s. 1(1)(b), s. 3(1)(b), RRA s. 1(1)(b).
2. The obstacles to this transplantation are discussed by B. Hepple, 'Judging Equal Rights' [1983] *Current Legal Problems* 71.

343. Requirement or condition. In the United States case law the concept of effects discrimination was first developed in the context of a practice of selection testing not related to the actual requirements of manual jobs in situations where past discrimination had the effect of disproportionately excluding blacks.[1] In Britain the concept is not limited to tests or to promotion rules. For example, it has been applied to an age requirement for executive officers in the civil service,[2] to the requirement that employees work full-time[3] (both of which have a disproportionate impact on women with child-care responsibilities), and to dress and appearance requirements that have a disproportionate impact on Sikhs.[4] Unlike the American case law in which attention is focussed on the employer's practices, the British legislation speaks of a 'requirement or condition' and this has been restrictively interpreted as meaning an absolute bar, rather than one of a set of flexible criteria which are weighed up in the final decision.[5]

1. *Griggs* v. *Duke Power Co.* 401 US 424 (1971).
2. *Price* v. *Civil Service Commission* [1978] ICR 2.
3. *Clarke* v. *Eley (IMI) Kynoch* [1983] ICR 165 (EAT); *Home Office* v. *Holmes* [1984] ICR 678 (EAT).
4. *Panesar* v. *The Nestlé Co.* (1980) IRLR 60; *Singh* v. *British Rail Engineering*, EOR No. 5, January/February 1986, p. 24.
5. *Perera* v. *Civil Service Commission (No. 2)* [1983] ICR 428 (CA)

344. The proportion who can comply is considerably smaller. This raises several questions. The first concerns the meaning of the words 'can comply'. It has been held that the test is not whether it is physically possible to comply, but whether the person can do so in practice, and consistently with his or her cultural identity.[1] Secondly, what amounts to a 'considerably lower proportion'? In particular, what is the relevant group of comparators and how much statistical evidence is required? British courts have generally been unwilling to embark on the detailed statistical exercises utilized by American courts, relying instead on a combination of elementary statistical evidence, common sense and intuition.[2] Indeed, the EAT has held that the relevant pool for comparison is a question of fact for the industrial tribunal, and has not provided any guidelines.[3]

1. *Price* v. *Civil Service Commission* [1978] ICR 2; *Mandla* v. *Dowell Lee, supra*.
2. *Price* v. *Civil Service Commission, supra; Perera* v. *Civil Service Commission, supra*.
3. *Kidd* v. *DRG (UK) Ltd.* [1985] ICR 405 (EAT).

345. Justification. Even if a requirement or condition has a disproportionate impact there is no unlawful discrimination if the respondent can show that it is 'justifiable' irrespective of the sex, race etc. of the complainant. In the United States the employer has to show 'business necessity', that the practice is 'necessary to the safe and efficient operation of the business' and that selection tests are 'job-related'.[1] In the early British cases the EAT decided that the term 'justifiable' required the tribunal to look at all the circumstances including necessity and the discriminatory effect of the requirement or condition.[2] But the Court of Appeal has equated 'justifiable' with 'reasonable'. The employer, it is said, must 'advance good grounds' 'acceptable to right-thinking people'.[3] The effect has been to reduce the issue to one of fact[4] which will be decided according to the views of the particular tribunal, not always with consistent results.[5] The burden of proof on the respondent has been diluted from the early notion of a 'heavy onus' to proof on the 'balance of probabilities'. The interplay between the unfair dismissal (above, para. 309) and discrimination jurisdiction has led the tribunals to respect a wide band of 'reasonable' managerial decisions, for example, in relation to dress and appearance regulations even where these cannot be said to be 'necessary'.

1. *Griggs* v. *Duke Power Co.* 401 US 424 (1971) at p. 431.
2. *Steel* v. *Union of Post Office Workers* [1978] ICR 181 at pp. 187–188.
3. *Ojutiku* v. *Manpower Services Commission* [1982] ICR 661 (CA). This was criticised by the EAT in *Clarke* v. *Eley (IMI) Kynoch Ltd.* [1982] IRLR 482 at p. 487.
4. *Mandla* v. *Dowell Lee* [1983] ICR 385 (House of Lords) at p. 395.
5. Compare *Kidd* v. *DRG* [1985] ICR 405 (EAT) where a requirement of full-time work to avoid redundancy selection was held to be justifiable, with *Clarke* v. *Eley (IMI) Kynoch Ltd.*, *supra*, where it was held to be unjustifiable; see too *The Home Office* v. *Holmes* [1984] IRLR 299 where the requirement of full-time work was not justified. See generally on part-time work para. 127, above.

346. The Acts also prohibit discrimination by *victimization*. This occurs where the respondent is shown to have treated the complainant less favourably than other persons because the complainant brought proceedings, gave evidence or information or alleged a contravention of the Race Relations Act, Equal Pay Act or Sex Discrimination Act.

§5. Areas of Unlawful Discrimination

347. The Sex Discrimination Act and the Race Relations Act make discrimination on any of the above grounds unlawful in certain defined areas of employment. These areas now cover most potential acts of discrimination but there are some loopholes. Among the main areas covered are selection arrangements, job offers, promotion, training, and other benefits. Dismissals are covered but since the burden of proof is on the complainant under this legislation, complainants are more likely to succeed under the unfair dismissals legislation (above, Ch. VII) where the burden of proof is on the employer. However, where the employee is dismissed before 2 years of continuous employment, the only remedy will be under the anti-discrimination statutes.

348. The Acts also outlaw discriminatory advertisements although only the Commissions can take legal action against these. Discrimination by partnerships of more than five partners in the admission or treatment of partners, by trade unions and professional and trade associations, and by training bodies and employment agencies are covered. Those who instruct or pressurise another to discriminate or knowingly aid discrimination are themselves guilty of an unlawful act.

§6. Exceptions

349. There are relatively few exceptions, but some of these are very important. One of the most litigated exceptions to the Sex Discrimination Act is that it does not apply to provisions in relation to death or retirement. This has been interpreted broadly to include anything which is 'part and parcel of the employer's system of catering for retirement'.[1] The rationale for this exception is the fact that the retiring age for the purposes of state pensions and for many other purposes remains at 65 for men and 60 for women, and although it is recognised that this may lead to blatantly discriminatory treatment, it is considered that the tradition of different retiring ages is deeply embedded in the legal structure and that it would be too expensive to sweep it away. The result, however, is that men and women are treated differently in a wide range of situations which may be central to their lives. For example, women over the age of 60 are not entitled to statutory redundancy pay whereas men remain entitled until 65, and it is lawful for an employer to offer women voluntary redundancy five years earlier than men.[2] The European Court of Justice has endorsed the right of Member States to decide their own pension ages,[3] but a recent European Court decision held that dismissal of a woman solely because she had reached State pensionable age infringed Directive 76/207.[4] Legislation is expected in 1986.

1. *Barber* v. *Guardian Royal Exchange Assurance Group*; *Roberts* v. *Tate & Lyle Food and Distribution Ltd.* [1983] IRLR 240 (EAT).
2. *Burton* v. *British Railways Board* [1982] ICR 329 (ECJ).
3. *Defrenne* v. *Sabena* [1978] ECR 1365 (ECJ).
4. *Marshall* v. *Southampton and South West Hampshire Area Health Authority (Teaching)* [1986] IRLR 140 (ECJ).

350. Other exceptions to the Sex Discrimination Act include employment as a midwife and jobs for which being a man or woman is a genuine occupational qualification, such as models, actors, toilet attendants, hospital and prison staff, and personal welfare counsellors. The Act also at present excludes employment for the purposes of a private household and employment with an employer with fewer than five employees, but the European Court of Justice has held that these exceptions infringe Community law.[1] The Government proposes to amend the Act in 1986 so that it will in future apply in these situations unless the employer's requirements are sufficiently intimate or private to require an employee of a particular sex.

1. *Commission of the European Communities* v. *United Kingdom* [1984] ICR 192 (ECJ).

351. The Race Relations Act has a narrower list of genuine occupational qualifications, including actors, models, personal welfare counsellors and jobs involving working in a place where food and drink is provided in a particular setting for which, in that job, a person of a particular racial group is required 'for reasons of authenticity' (*e.g.* Chinese restaurants).

§7. 'Reverse' Discrimination and Positive Action

352. Nothing in the legislation requires a 'reverse' discrimination in favour of women, married persons or blacks. Indeed, the definition of discrimination means that, apart from a few exceptions, such discrimination is itself now unlawful. One exception is in respect of discriminatory training and education, but a number of detailed conditions must be satisfied. 'Positive' action, to encourage applicants for jobs and trade union membership by women and blacks, and to provide them with training to help fit them for particular jobs, where their numbers have been disproportionately few during the past twelve months, is regarded as essential if equal employment opportunity is to be made a reality.[1] Another exception is that trade unions and similar bodies may reserve seats on elective bodies for members of one sex. The most important form of 'reverse' discrimination, which is not affected by the Sex Discrimination and Equal Pay Acts, is the protective legislation which applies to women. We have seen (para. 183, above) that much of the 19th century legislation relating to the hours of work, holidays and safety of women remains in force, with certain modifications, and that underground work by women is generally prohibited. The EOC and the Health and Safety Commission are obliged to keep this legislation under review. The Government plans in 1986 to abolish all the restrictions of women's hours of work in factories, despite objections from the TUC that such legislation is still required to protect women in view of their position in the family, which may require longer-term social changes before the legislation can be repealed.

1. See CRE, *Positive Action and Equal Opportunity in Employment*, London, 1985

§8. Enforcement

353. The experience under the Race Relations Act 1968 was regarded by some as proof that investigation of all individual complaints by a public agency was 'costly and wasteful' and as creating 'resentment and hostility' among those whom it was designed to assist because they were denied direct access to the courts.[1] On the other hand, it was argued that private individuals did not have the resources to find and prove discrimination, and that it was through individual casework that patterns of discrimination emerged. The new Acts try to meet these points by allowing both individual enforcement, in some cases with the assistance of the Commissions, and also action against discriminatory practices by the Commissions.

1. *Equality for Women*, Cmnd. 5724, 1974, para. 28; *Racial Discrimination*, Cmnd. 6234, 1975, paras. 40, 41.

354. An individual may complain to an industrial tribunal within three months of the alleged discriminatory act (the period may be extended) and the EOC and CRE may, in their discretion, assist individuals for example by giving advice, procuring settlements, arranging for legal assistance or representation. Officers of ACAS have to attempt conciliation encouraging use, where appropriate, of voluntary industrial grievance procedures. The most serious obstacle facing the complainant is that of proving unlawful discrimination, although a procedure does exist by which the complainant may obtain information from the respondent to help him or her to decide whether or not to institute proceedings and, if he or she does, to assist in presenting a case. The remedies which the tribunal may award are less effective than those to be found in corresponding American legislation. The tribunal may (1) make an order declaring the rights of the parties; (2) award compensation (with a maximum of £8,000 including a sum in respect of hurt feelings); and (3) recommend that the respondent take within a specified period action appearing to the tribunal to be practicable for the purpose of obviating or reducing the adverse effect of the unlawful discrimination on the complainant. There is no power to order reinstatement or re-engagement or that the next job be offered to the complainant, although these measures may be recommended. If a recommendation is not complied with, without reasonable justification, the amount of compensation awarded may be increased, but not so as to exceed the overall limit of £8,000. In 1983, only 24 awards of compensation under the Race Relations Act were made by tribunals and the median award was between £300–£399. Twenty-six awards were made under the Sex Discrimination Act in 1983, the median award being between £500–£749.[1] (The relationship with unfair dismissal claims is discussed, above para. 318. The power of the Commissions is discussed in paras. 75–76, above.)

1. *Employment Gazette*, vol. 92, December 1984, p. 540.

§9. EQUAL PAY

355. The Equal Pay Act 1970 and the Sex Discrimination Act 1975 are mutually exclusive, in that the former applies only to discrimination relating to payment of money or other terms under the contract (including terms such as holidays, holiday pay, hours and sick pay), while the latter applies only to matters not included in a contract. Although the Acts are intended to be read as a code, there is a discrepancy between them, in that the Equal Pay Act requires a comparison to be made with a specific member of the opposite sex in the same employment whereas the Sex Discrimination Act covers situations where there is no comparable member of the opposite sex, *i.e.* a 'hypothetical' male. This has proved to be a serious limitation on the impact of the Equal Pay Act since, as has been pointed out above, many women work in predominantly female occupations or grades and are thus unable to find a suitable comparator. Moreover, the area of comparison which a woman may draw with a man's job is limited to a man in the same employment, that is employed by one employer or an associated employer at the same establishment in Great Britain. A comparison may be drawn with other establishments elsewhere in Britain only if common terms of employment are observed in those establishments. It is unusual for plants in different parts of the country to share common terms in this way. References in the Act to women apply equally to men and *vice versa*.

356. The Equal Pay Act entitles a woman to claim equal treatment with a man in three situations. First, it allows a woman the right to equal treatment when employed on work of the same or a broadly similar nature to that of a man in the same employment. In making the comparison, regard must be had to the frequency or otherwise with which any differences between their work occur in practice, as well as the nature and extent of the differences. This is a necessarily limited basis of comparison, and has been narrowly interpreted by tribunals and courts. Secondly, a woman is entitled to equal treatment with a man if her job and his have been given an equal value under a job evaluation study (JES). A 'job evaluation' is defined as a study undertaken with a view to evaluating jobs to be done by all or any employees in an undertaking or group of undertakings, where the evaluation is made in 'terms of the demands made on the worker under various headings (for instance effort, skill, decision)'.[1] The basis of comparison is also limited in that the employer is not obliged to undertake such a study. Although a recent survey found that about one-quarter of establishments have job evaluation studies, it also found that establishments with a predominantly female workforce were less likely to utilize such studies.[2] Even where a JES does exist, it may give disproportionate weight to traditionally 'male skills' such as physical strength or experience.

1. Eq.P.A. s.1(5).
2. W. Daniel and N. Millward, *Workplace Industrial Relations in Britain*, pp. 203–205.

357. The third and residual basis of comparison allows a woman to claim equal treatment with a man doing work of equal value.[1] This was introduced in 1983 as a result of infringement proceedings under Article 119 of the Treaty of Rome.[2] It is broader than the first two methods, since it does not require like work, nor does it rely on an employer-initiated job evaluation exercise. However, a claim for equal value cannot be made if a job evaluation study has been carried out unless the existing study can be shown to be discriminatory. If the tribunal is satisfied that there are reasonable grounds for determining that the work is of equal value, or that the existing JES is discriminatory, it may appoint an independent expert, one of a panel appointed by ACAS, to conduct a job evaluation exercise. The expert is given considerable discretion, the only guidelines being that the evaluation should be carried out according to the demands made on the employee, rather than using other methods of job evaluation such as market value or marginal productivity. The expert's report is only challengeable on limited grounds. The equal value provisions have been successfully used to establish entitlement to equality of pay between a female canteen worker and three skilled manual workers in a shipyard,[3] female ship packers and a male labourer[4] and a house-mother and a house-father.[5] However, the provisions are still limited in that the woman must find a comparator in the same employment doing work of the same value. There is still no redress for women on an admittedly lower grade where the differential with the next grade is disproportionately large, or for a woman in a segregated establishment.

1. Equal Pay (Amendment) Regulations 1983, SI 1983, No. 1794.
2. *Commission of the European Communities* v. *United Kingdom* [1982] ICR 578 (ECJ)
3. *Hayward* v. *Cammell Laird Shipbuilders Ltd.* [1984] IRLR 463.
4. *Wells* v. *F. Smales & Son Fish Merchants* EOR, No. 2, July/August 1985, p. 24.
5. *Scott* v. *Beam College*, EOR, No. 4, November/December 1985, p. 6.

358. Where a woman has established the relevant comparison, it is still open to the employer to argue in defence that the difference in pay was genuinely due to a material factor, other than the differences of sex.[1] In the case of 'like work' and 'work rated as equivalent', the material factor must be a 'material difference between the woman's case and the man's', whereas in the case of work of equal value, it need not be. The significance of this distinction lies in the extent to which the employer is entitled to justify the discrepancy by reference not to personal merits, but to broader market factors. The case law prior to the introduction of the equal value provisions had interpreted the reference to a 'material difference between her case and his' to mean that the employer's defence was limited to personal factors such as merit and experience.[2] The specific omission of these words in the defence to the new equal value provisions suggests that the intention was to allow market forces to justify a discrepancy. In any case, the principle is being eroded even in the context of like work and work rated as equivalent, for example in cases where there is no intention to discriminate,[3] or where successive employees are being compared.[4] The market forces defence is potentially a significant limitation on the impact of the Equal Pay Act particularly where 'women's work' is undervalued by the market due to traditional stereotypes, inferior training or responsibilities for child-care. This is mitigated to some extent by the principle that the employer must show, not just an intention to achieve an objective, but that the difference in pay actually achieved that objective.[5]

1. Section 1(3), Eq.P.A. 1970.
2. *Clay Cross (Quarry Services) Ltd.* v. *Fletcher* [1979] ICR 1 (CA).
3. *Jenkins* v. *Kingsgate (Clothing Productions) Ltd. (No. 2)* [1981] ICR 715 (EAT).
4. *Albion Shipping Agency* v. *Arnold* [1982] ICR 22 and see *Rainey* v. *Greater Glasgow Health Board* [1984] IRLR 414 (Court of Session).
5. *Jenkins* v. *Kingsgate (Clothing Productions) Ltd., supra.*

359. Unlike the Sex Discrimination Act, the Equal Pay Act does not explicitly include the concept of indirect discrimination. However, it has been held by the EAT that the Equal Pay Act 'operates to counteract all discrimination, whether direct or indirect and whether intentional or unintentional; it looks at the effect of the contractual terms, not whether they were expressed in overtly discriminatory words or with any particular intention'.[1]

1. *Jenkins* v. *Kingsgate (Clothing Productions) Ltd. (No. 2), supra,* at p. 724. This goes beyond the interpretation placed on Article 119 of the Treaty of Rome by the European Court of Justice: [1981] ICR 592.

360. The individual may enforce the right to equal treatment through a statutory term in the contract of employment (called the 'equality clause'). The claim may be referred to the industrial tribunal either by the employee, or by the employer, and in exceptional cases (so far never used) by the Secretary of State. The tribunal may award up to two years' arrears of pay and damages for breach of an equality clause. The proceedings must be instituted within 6 months of the termination of the woman's employment. Claims in respect of like work and work rated as equivalent under a JES follow a similar procedure to the tribunal proceedings (see above, Introduction, para. 80), but where there is an equal value claim a much more complicated and lengthy procedure has to be followed. This includes a compulsory preliminary hearing to weed out cases where there is no reasonable prospect of success.

361. Section 3 of the Equal Pay Act is concerned with collective agreements, employers' pay structures and wage regulation orders which contain provisions applying specifically to women only or to men only. There is no need to find a comparator as in the earlier sections. Since this is a collective rather than individual matter, complaints may be referred to the Central Arbitration Committee (see above, Introduction, para. 72) by the parties to a collective agreement or by the Secretary of State, rather than by individuals to an industrial tribunal. Until 1980, the CAC interpreted its powers under this section broadly, scrutinizing provisions which in effect applied predominantly to women, even if there was no explicit reference to women, and re-organising grading structures to ensure that *de facto* 'women's only' grades did not receive disproportionately low pay.[1] However, the High Court held in 1980 that the CAC's powers were limited to removing or amending provisions which explicitly referred to women.[2] As overtly discriminatory collective agreements and pay structures become less common, the CAC's jurisdiction under section 3 has all but dried up. In fact, only three references were received between 1981 and 1984. Following infringement proceedings in the European Court of Justice, the UK is now obliged to introduce legislation requiring that any provision contrary to the principle of equal treatment in a collective agreement is declared void or amended.[3] The Government has proposed a very limited amendment to the Act which would avoid discriminatory terms in collective agreements. Only direct discrimination is, however, to be covered, and if the clause is incorporated into the individual contract of employment, it will remain in force until the relevant agreement has been renegotiated.[4] It remains to be seen whether such an amendment fulfils the requirements of the EEC Equal Treatment Directive.

1. See P. Davies, 'The CAC and Equal Pay' [1980] *Current Legal Problems* 165.
2. *R* v. *CAC ex p., Hy-Mac* [1979] IRLR 461 (QBD)
3. *Commission of the European Communities* v. *United Kingdom* [1984] ICR 192.
4. Department of Employment, Consultative Document, September 1985.

362. The Equal Pay Act applies to persons employed on contracts of service or contracts personally to execute any work or labour. As in the case of the Sex Discrimination Act, one of the most important exceptions is the exclusion from the ambit of the Act of any 'terms and conditions related to death or retirement or any provision made in connection with death or retirement', and like the Sex Discrimination Act, this exception has been broadly construed (above, para. 349). This has been mitigated to some extent by the operation of EEC law, by virtue of which the Act, as impliedly amended by Article 119 of the Treaty of Rome, has been held not to exclude contributions to retirement pension schemes paid by an employer as an addition to gross salary.[1] The Equal Pay Act does operate in relation to terms relating to membership of an occupational pension scheme, but excludes terms 'affected by compliance with the law regulating the employment of women', and 'any special treatment accorded to women in connection with pregnancy or childbirth'. The latter prevents any complaint by men who do not receive paternity leave comparable to the maternity leave granted to female employees.

1. *Worringham* v. *Lloyds Bank Ltd.* [1981] ICR 558 (ECJ).

§10. REFORM

363. In 1985, the CRE made a number of wide-ranging proposals for the reform of the Race Relations Act.[1] These include a stronger and simpler definition of indirect discrimination, a shift to the respondent of the burden of disproving racial discrimination when less favourable treatment has been shown, a specialist division of the industrial tribunals to deal with discrimination cases, and the right to conduct formal investigations (see para. 76, above) on a more extensive basis. The CRE has also asked for powers to require ethnic record-keeping monitoring, which at present is voluntary under the Code of Practice. As long ago as 1980, the EOC presented a comprehensive list of proposed amendments to the Sex Discrimination and Equal Pay Acts[2] but these have not been implemented. These included a shift in the burden of proof to the alleged discriminator under the Sex Discrimination Act, and to enable a woman to compare her work with that of a 'hypothetical' male counterpart under the Equal Pay Act. It may be that reforms of this kind could improve the effectiveness of anti-discrimination law, but the wider goal of equal opportunities can only be achieved through programmes of positive action.

1. CRE, *Review of the Race Relations Act 1976: Proposals for Change*, London 1985.
2. EOC, *Annual Report* 1980, Appendix 5, London 1981; see too Katherine Scorer and Ann Sedley, *Amending the Equality Laws*, London, NCCL, 1983.

Chapter IX. Competition by Former Employees

364. This is a subject entirely regulated by rules of public policy formulated by the courts. Since early times restraints against competition have been regarded as void, and those who tried to control business competition were once even liable to imprisonment. It was however recognised that an employer might be unwilling to train apprentices if he could not restrain them from competing with him at the end of their time. In 1711, the rule was formulated that a restraint was *prima facie* valid if it did not extend over the whole country and was the result of a bargain between the parties. Since then, the rule has been changed in various ways and the modern doctrine is that restraints of trade are *prima facie* void but they can be justified if they are reasonable and are not contrary to the public interest. Moreover, a restraint may extend over the whole country or even the whole world, provided that this is reasonable and in the public interest.[1]

   1.*Nordenfelt* v. *Maxim Nordenfelt Guns & Ammunition Co.* [1894] AC 535.

365. We have seen (above, para. 169) that the duty of faithful service obliges an employee not to disclose trade secrets of the employer or his confidential information so long as the employment lasts. The duty not to disclose secrets or information may even continue after the employment has ended, and no covenant is needed for this purpose. However, this duty is more restricted than that imposed on the employee while the employment lasts. The obligation not to use or disclose information might cover secret processes or manufacture, or designs or special methods of construction, and other information of a sufficiently high degree of confidentiality as to amount to a trade secret. The obligation, after the employment has ended, does not extend to information only 'confidential' because the employee was told to keep it confidential and it remained in the employee's head and became part of his skill and knowledge. If the employer wishes to protect this latter kind of information after the employment has ended, he must enter into a restrictive covenant.[1] Another reason for a covenant is that there is no general restriction on an ex-employee canvassing or doing his business with customers of his former employer. The doctrine of restraint of trade then becomes relevant.

   1. *Faccenda Chicken Ltd.* v. *Fowler The Times*, 11 December 1985, CA.

366. The interests which an employer can protect by a covenant of this kind are narrowly defined. The employer cannot protect himself simply on the ground that competition by the ex-employee will harm the business in which he once worked. It has been suggested that the reasons for this are that the employer pays only for the services he receives and not for restraints against future competition, and that the employee is not an equal bargaining partner who is capable of protecting his own interests. Whatever the reasons it seems clear that an employer may expressly protect his trade secrets and confidential information (which, as we have said, might be impliedly protected anyway, but an express covenant puts it beyond doubt) and probably his 'know-how'. The employer may only restrain the employee from soliciting customers after leaving the employment if the employee's position enabled him to gain influence over them, *e.g.* a sales representative or hairdresser's assistant.

367. In order to be regarded as reasonable the covenant must not go beyond what is necessary to protect the employer's interests. In this regard the courts have distinguished between 'area covenants' and 'solicitation covenants'. The former prohibit *working* in a particular area, the latter prohibit *soliciting* former customers. The courts are more inclined to uphold solicitation covenants than area covenants, but an area covenant may be upheld provided that the area covered is not too large. Similarly a restraint for an excessive *length of time* will not be upheld, nor will one which restrains an activity which bears no relation directly to the business of an employer, such as a tailor being restrained from working as a seller of shoes.

368. Even if the restraint is reasonable, it may still be held to be against the public interest. This has rarely been used as a ground for invalidity and has been strongly criticised by academic writers largely because the court is unlikely to pay much attention to general economic conditions, such as whether large-scale unemployment renders restraints unreasonable and in the public interest.[1] In one case (1967)[2] a restraint contained in the rule of a pension fund to which an employee had agreed as a term of his employment was struck down as not being in the public interest. The rule which was held to be invalid stated that the employee would lose his pension if he engaged in any competitive activity. Instead of using the ground of public interest, the court could have decided that the employer had no sufficient 'interest' to protect or that the restraint was not reasonable.

1. A. L. Goodhart, *Law Quarterly Review* Vol. 49, p. 465.
2. *Bull* v. *Pitney-Bowes Ltd.* [1967] 1 WLR 273.

Chapter X. Inventions by Employees

369. The law relating to inventions, patents and copyrights is a highly specialised subject which, in England, is practised by patent agents and a small number of specialist solicitors and barristers. Nevertheless, since three-quarters of all patented inventions are produced by employees in the course of their employment, the area is one of potential importance to collective bargaining and some trade unions organising research and engineering workers have been active in seeking rewards for employee inventors.

370.[1] Before the Patents Act 1977 came into operation there were often express contractual terms requiring research workers and similar employees to assign to the employer any rights accruing to the employee from his inventions. Even if there was no express term the employee could be held by the courts to be the trustee of the invention for his employer's benefit, or, if there was no trust it could be held that there was an implied term in the contract vesting the benefit of the invention in the employer. In those circumstances the employee was not entitled to any reward, at common law. An attempt to improve the position of the employee inventor was made by the Patents Act 1949, section 56(2) of which provided that the court or Comptroller of Patents could order the apportionment of the benefit of an invention between an employer and his employee, unless satisfied that one or other was entitled to the benefit to the exclusion of the other. This section was given a narrow interpretation in *Sterling Engineering Co. Ltd.* v. *Patchett*[2] which decided in effect that the beneficial distribution of patent profits between employer and employee could take place only where *both* parties were entitled to the patent at law, a situation which has arisen in only one reported case, and that in 1905. The decision also supports the view that, at common law, it is an implied term in every contract of employment that inventions produced in the course of employment become the property of the employer. This remains the law in respect of all inventions made before the coming into operation of the Patents Act 1977, and for certain inventions where the employment was not connected with the United Kingdom at the time of making the invention.

1. This and the following paragraphs are reprinted with permission of Sweet & Maxwell Ltd. from Hepple and O'Higgins, *Employment Law*, 4th ed. (London, 1981).
2. [1955]AC 434.

371. The Patents Act 1977 replaces the earlier law, in respect of inventions made after the Act comes into operation, principally in respect of (1) the ownership of inventions; (2) the right of the employee to be rewarded; (3) the amount of the reward; and (4) the exclusion by express contract of the statutory rights.

(1) *Ownership of inventions.* Section 39(1) provides that, notwithstanding anything in any rule of law, an invention made by an employee belongs to the employer if

'*(a)* it was made in the course of normal duties of the employee or in the course of duties falling outside his normal duties, but specifically assigned to him,

and the circumstances in either case were such that an invention might
reasonably be expected to result from the carrying out of his duties; or
(b) the invention was made in the course of the duties of the employee and at
the time of making the invention, because of the nature of his duties and the
particular responsibilities arising from the nature of his duties he had a
special obligation to further the interests of the employer's undertaking.'

Any other inventions belong to the employee. The first limb of section 39(1)
appears to be more favourable to the employee than the old common law test of
ownership, because factors such as the employee's status, the use made by him
of the employer's facilities and his skills and qualifications are no longer
relevant to this question, although they may affect the size of the employee's
award. The relevant criteria under the first limb are (1) were the inventor's
duties of employment linked to the invention? and (2) was it reasonably
expected that invention would result from the performance of those duties? It
has been held that an employee's 'normal duties' are those which he was
actually employed to do. So the manager of a valve department, who was not
employed to design and invent but only to effect sales of the company's valves
and ensure after-sales service, was entitled to keep his invention of a new kind
of valve.[1] The second limb of section 39 appears to codify the common law rule
that the invention belongs to the employer where the employee was employed
to make inventions of that sort, as where he is a consultant of the employer
company's managing director.

1. *Reiss Engineering Co. Ltd.* v. *Harris* [1985] IRLR 232, High Court.

372. (2) *The right of the employee to be rewarded.* An employee whose
invention is exploited by his employer may apply to court or to the Comptroller
of Patents for an award of compensation under section 40. He is entitled to do
so whether the invention belongs to employer or employee, but the requirements are different in each case. (a) Where the invention belongs to the
employer, the employee must show that (i) he made the invention; (ii) a patent
has been granted; (iii) the patent is (having regard among other things to the
size and nature of the employer's undertaking) of 'outstanding benefit' to the
employer; and (iv) by reason of those facts it is 'just' that the employer should
compensate the employee. (b) Where the patented invention belongs to the
employee, and the rights in the invention or patents or application for a patent
have been assigned to the employer, or an exclusive licence granted to the
employer, then all the employer need show is that (i) the benefit derived by the
employee is inadequate in relation to the benefit derived by the employer from
the patent; and (ii) by reason of those facts it is 'just' that the employer should
compensate the employee in addition to that benefit.

However, in both these cases, the employee's statutory rights do not apply if
there is a 'relevant collective agreement' (*i.e.* made between a trade union to
which the employee belongs and the employer or an association to which the
employer belongs) providing for the payment of compensation 'in respect of
inventions of the same description as that invention to employees of the same
description as that employee'. The restrictions on contracting-out (below) do

not apply to such collective agreements. While it is expected that collective agreements will improve on the statutory rights there is nothing in the Act to prevent less favourable compensation arrangements by virtue of a collective agreement. In such a case the employee could protect himself only by resigning from the union but he would need to do so *before* the invention is made.

373. (3) *The amount of the reward.* Section 41(1) provides that the employee must receive an award of compensation which secures for him ' . . . a fair share (having regard to all the circumstances) of the benefit which the employer has derived, or may reasonably expect to derive, from the patent or from the assignment, assignation or grant to a person connected with the employer . . .'

A compensation order may be varied, discharged, revised or suspended. Among the relevant criteria in determining what is a 'fair share' are (i) the nature of the employee's duties, his remuneration and other employment advantages; (ii) the effort and skill he devoted to making the invention; (iii) the effort, skill and advice contributed by others; (iv) the contribution made by the employer by the provision of advice, facilities and other assistance, by the provision of opportunities and by his managerial and commercial skills and activities.

(4) *Exclusion by express contract of the statutory rights.* Section 42(2) renders unenforceable any term in a contract which diminishes the employee's rights in inventions made after the date of the contract. This applies to Crown employees as it does to other employees, and even to contracts made with some person other than the employer (*e.g.* a Research Council) at the request of the employer or in pursuance of the employee's contract of employment.

189

Part II. Collective Labour Relations

Chapter I. Trade Union Freedom

§1. GOVERNMENT POLICIES

374. The United Kingdom has ratified ILO Convention No. 87 (1948) on Freedom of Association, Convention No. 98 (1949) on the Right to Organise and Collective Bargaining, Convention No. 151 (1978) on Protection of the Right to Organise in the Public Service, and Convention No. 135 (1972) Concerning Protection and Facilities to be Afforded to Workers' Representatives in the Undertaking. It has also accepted the obligations in Article 11 of the European Convention on Human Rights and Fundamental Freedoms, which include the right to form and join trade unions, and Article 5 of the European Social Charter on the right to organise. These obligations are not directly enforceable as part of domestic law (for the reasons explained above para. 19), but before the 1980s successive governments sought to achieve international standards first by acting as a model employer in this respect, and secondly, since 1971, by legislation. There have been three main occasions on which direct complaints have been made to the ILO Governing Body Committee on Freedom of Association from the United Kingdom. The first was by the National Union of Bank Employees in 1962 and led to the setting up of an official inquiry in the United Kingdom which made suggestions for the improvement of trade union recognition by the Banks.[1] The second occasion arose from the Government's refusal in 1981 of access to arbitration in accordance with a Civil Service Arbitration agreement made in 1925. The ILO Governing Body's Committee on Freedom of Association in its finding[2] stressed the importance of access to independent arbitration but without any direct impact on the Government's policy. Thirdly, in 1984, a complaint was made by the Council of Civil Service Unions concerning the prohibition of trade unions at the Government Communications Headquarters (GCHQ) (below, para. 375). The Committee on Freedom of Association held[3] that the UK Government had contravened its obligations. No action has, however, been taken by the Government to remedy this contravention. The relevant trade unions have lodged a petition with the European Commission on Human Rights complaining that the UK Government has contravened Article 11 of the Convention. In a different case, concerning the closed shop operated by British Rail, the European Court held that the UK had contravened Article 11 (see below, para. 382).

1. Report of the Inquiry (Chairman: Lord Cameron) Cmnd. 2202, 1963.

2. ILO Governing Body, 211th Report of the Committee on Freedom of Association, 1981, Case No. 1038.
3. ILO Governing Body, 234th Report of the Committee on Freedom of Association, 1984, Case No. 1261.

375. From 1906 until 1979 there was an official policy of *encouraging* public service employees to join trade unions (apart from the police whose freedom of association is strictly limited by law). In this, governments were a model employer. From 1946 until repealed in 1983, the Fair Wages Resolution of the House of Commons in effect required government departments to include in their contracts with suppliers a clause which provided that 'the contractor shall recognise the freedom of his workpeople to be members of trade unions'. However, the Conservative Government, in power since 1979, has moved away from this traditional policy. The Fair Wages Resolution was repealed in 1983 and the official encouragement to civil servants to join the appropriate trade unions was removed from the staff handbook. The most striking sign of the new policy direction was the Prime Minister's decision in January 1984 that trade union membership at the intelligence gathering unit, Government Communications Headquarters (GCHQ), posed a threat to national security. Without advance warning or consultation, the government banned the trade unions which had been firmly established there since the inception of GCHQ. It is now a condition of service of all civil servants employed at the intelligence gathering unit that they will not belong to a trade union or staff association, other than the internal, management-sponsored staff association which has subsequently been established. A legal challenge to this unilateral change in conditions of service was unsuccessful.[1] The unions argued that the failure to consult them before the decision was a breach of natural justice, rendering it void. This contention was upheld by Glidewell J., but dismissed by the Court of Appeal and the House of Lords. The Law Lords unanimously held that the long history of encouragement of trade union membership and consultation over terms of employment gave rise to a duty to consult trade unions before making important changes. However, this duty was outweighed by the interests of the state in national security. The Law Lords did not require the Prime Minister to provide evidence of the alleged threat to national security beyond proving that the real reason for her action was her genuine fear of such a threat. The issue whether the decision to ban trade union membership was necessary in the interests of a democratic society for the protection of national security, subject to the margin of appreciation, which gives the state a discretion, will now be argued in proceedings under the European Convention on Human Rights (para. 374, above).

1. *Council of Civil Service Unions* v. *Minister for the Civil Service* [1984] 3 All ER 935, HL; see too para. 94 on the basis for the judicial review of government actions in this field.

§2. The Right to Belong to and Participate in the Activities of an Independent Trade Union

376. A statutory right to belong to a trade union of one's choice was introduced for the first time in Great Britain by the Industrial Relations Act 1971. After the repeal of that Act there was no comprehensive legal guarantee of the right to organise. Instead three individual legal rights were introduced to protect trade union membership and activity at the workplace. These individual rights were consolidated in the Employment Protection (Consolidation) Act 1978. The first of these is that officials and members of independent trade unions have the right to time off to participate in union activities. (This is discussed in Part I, paras. 188 and 189.) The second is that every employee has the right not to be unfairly dismissed by reason of membership of, or activities, at an appropriate time, in an independent trade union.[1] The third is that every employee has the right 'as an individual' not to be penalised for, or deterred or prevented from joining an independent trade union or taking part in its activities at an appropriate time, by sanctions short of dismissal imposed by the employer.[2] There is no upper age limit or qualifying period of service for claiming these rights.

1. EPCA 1978, s. 58 as amended.
2. EPCA 1978, s. 23 as amended.

377. A number of points may be made about the second and third of these rights. The first is that they belong to *individuals*. Although they protect a *collective* freedom, they cannot be enforced by the trade union, but only by the employee against his employer. Although the union may be expected to support the individual in any action he takes, it may be a weakness of this approach that the individual is more likely than a trade union to be deterred from bringing an action against the employer, especially during the subsistence of the employment relationship. A second point is that the right (like a complaint of unfair dismissal) is limited to those who are *employees* (above, para. 114). Surprisingly, the legislation introduced by the Labour Government in 1975 narrowed the protection given in this respect by the Industrial Relations Act. The present Act does not protect *workseekers* or those who are not employees, for example 'self-employed' construction workers. Moreover it has been held that an employee is not protected against dismissal for trade union activities in a *previous* job.[1] In these respects, British legislation plainly falls short of the ILO standards.

1. *City of Birmingham District Council* v. *Beyer* [1977] IRLR 210.

378. A third point is that the right to belong is not unlimited. It is a right to belong to an *independent trade union* (see para. 416, below) and so properly excludes employer-dominated 'company unions'. Moreover, where there is a valid 'union membership agreement' (certain types of closed shop) it must be the trade union or unions named in that agreement (see below, para. 389). So it is not always a right to belong to the union of one's choice. However, if there is no 'union membership agreement' then the employee may belong to any union

and not necessarily the union which the employer recognises for collective bargaining purposes.

379. A fourth point is that the ambit of legitimate trade union activities has been severely limited by judicial interpretation. The House of Lords has held that the protected activities are only those not requiring the employer's assistance or those normally available to employees or those requiring him to submit to no more than trifling inconvenience. So use of a canteen outside working hours while the employees are permitted to be on the premises is protected but not necessarily use of a notice board.[1] Moreover, the Court of Appeal has decided that the employee is protected only if the employer's action is a response to the individual's activities as part of a trade union and not in respect of a general reprisal against the union itself. So a management decision to dismiss employees as a direct response to a union's request for recognition, after the employees had joined the union, was not unlawful.[2] At the same time the EAT has excluded an employer's action against employees who presented a petition about safety at work on the grounds that they were acting as individual members of a trade union rather than as part of the activities of the trade union.[3] In other words, only where the employer's action is taken against employees for their *individual* participation in the *collective* activity does the legislation provide any remedy. Finally it is to be noted that the right to participate is confined to activities at 'an appropriate time'. This in effect means times outside working hours, or times when the employee is on the employer's premises with permission but is not required to be at work (*e.g.* during meal breaks). While the employee is at work the employer's permission is required.[4]

1. *Post Office* v. *Union of Post Office Workers* [1974] ICR 378, HL.
2. *Carrington* v. *Therm-a-Stor Ltd.* [1983] ICR 208, CA.
3. *Chant* v. *Aquaboats Ltd.* [1978] ICR 643, EAT.
4. EPCA 1978, ss. 23(2), 58(2).

380. The employee's remedy for breach of these rights is to make a complaint to an industrial tribunal within three months of the act complained of. In the case of unfair dismissal, the special procedure of 'interim relief' is available to continue the employee's contract of employment until his or her rights are determined (see Part I, para. 316, above). Where reinstatement or re-engagement is not ordered, there is a minimum *basic* award of compensation, and also a *special* award (see Part I, paras. 314 and 315 above). These relatively high levels of compensation were introduced by the Employment Act 1982, and were mainly intended to deter closed shop dismissals (see para. 392, below). It remains to be seen whether they will provide a deterrent against the victimisation of trade unionists. Between 1979 and 1982, an average less than 15 per cent of employees who complained of unfair dismissal on grounds of trade union membership and activities[1] won their tribunal cases. In the case of action short of dismissal, the tribunal may grant a declaration as to the employee's rights and may award compensation for the loss sustained (*e.g.* loss of earnings) and also in respect of 'the infringement of the complainant's rights' (a statutory penalty not limited in amount).

1. L. Dickens *et al., Dismissal: A study of unfair dismissal and the industrial tribunal system* Oxford, 1985, pp. 245–247.

§3. THE RIGHT NOT TO BELONG

381. The right not to belong to a trade union has frequently been treated differently from the right to belong. The question is of particular relevance where membership of a trade union is a precondition for obtaining or retaining employment (the 'closed shop'). (The closed shop is dealt with below, para. 386.) It has been argued that whereas freedom of association is essential to the protection of workers in a pluralist society, the right not to belong is of a different character and may lead to disruption of orderly industrial relations. The Donovan Commission, for example, argued that 'the two are not truly comparable. The former condition [the right not to belong] is designed to frustrate the development of collective bargaining, which it is public policy to promote, whereas no such objection applies to the latter'.[1]

1. Report of the Royal Commission on Trade Unions and Employers' Associations Cmnd. 3623, 1968, para. 599, and see generally R. Lewis and B. Simpson (1982) 11 *Industrial Law Journal* 227; *cf.* Industrial Relations Act 1971, s. 5.

382. A persistent argument against the closed shop centres around the alleged threat to individual freedom. The debate about whether the right to freedom of association is infringed by the closed shop depends to some extent on whether freedom of association is seen as an aspect of individual autonomy, or as a social right, to which exclusively individual interests are to some extent subordinate. One question which arises is whether the closed shop infringes Article 11 of the European Convention on Human Rights and Fundamental Freedom, which states that freedom of association should not be subject to any restrictions except such as are prescribed by law and are necessary in a democratic society for the protection of the rights and freedoms of others. In the discussions leading up to the formulation of Article 11, it was explicitly agreed that it would be undesirable to include a right not to be compelled to join a union parallel to the right to join a union. In 1981, this question was raised directly before the European Court of Human Rights.[1] Three former employees of British Rail complained that their rights under Article 11 had been infringed when they were dismissed for refusal to belong to the unions with which British Rail had concluded a union membership agreement. Although the Court refused to review the closed shop system as such, it upheld the applicants' complaint in the particular circumstances of the case. The fact that the closed shop had been imposed on the applicants after their employment had begun and under the threat of dismissal was held to be an unacceptable infringement of their freedom of association. In addition, the Court held that the applicants' freedom of association had been infringed by the limitation on their choice of which union to join. The implications of the judgment are

ambiguous.[2] Since the majority of the Court declined to find a general
'negative right to dissociate' it is difficult to see what right the compulsion to
join violated. Moreover, 'freedom of choice' is meaningless where, as in this
case, there was effectively only one union the men could join. Freedom to
choose does not logically imply a freedom not to join *any* union.[3]

1. *Young, James and Webster* v. *United Kingdom* [1981] IRLR 408 (ECHR).
2. M. Forde, (1982) *Industrial Law Journal* vol. 11, p. 1 at pp. 4–5.
3. See F. Prondzynski (1982) *Cambridge Law Journal* 256.

383. The Industrial Relations Act 1971, reflected an individualist philosophy by conferring a general right not to associate, in parallel with the new
right to associate. This clashed with the collectivist aims of trade unions, most
of whom had in any case refused to register as required by the Act. Competition for members developed between unregistered TUC unions and new or
splinter unions who utilised the new rights as a platform to organise. As a result
stable bargaining arrangements were threatened with disruption. After the
repeal of the 1971 Act, the right not to belong to a union was recognised in only
two specific instances, by legislation enacted between 1974–1976. First, there
was a right not to be compelled to be a member of a non-independent
(employer-dominated) trade union. Secondly, where a closed shop existed, an
employee who genuinely objected on grounds of religious belief to being a
member of any trade union whatsoever was protected from dismissal on
grounds of non-membership.

384. The Conservative Government elected in 1979 took the view that the
right not to belong to a trade union was equivalent to the right to belong. This
was reinforced by the view that the closed shop was an unwarranted restriction
on individual freedom of choice, and an unnecessary fortification of trade
union power, distorting the free market (see Introduction, para. 64). The
statutory protections of the right to belong have therefore been expanded to
include similar protections for the right not to belong. Thus the right not to be
unfairly dismissed for membership of a trade union has been extended, so that
it is automatically unfair to dismiss an employee where the principal reason for
dismissal was his or her non-membership of or refusal to belong to a particular
or any trade union.[1] Specific provisions operate where there is a closed shop
(see below). As in the case of trade union membership, dismissal for non-
membership attracts very high levels of compensation, particularly where
reinstatement has been ordered and not complied with (see Part I, paras. 314
and 315, above). Similarly, employees are protected from action short of
dismissal compelling them to be or become a member of any trade union or a
particular trade union, or to enforce a requirement to make a payment as an
alternative to joining a trade union.[2] In addition, interim relief is available to
those dismissed for non-membership in the same way as for membership (see
para. 316, above).

1. EPCA 1978, s. 58(1)(c) and see above, para. 305 (automatically unfair reasons for
   dismissal).
2. EPCA 1978, s. 23(1)(c). For closed shop provisions see below, para. 390.

385. A further significant innovation of the Employment Acts 1980 and 1982 was the introduction of a right to include the trade union as a third party or co-defendant in proceedings against the employer for unfair dismissal or action short of dismissal.[1] Both the employer and the employee have the right to join the trade union as a party to the proceedings if it is claimed that the union took industrial action or threatened to do so in order to put pressure on the employer to dismiss the employee or take action short of dismissal. The tribunal may then make an award against the union only, or against both the employer and the union.

1. EPCA 1978, ss. 26A, 76A.

§4. The Closed Shop

386. The closed shop has been defined as a 'situation in which employees come to realise that a particular job is only to be obtained and retained if they become and remain members of one of a specified number of trade unions'.[1] The closed shop is normally maintained by unions threatening to take industrial action unless the employer dismisses or refuses to employ non-members. The phenomenon takes many different forms. A distinction is sometimes drawn between the *pre-entry closed shop*, in which a worker cannot apply for a job unless he is a union member, and the *post-entry closed shop* (called the 'union shop' in America), in which the worker is required to join a union within a stated period after having taken up the job. In Britain, the line between these two is often blurred in practice. Another distinction is between the requirement that the worker should become a member of any union or that he should belong to a specified union, or even a section of a specified union. Closed shops of all these varieties are found in Britain.

1. W. E. J. McCarthy, *The Closed Shop in Britain*, Oxford, 1964. This definition was followed by the Royal Commission on Trade Unions & Employers' Associations, Cmnd. 3623, 1968, para. 588.

387. The function of the closed shop has changed over the years. In a major study published in 1964, McCarthy found that the closed shop was a response by unions and workers to certain organisational problems, such as high turnover, scattered workforces, inter-union competition and the existence of an alternative workforce which might undermine industrial action. The closed shop assisted unions in establishing and maintaining membership, in disciplining the members, and (in the case of a pre-entry closed shop only) in controlling an alternative workforce.[1] Recent studies show, however, that in the 1970s the closed shop became less an instrument of employee control and more an instance of joint trade union and employer regulation in the interests of orderly industrial relations.[2] Employers not infrequently regarded the closed shop as a useful means of preventing inter-union disputes, of ensuring that collective bargaining arrangements cover all workers, and of maintaining effective discipline by union officials over the workforce. Indeed, during the period 1971–1974 when the closed shop was prohibited by law, it appears that employers and trade unions colluded to maintain closed shops in existence. Moreover, closed shop agreements are now more likely to be formal and in writing than they were 20 years ago.

1. McCarthy, *op. cit.*
2. S. Dunn and J. Gennard, *The Closed Shop in British Industry*, London, 1984; and Ch. 4 in *Industrial Relations and the Law in the 1980s: Issues and future Trends* (eds. P. Fosh and C. R. Littler), London, 1985.

388. By the end of the 1970s, closed shop arrangements covered about a quarter of the workforce, more than 5.2 million people.[1] About 800,000 of these (4 per cent of the workforce) were in pre-entry closed shops, nearly all of these having been established in the era of craft unionism and in industries, such as merchant shipping, dock work and acting, in order to counteract the employers' use of a plentiful supply of casual non-union labour.[2] In the early 1960s post-entry closed shops covered 3 million people (12 per cent of the workforce), and were concentrated in a few industries, in particular engineering and coalmining.[3] By the end of the 1970s, the number in post-entry closed shops had grown to at least 4.5 million, an increase of over 50 per cent since the early 1960s. Post-entry closed shops had emerged in industries where they were little known previously, such as food, drink, clothing, footwear and chemical manufacture, local authorities and the nationalised industries.[4] However, even before the Conservative Government's Employment Acts of 1980 and 1982 (below) had begun to take effect, the closed shop had reached a point of stagnation and decline. By mid-1982, it had fallen by 13 per cent to approximately 4.5 million in both pre- and post-entry closed shops.[5] The shrinking of industries such as coalmining, steel, shipbuilding, clothing, footwear, vehicles and railways where the closed shop was widespread, has not been compensated by extension in other industries. The continuation in these economic trends, with an overall decline in union membership, coupled with the impact of the Employment Acts 1980 and 1982, means that the closed shop has continued to decline since 1982.

1. J. Gennard *et al.*, (1980) 88 *Employment Gazette* 16.
2. *Ibid.*
3. McCarthy, *op cit.*, pp. 14–22.
4. Gennard *et al.*, *op cit.*
5. Dunn and Gennard, *op cit.*, p. 147.

389. Successive governments have displayed differing attitudes to the closed shop. It remained outside the scope of legal regulation until the Industrial Relations Act 1971 directly challenged the practice by making all pre-entry closed shop agreements void and allowing the post-entry closed shop only in two exceptional situations (the 'agency' shop and the 'approved closed shop'). The legitimacy of the closed shop was subsequently recognised by the Trade Union and Labour Relations Acts 1974–1976 in that a dismissal for refusing to belong to a union was deemed fair if there was a 'union membership agreement' made with an independent trade union, under which employees had to belong to a trade union. A limited exception was provided in the case of employees who genuinely objected to union membership 'on grounds of religious belief'. With some amendments, this remained the legal framework until 1980. The Employment Acts 1980 and 1982 amended the legal framework in order to undermine the closed shop as far as possible without outlawing it directly. Although dismissal of a non-member where there is a union membership agreement remains possible, the Employment Acts 1980 and 1982 have introduced so many exceptions that in most cases the dismissal will in fact be unlawful.

390. For the purposes of the statute, a closed shop is referred to as a 'union membership agreement'. This is defined as an agreement between employers and one or more independent trade unions, which relates to employees of an identifiable class and has the effect in practice of requiring employees of that class to be or become members of the union or unions who are parties to or specified in the agreement.[1] Where there is a union membership agreement as so defined, a dismissal for non-membership of a specified union will be unfair in the following situations. First, such a dismissal will be unfair unless the union membership agreement has been approved by a secret ballot within the five years preceding the relevant dismissal.[2] The level of support required in a ballot is unusually high. Union membership agreements which take effect after 15 August 1980 require the approval of at least 80 per cent of those entitled to vote. For union membership agreements which took effect before that date (the vast majority of closed shops), and for all second and subsequent ballots, a majority of 80 per cent of those entitled to vote or 85 per cent of those voting is required. These provisions came into effect on 1 November 1984. The TUC's official policy has been to refuse to recommend ballots to test the closed shop, but some ballots have been held, with mixed results.

1. TULRA 1974–1976, s. 30(1).
2. EPCA 1978, ss. 58(3) and 58A as mended and substituted by EA 1982, s. 3.

391. Secondly, a dismissal will be unfair if the employee 'genuinely objects on grounds of conscience or other deeply held personal conviction to being a member of any trade union whatsoever or of a particular trade union'.[1] This may encourage factionalism, since protection has been judicially interpreted to extend beyond employees who have fundamental objections to unionism in general to include those who disagree with the particular policies being pursued by the union at the time.[2] Thirdly, it is unfair to dismiss an employee who has not been a member of a union specified in the union membership agreement at any time since the agreement took effect. Fourthly, where the union membership agreement took effect after 14 August 1980, it is unfair to dismiss a relevant employee who has not been a member of the union at any time since the day on which the ballot approving the closed shop was held. Fifthly, it is unfair to dismiss an employee who has been excluded or expelled from the union, and has initiated proceedings or obtained a declaration that such exclusion or expulsion was unreasonable by virtue of section 4 of the Employment Act 1980 (see below, para. 393).[3] Finally, the statute protects employees who are subject to a written (usually professional) code of conduct which prevents them from taking industrial action.[4]

1. EPCA 1978, s. 58(4).
2. *Home Delivery Ltd.* v. *Shackcloth* [1985] ICR 147, EAT at 154; *McGhee* v. *Midland British Road Services Ltd.* [1985] ICR 503 (EAT).
3. EPCA 1978, s. 58(7).
4. EPCA 1978, s. 58(8).

392. The restrictive effect of the above provisions is further reinforced by the very high levels of compensation available in cases in which a dismissal is unfair by virtue of these provisions (see Part I, paras. 314 and 315, above), and the possibility of using the interim relief procedure (above, para. 316) to continue the contract of employment until a tribunal has resolved a complaint. As described above, para. 385, it is possible for either the applicant or the employer to join the trade unions as a respondent or third party in unfair dismissal proceedings, where the dismissal has taken place as a result of pressure by the union. These provisions are particularly appropriate to closed shop situations, where direct or indirect threats of industrial action are often necessary to preserve the closed shop. The tribunal may then award compensation against the union, or against both the union and the employer.

§5. Exclusion or Expulsion from the Union

393. In a further important innovation, the Employment Act 1980 provided a right not to be unreasonably excluded or expelled from a trade union where a union membership agreement is in operation.[1] An employee who has been excluded or expelled from a union in these circumstances has the right to complain to an industrial tribunal, which may declare that the exclusion or expulsion was unreasonable. The statutory provisions give little credence to the union's interest in autonomy in respect of its internal procedures. Thus there is no requirement that workers first exhaust internal complaints or appeals procedures before applying to a tribunal. Nor is it sufficient for the expulsion or exclusion to be consistent with the union's own rules; such an exclusion or expulsion may nevertheless be considered unreasonable by the tribunal. Conversely, the union's actions are not necessarily unreasonable simply because they contravened the union's rules. (This may be contrasted with the strict common law requirements that a trade union abide by its own rules – below, para. 424.) It has been held that it is not necessary for the applicant to show that he or she was denied a particular job; it is sufficient to be seeking work in the particular field of industry to which the closed shop relates.[2]

1. EA 1980, ss. 4–5.
2. *Clark* v. *NATSOPA (Sogat '82)* [1985] IRLR 494 (EAT).

394. If the union does not admit or re-admit the person after a tribunal has declared his or her complaint to be well-founded, he or she may apply for compensation to the Employment Appeal Tribunal, which must award such compensation as it considers just and equitable in the circumstances. This includes loss of earnings, loss of earning opportunity in the industry where the closed shop operates, and non-pecuniary loss, such as injury to feelings and upset in the person's personal life resulting from the refusal of membership.[1] The award may be reduced if the applicant caused or contributed to the refusal or exclusion and the applicant has the duty to mitigate his or her loss. If the person has been admitted or re-admitted, he or she may apply to an industrial tribunal for compensation for any loss sustained in consequence of the refusal or expulsion complained of. (The common law controls on the relationship between unions and their members are described below, para. 424).

1. *Howard* v. *NGA* [1985] ICR 101 (EAT). Compare unfair dismissal, where compensation for injury to feelings is not *per se* compensatable.

§6. THE TUC'S INDEPENDENT REVIEW COMMITTEE

395. In 1976, the TUC established a voluntary committee, the Independent Review Committee (IRC), as an alternative to the legal control of internal trade union affairs where a closed shop exists. Its terms of reference are 'to consider appeals from individuals who have been dismissed, or given notice of dismissal, from their jobs as a result of being expelled from, or having been refused admission to, a union in a situation where trade union membership is a condition of employment'.[1] In contrast with the statutory provisions (para. 393, above), the IRC will not consider a complaint before the individual has exhausted all internal procedures of his or her own union and an attempt has been made to settle the matter by agreement. If this fails, the IRC may make a recommendation to the union concerned. A majority of TUC affiliated unions have agreed to abide by the recommendations of the Committee (which consists of Professor Lord Wedderburn, Lord McCarthy and Mr. George Doughty). The IRC attaches great importance to conciliation in its work, both before and after a full hearing.[2] It has no power to award compensation, and although it has had some success in achieving admission or re-admission into membership of the union, it has had little success in securing reinstatement into employment. Twenty cases reached a full hearing between 1976 and 1981. Since the enactment of a statutory right to appeal to an industrial tribunal on a complaint of unreasonable exclusion or expulsion, an applicant has had an alternative remedy to that supplied by the IRC, and one which includes a possible remedy of compensation (above, para. 394). On the other hand, the IRC has the advantage of greater flexibility of procedure and is more likely to find a compromise which is acceptable to both union and applicant.[3]

1. TUC Report, 1976, p. 94.
2. See K. D. Ewing and W. M. Rees (1981) 10 *Industrial Law Journal* 84.
3. *Ibid*.

§7. UNION-ONLY PRACTICES

396. One way of supporting union membership and recognition, apart from the closed shop, is the 'union-only' or 'recognition-only' practice, whereby contracts for the supply of goods or services are made subject to the condition that the suppliers' employees are trade union members, or that the supplier recognises, negotiates or consults with a union. For example, some local authorities controlled by the Labour Party allow only fully unionised firms on to their tender lists. As part of the present government's strategy of preventing such aids to the maintenance of union membership, the Employment Act 1982 contains provisions preventing such practices.[1] This is done in three ways. First, a clause imposing either a union-only or a recognition-only requirement in a contract for the supply of goods or services is made void. Secondly, a right to sue for breach of statutory duty is created when a person is excluded from a list of supplies, or from those from whom tenders are invited, or when a supply contract is terminated, or when no supply contract is entered into with a person, on the grounds that that person does not recognise, bargain with or consult unions, or the work to be done under the contract is likely to be done by non-unionists. Any person adversely affected has the right to sue. These would include, for example, a sub-contractor to the supplier affected, or an employee made redundant by that supplier. Thirdly, the Act lays down certain circumstances in which industrial action intended to put pressure on employers to maintain union-only or recognition-only practices is not protected from civil liability by the immunities afforded to other types of industrial action (see Ch. IV, paras. 484–502, below). Like the other recent legislation this reflects the clear 'preference for non-unionism' in government policy since 1979.[2]

1. EA 1982, ss. 12–14.
2. J. Clark and Lord Wedderburn in *Labour Law and Industrial Relations: Building on Kahn-Freund*, Oxford, 1983, p. 143.

Chapter II. Trade Unions and Employers' Associations

§1. TRADE UNION MEMBERSHIP

397. After many years of steady growth, trade union membership in Britain has declined steeply since 1979.[1] In 1984, there were 11.08 million trade union members, a drop of 17 per cent from the 1979 peak of 13.3 million. During the same period, employment in the United Kingdom fell by 8 per cent. Trade union density has been particularly badly affected by the decline in employment in manufacturing industries, where there is a traditional concentration of union members, and where the largest falls in membership occurred. At the same time, there was some increase in membership in service industries, such as banking, finance and insurance.

1. Figures in this and subsequent paragraphs come from *Employment Gazette*, vol. 94, January 1986, pp. 28–30; see for a full discussion G. S. Bain and R. Price, Ch. 1 in *Industrial Relations in Britain* (ed. G. S. Bain), Oxford, 1983.

§2. TRADE UNION STRUCTURE

398. In recent years, there has been a trend towards concentration of union membership into fewer and larger unions. Whereas at the start of the 20th century, there were 1,323 trade unions, this had fallen to 519 in 1973, and to 371 in 1984. More than half the total membership in 1984 was covered by the largest 7 unions and there were 21 unions each with 100,000 or more members. At the same time, there remain a large number of very small unions. In 1984, over half of all trade unions had fewer than 1,000 members each; together they accounted for only 0.5 per cent of the total membership of all unions. The process of concentration has been stimulated by a number of pressures including the difficulties faced by smaller unions in remaining solvent in the face of inflation and falling membership, changes in technology which have eroded traditional crafts and skills, and the active policy of expansion adopted by some unions. Hyman comments that 'two decades ago the pattern of British union membership differed little from the structure consolidated around the turn of the century: dominated by a handful of general, ex-craft and single industry sections of 19th century British capitalism. Unionism in the 1980s is far more broadly based: a reflection in part of the decline of traditional strongholds and the growth of "tertiary" employment, in part of increased density in areas of former weakness, particularly in the public sector. Occupational shifts in employment and unionisation have led to the current prominence of "white-collar" organisations. The number of women trade unionists has doubled: out of every ten union members today three are women as against two in 1960'.[1]

1. R. Hyman, Ch. 2 in *Industrial Relations in Britain* (ed. G. S. Bain), Oxford, 1983, pp. 35–36.

399. Three principal categories of trade union structure are to be found in Britain – *craft, industrial* and *general*. But these categorizations have to be used with caution because many of the larger unions spill over the categories. The *craft* unions, organising those with a particular skill, are particularly important in printing, engineering, shipbuilding and construction industries. Some unions have been regarded as *craft* unions, although skills are learned through a process of promotion from labourer to skilled worker rather than through an apprenticeship system, and the union may in fact also be an *industrial* one because it covers most workers in an industry. An example is the major steel industry union, the Iron & Steel Trades' Confederation.

400. The nearest to an *industrial* union in Britain is the National Union of Mineworkers, which until a breakaway Union of Democratic Mineworkers was formed in 1985, included the vast majority of the National Coal Board's employees, manual and clerical and some supervisory, although most of the latter belong to a separate union. Others with a claim to the description of 'industrial' include the Union of Communications Workers, the National Union of Railwaymen, and the Banking, Insurance and Finance Union.

401. The *general* unions, who organise workers regardless of skill or industry, whatever the job they perform, include the Transport & General Workers' Union and the General Municipal Boilermakers and Allied Trades Union. In some industries these unions organise nearly all the workers in the industry; in some they organise only certain occupations or gradings; in some they cover white-collar employees; in some they compete with other unions. They are spread over nearly all industrial groups. The main production workers' unions, the Amalgamated Union of Engineering Workers and the Electrical, Electronic, Telecommunications and Plumbing Union, are also to be found in nearly every industrial group, including not only the majority of skilled maintenance workers but, increasingly, less well-skilled workers of all grades of skill. Consequently, there is an overlap between the avowedly general unions and these former skilled craft unions. All these large unions are showing increasing interest in technicians and white-collar employees, in many cases competing for membership with organisations like the Association of Scientific, Technical and Managerial Staffs.

§3. TRADES UNION CONGRESS

402. The Trades Union Congress (TUC), formed in 1868, lacks the power of some central trade union organisations in other countries, but it is almost unique in Western Europe as a single trade union federation to which all major unions are affiliated covering, by 1984, 9.86 million workers, about 90 per cent of total trade union membership.

403. The TUC has power under its Constitution to intervene in jurisdictional disputes between affiliated unions. A set of principles for avoidance of inter-union disputes was first laid down by the TUC in 1924 (the Hull Main Principles) and revised at the annual Conference held in 1939 at Bridlington.

The so-called 'Bridlington' principles (which have been subsequently revised) advise unions to reach agreement on spheres of influence, recognition of membership of other affiliated bodies, and transfers of members. The Principles prohibit a TUC-affiliated union from commencing organisational activities in any grades of workers in which another TUC union has organised a majority of the workers and negotiates on behalf of those workers. Majority membership may not, however, be required in order to protect a union where organisation has been 'exceptionally difficult'. The Principles also provide that no affiliated union should accept a member of another affiliated union into membership without inquiry. If the reply indicates that he is under discipline, or in arrears of subscriptions, or that there is a trade dispute (*i.e.* industrial action) in progress, the application should not be accepted.

404. The TUC Disputes Committee deals with complaints from affiliated unions concerning alleged breaches of the Bridlington Principles. According to revised TUC rules adopted at the 1976 Annual Conference, a fair hearing must be given, and Awards of the Committee are 'binding' when issued. They are probably not binding in law, however, because of the general view that the TUC Constitution and the Bridlington Principles are not 'intended to create legal relations'. Legal problems do, however, arise when an affiliated union is required by an Award to expel a member who has been recruited contrary to the Bridlington Principles. At common law a union may expel a member so long as the rules permit this. Nearly all affiliated unions now have a rule which states that the Executive Committee may by giving 6 weeks' notice in writing terminate the membership of any member if necessary to comply with a decision of the Disputes Committee of the TUC. This model rule was the subject of litigation in 1975,[1] when the High Court decided in effect that before a union may expel a member under this rule there must be a *valid* decision of the Disputes Committee within the terms of reference of the Committee and the Principles must in fact have been breached. Moreover the TUC General Council must act within its powers in enforcing the decision. Although the 1976 and 1979 TUC Conferences amended TUC rules in order to limit the opportunities for the courts to intervene as they did in this case, the notion that the rules are outside the ambit of legal relations can no longer be accepted. TUC Disputes Committee rulings may also come into conflict with a member's right not to be unreasonably expelled (see para. 393, above), and dismissal or action short of dismissal of an employee who refuses to accept a TUC ruling may in some circumstances be unlawful (see para. 391, above).

1. *Rothwell* v, *APEX* [1976] ICR 211; and see *Cheall* v. *APEX* [1983] ICR 398, where the House of Lords held that the Bridlington Principles are not contrary to public policy.

§4. TRADE UNION AMALGAMATIONS

405. Working arrangements between trade unions in order to avoid inter-union disputes, encouraged by the Bridlington Principles, is one way in which the harmful consequences of multi-unionism can be combatted. Another way is through the formation of federations of trade unions in certain industries, such as the Confederation of Shipbuilding & Engineering Unions and the Printing & Kindred Trades Federation. These federations handle negotiations in several industries and adopt joint policies. A further form of co-operation in particular industries where Joint Industrial Councils exist (see Ch. IV, below) is that achieved by the holding of joint meetings and the appointment of a joint secretariat by all the unions which sit on the 'workers' side' of such Councils.

406. Reformers have, however, tried to reduce multi-unionism by amalgamations between unions. The total number of unions has fallen and this process is likely to continue (see para. 398, above). Amalgamations have played an important role in this. Legislation has existed since 1876 to facilitate amalgamations, and the requirements were eased first in 1917 and then by the Trade Unions (Amalgamations) Act 1964, as amended by the Employment Protection Act 1975. The Act provides for mergers in two ways, by amalgamation and by transfer of engagements. The first method requires the consent of the majority of those voting in each amalgamating union, while the second method requires a vote only of the members of the transferor union. Certain minimum standards are laid down for the conduct of the ballots so as to ensure that every member has a proper opportunity to vote and that he has full knowledge of the terms. Complaints may be made to the Certification Officer with a right of appeal on questions of law to the Employment Appeal Tribunal.

407. The result of amalgamations has not, however, been to simplify union structure. On the contrary it has helped to produce several large unions which cover nearly all industries – such as the Transport & General Workers' Union, the Amalgamated Union of Engineering Workers, the General Municipal Boilermakers and Allied Trades Union, and the Electrical, Electronic, Telecommunications & Plumbing Union. In the words of Professor Clegg the 'consequence has not been a rationalisation of trade union structure, but increasing complexity'.[1]

    1. H. A. Clegg, *The Changing System of Industrial Relations in Great Britain*, London, 1979, p. 177.

§5. Definition and Objects of a Trade Union

408. For legal purposes a workers' organisation is a 'trade union' only if it satisfies the definition in section 28 of the Trade Union and Labour Relations Act 1974. This lays down that the organisation (which may be temporary or permanent) must: (1) consist wholly or mainly of workers of one or more descriptions; and (2) be an organisation whose principal purposes include the regulation of relations between workers of that description or those descriptions and employers or employers' associations. It will be seen that although the definition is wide enough to cover an *ad hoc* negotiating committee, the organisation must be directly involved in negotiation with employers: a body whose sole concern is to support strike action or to exert political influence is not a 'trade union'.

409. The definition does not, however, *limit* the purposes of a trade union. A trade union may include in its rule book (constitution) any lawful purposes at all, including political objects. Many unions do in fact include the socialisation of the means of production, or support for the Labour Party, among their objects. In this respect the definition of a 'trade union' in the Industrial Relations Act 1971, as re-enacted in section 28 of the 1974 Act, clears up a long-standing controversy as to whether objects other than labour-management relations could be validly pursued by a trade union.

§6. EXPENDITURE ON POLITICAL OBJECTS

410. There is, however, one limitation on the freedom of trade unions to support political objects. In the *Osborne* case in 1909,[1] the House of Lords decided that it was beyond the powers of a trade union to levy a contribution on members to support the Labour Representation Committee, the forerunner of the Labour Party. The Trade Union Act 1913 effectively overruled this by permitting a trade union to have any lawful objects. At the same time the Act laid down a complicated set of conditions which must be observed before the union may expend funds on political objects. The purpose of these conditions is to protect political dissentients within the union. The 1913 Act was substantially amended by the Trade Union Act 1984.

    1. *Amalgamated Society of Railway Servants* v. *Osborne* [1910] AC 87; see generally on this subject K. D. Ewing, *Trade Unions, the Labour Party and the Law*, Edinburgh, 1982.

411. If a union wishes to expend money on 'political objects' as defined by the Act, it must set up a separate fund (the 'political fund') for that purpose. Such a fund may only be set up if a majority of the members of the union vote in favour of the fund in a secret ballot. Prior to 1984, no further ballots were required to maintain the fund. The Trade Union Act 1984, however, obliges the union to win majority support for the continuation of the fund in a ballot held every 10 years. For unions which have had a political fund for more than 9 years at the commencement of the Act (31 March 1985), a new ballot must be conducted within 12 months of that date. The Act also provides for several controls over the operation of the political fund. In particular, the Certification Officer (above, para. 78) must approve the rules governing the fund.

412. If no ballot has been held, or a majority of members has voted against the formation of a political fund, the union cannot spend money on 'political objects' as defined by the Act. Thus the definition of political objects is crucial. This definition, as revised and expanded by the 1984 Act, includes the expenditure of money, directly or indirectly, on 'party political' matters such as contributions towards a political party, or provisions of a service or property for use by that political party, as well as the selection of candidates and the maintenance of holders of political office. In addition, a meeting or conference whose main purpose is the transaction of business in connection with a political party must be funded from the political fund, as must any advertising, literature, film or sound recording whose main purpose is to persuade people to vote or not to vote for a political party or candidate.[1] This last provision has led to fears that a union without a political fund would not be able to conduct campaigns which oppose Government policy even on matters which directly affect its members such as privatization of State enterprises which may affect members' jobs.

1. Trade Union Act 1913, s. 3(3) as amended.

413. If a political fund has been approved, union members will usually be charged a political levy, unless they choose to 'contract out'. The Government has thus far refrained from implementing suggestions that members be required to 'contract in' to political subsidies. However, members must be notified of their right to contract out and they are protected against discrimination if they do so. A complaint may be made to the Certification Officer for breach of the rules with a right of appeal on questions of law to the EAT. In addition, the TUC has issued a Statement of Guidance which encourages trade unions to ensure that no obstacles are placed in the way of members wishing to contract out, but it is possible that the government will legislate in 1986 to prevent the use of the check-off for the payment of the levy. Section 18 of the Trade Union Act 1984 already requires an employer to ensure that a political contribution is not deducted from the emoluments of a contracted-out worker who has certified that he has notified the union of his objection to contributing to the political fund and gives the worker a right to sue the employer in the county court or sheriff court.

414. Although the statute does not refer to any particular political party, the Labour Party is the chief beneficiary of most political funds. As at 31 December 1984, 53 trade unions (comprising 8,063,000 members) and one employers' association maintained political funds, with a total income of £8.4 million. Roughly 75 per cent of all members of unions with political funds contributed to the fund.[1] Most of these unions are required to ballot their members before 31 March 1986. By the end of 1985, 85 per cent of the unions with political funds had conducted ballots and all of these had resulted in impressive majorities in favour of retaining these funds. Paradoxically, and to the surprise of the Conservative Government which expected the ballots to weaken the Labour Party, the campaigns preceding the ballots increased political awareness among union members, and ten unions which until now have not had political funds have decided to conduct ballots on setting them up.

1. Annual Report, Certification Officer, 1984.

§7. Legal Classifications of Trade Unions

415. A list of trade unions is maintained by the Certification Officer (see para. 78). This system of listing is sharply to be distinguished from the *registration* which existed under the Industrial Relations Act 1971; registration was a pre-condition for the exercise of many collective bargaining rights and it carried with it a high degree of control of internal trade union affairs. The Trade Union and Labour Relations Act 1974 abolished registration, and listing is automatically granted to any organisation which is a 'trade union' as defined in the Act, provided it complies with some simple formalities. The main advantages of listing are that a *listed* union may be able to obtain relief from tax on the income from its benefit funds, and it may seek a certificate of independence (next para.). There is a right of appeal on questions of fact and law from the Certification Officer's decision to refuse to list, or his removal from listing, of a trade union.

416. It is crucial for a trade union which is listed to obtain a *certificate of independence* in order to exercise a number of rights or to secure those rights for its members and officials. The certificate is conclusive proof that a trade union is independent. It is needed by a trade union in order to (1) enforce a right to disclosure of information; (2) secure rights for individuals to participate in trade union activities and membership; (3) secure rights for individuals to claim time off for union activities; (4) make a union membership agreement so as to permit an employer to fairly dismiss non-members; (5) be consulted in respect of collective redundancies; (6) appoint safety representatives; (7) be consulted about occupational pension schemes; (8) be consulted in respect of transfers of undertakings; and (9) obtain funds for ballots from the Certification Officer. The definition of 'independent trade union' in section 30(1) of the Trade Union and Labour Relations Act 1974 is one which –
'(a) is not under the domination or control of an employer or a group of employers or one or more employer associations;
(b) is not liable to interference by an employer or any such group or association (arising out of the provision of financial or material support or by any other means whatsoever) tending towards such control'. The decision whether or not a trade union falls within this definition is in the sole discretion of the Certification Officer, with a right of appeal on questions of fact or law to the Employment Appeal Tribunal.

417. A special category of organisations enjoying, broadly speaking, the same rights as trade unions are *special register bodies*. Unlike ordinary trade unions these are corporate bodies, that is either companies registered under the legislation relating to limited liability companies or incorporated by royal charter or letters patent. Such bodies are found mainly in the public services – such as the Royal College of Nursing – and their principal purposes are to maintain professional standards, but they have become involved in recent years to an increasing extent in negotiating terms and conditions of employment with employing authorities, often in competition with ordinary trade unions. In order to protect these bodies, the Industrial Relations Act equated them with trade unions for most purposes. This special position was retained by the Trade Union and Labour Relations Act 1974. However, those special register bodies whose *principal* purposes do not include labour-management relations may not be listed or seek a certificate of independence. In the private sector such bodies are of relatively little importance.

§8. LEGAL STATUS OF TRADE UNIONS

418. Trade unions are not corporate bodies (with the exception of special register bodies, above). However, the courts have treated trade unions in the same way as corporate bodies for many purposes. For example, in the *Taff Vale* case,[1] the House of Lords held that a trade union registered under the Trade Union Act 1871 could be held liable in tort (delict) for the acts of its officials in the course of a strike. Similarly, in the *Osborne* case,[2] the *ultra vires* doctrine was applied to trade unions as quasi-corporate bodies. Parliament intervened in the Trade Disputes Act 1906 to give trade unions a complete immunity from actions in tort (removed from 1971–1974 and again since 1982, below, para. 420) and in the Trade Union Act 1913 to override the *Osborne* decision, but neither statute resolved the underlying question of the status of trade unions.

1. *Taff Vale Railway Co.* v. *ASRS* [1901] AC 426.
2. *Amalgamated Society of Railway Servants* v. *Osborne* [1910] AC 87 (HL), above, para. 410.

419 Trade unions were given corporate status for the brief currency of the Industrial Relations Act 1971, but restored to unincorporated status by the Trade Union and Labour Relations Act 1974. The 1974 Act did, however, resolve some of the practical problems which flow from the unincorporated character of trade unions. The Act provides that (i) trade unions are capable of making contracts; (ii) all the property belonging to a union must be vested in trustees in trust for the union; (iii) trade unions are capable of suing and being sued in their own names; (iv) trade unions are amenable to criminal prosecution in their own names; and (v) judgments, awards, and orders may be enforced against any property held in trust for the union.[1] Nevertheless, some problems remain unresolved. Trade unions are not corporate bodies for the purposes of maintaining a defamation suit,[2] but the doctrine of *ultra vires* applicable to incorporated bodies has been held applicable to trade unions (see further para. 430, below).[3] Similarly, trade unions have been held to be subject to the rule in *Foss* v. *Harbottle*,[4] by virtue of which only the association, not the individual member can sue for wrongs done to the association or for internal irregularities, unless a member's individual rights have been breached, or the acts done were fraudulent or *ultra vires*.[5]

1. TULRA 1974, s. 2(1).
2. *EEPTU* v. *Times Newspapers* [1980] QB 585 (QBD).
3. *Hopkins* v. *National Union of Seamen* [1985] ICR 268 (Ch.D.); *Thomas* v. *National Union of Mineworkers* [1985] 2 All ER 1 (Ch.D.); *Taylor* v. *National Union of Mineworkers* [1985] IRLR 99 (Ch.D.); see Wedderburn (1985) 14 *Industrial Law Journal* 127.

4. (1843) 2 Hare 461.
5. *Cotter* v. *National Union of Seamen* [1929] 2 Ch. 58.

§9. LIABILITY OF TRADE UNIONS IN TORT

420. For much of the 20th century, trade unions were given statutory immunity from liability in tort.[1] The immunity enjoyed by trade unions was broader than that afforded to individuals in respect of acts in contemplation or furtherance of a trade dispute (below, para. 484). The immunity of trade unions was not confined to specific torts, nor to acts taken in contemplation or furtherance of a trade dispute. Thus liability for torts committed in the course of industrial action attached to the individual organisers rather than the union, although the union generally supported its officials financially in the conduct of the case and the satisfaction of any judgment. One of the most significant changes brought about by the Employment Act 1982 was to remove this immunity, leaving trade unions, like individuals, exposed to tort action unless the more limited immunities in section 13 of the Trade Union and Labour Relations Act 1974 (as amended) applied (below, para. 485). Further restrictions were imposed by the Trade Union Act 1984, by virtue of which section 13 immunities would be of no avail to a union which had engaged in industrial action without conforming with the statutory balloting requirements (below, para. 493). Both these provisions have had dramatic implications for labour relations.

1. Trade Disputes Act 1906, s. 4, repealed by the Industrial Relations Act 1971. A more limited but still extensive immunity was contained in TULRA 1974, s. 14 (repealed in 1982).

421. Since a trade union can act only through its officials and members, it is necessary to determine in what circumstances trade unions will be held liable for the tortious acts of their members. At common law, a broad concept of trade union liability for actions of its members was established by the House of Lords in the famous case of *Heaton's Transport (St. Helens) Ltd.* v. *TGWU*,[1] where a trade union was held liable for the unofficial acts of shop stewards, on the basis that shop stewards have general authority and discretion to act on the trade union's behalf. The trade union could only escape liability if it had expressly forbidden its members to take particular actions, possibly by disciplining members or withdrawing shop stewards' credentials. This could put trade unions in the difficult position of having to '"police" collective agreements and the law as against its own members'.[2] The Employment Act 1982 and Trade Union Act 1984 do not rely on common law principles of vicarious liability, but set out a statutory sheme whereby a union is liable if and only if the tortious act was 'authorised or endorsed by a responsible person'.[3] There are five categories of 'responsible person', namely: (i) the principal executive committee; (ii) the president or general secretary; (iii) persons empowered by the rules of the union to authorise or endorse industrial action; (iv) employed officials of the union; and (v) any committee of the union to whom an employed official regularly reports. In the first two cases, the union is liable even if the rules do not empower this committee or these persons to authorise industrial action, but the union can escape liability in the last two cases if the officer or committee is prevented by the rules from authorising industrial action, or if their actions are repudiated by the executive committee, president or general secretary of the union. It is not yet clear what amounts to 'authorisation' or 'endorsement', although it appears that unions are not required positively to instruct their members to return to work. The thrust of these new rules on vicarious liability has been to put pressure on union leaders to repudiate spontaneous action by members. Clark and Wedderburn commented that 'wedges will inevitably be driven between stewards and full-time officials, between both of them and the executive and the two top officers, and between all of them (as 'responsible persons') and the membership'.[4] Experience since this was written suggests that the prospect of union liability has encouraged a significant number of employers and third parties to bring actions in tort.[5]

1. [1972] ICR 308, HL.
2. O. Kahn-Freund, 'The Industrial Relations Act 1971 – Some retrospective reflections' (1974) 3 *Industrial Law Journal* 186 at p. 188.
3. EA 1982, s. 15(2).
4. J. Clark and Lord Wedderburn in *Labour Law and Industrial Relations: Building on Kahn-Freund*, Oxford, 1983, p. 204.
5. S. Evans, (1985) 23 *British Journal of Industrial Relations* 133.

422. In order to avoid the risk of bankruptcy, section 16 of the Employment Act 1982 limits the amount of damages which may be awarded against a union in a tort action. The maximum in any single proceedings in favour of each plaintiff is £10,000 if the union has less than 5,000 members, £50,000 if it has 5,000 but less than 25,000 members, £125,000 if it has 25,000 but less than 100,000 members and £250,000 if it has 100,000 or more members. The amounts may be varied from time to time. A trade union's provident benefit funds and political fund (if it has one) are protected, as are the private property of the union's trustees, officials and members. But no property is safe, nor are there any limits in respect of the enforcement of fines imposed for contempt of court, *i.e.* refusal to obey a court order. Nor do the limits on damages include the legal costs which the unsuccessful union is likely to have to pay. The possibility of a single strike with a small employer causing severe financial damage to a union is illustrated by the Stockport Messenger action in 1983 against the National Graphical Association as a result of which the union may lose as much as one-tenth of its assets. The damages against the union were assessed at £131,051 plus interest (which included aggravated and exemplary damages in addition to proved losses).[1] When this was added to the £675,000 fines for contempt of court for non-compliance with an injunction, and legal costs of sequestration, it was estimated in December 1985[2] that the union had lost over £1 million. In addition, six other newspaper proprietors were still pursuing damages claims for £1.1 million in respect of strike action taken at their plants in support of the Stockport Messenger strike.

1. *Messenger Newspaper Group Ltd* v. *NGA* [1984] IRLR 397.
2. *Financial Times*, 27 December 1985.

423. Failure by the union to pay damages or fines for contempt of court exposes the union to the risk of sequestration of its assets,[1] the effect being to deny the union and its officers any control over its funds and premises until the court judgments have been satisfied and the union has 'apologized' to the court or otherwise 'cleared' its contempt. During the miners' strike of 1984–1985 when the funds of the National Union of Mineworkers were sequestrated it proved difficult to locate all the assets, some of which had been moved out of the jurisdiction. The court removed the union's trustees from office and replaced them by a court-appointed receiver. Nine months after the ending of the strike, the union, once the most powerful in Britain, was split, its assets severely depleted and still in the hands of the receiver, although the sequestration was ended. It was estimated that the cost of the union's defiance of the court was about £1.4 million, at that stage.[2]

> 1. This occurred in the *Stockport Messenger* dispute (above); and also against the South Wales Area of the National Union of Mineworkers followng *Richard Read (Transport) Ltd.* v. *NUM (South Wales Area)* [1985] IRLR 67 in tort actions. The actions against the National Union of Mineworkers arose out of breach of union rules, see below, para. 430.
> 2. *Financial Times*, 15 November 1985.

§10. TRADE UNION RULES

424. Trade union government in Britain depends in part on what is written down in the formal rules and in part on unwritten but well-understood procedures ('custom and practice'). Rule books differ widely and display varying degrees of precision. Moreover, the courts have recognised that the rules are not the constitution; they are capable of modification by the proof of custom and practice. The TUC, in words which were adopted in a leading case by the House of Lords, has said that: 'Custom and practice may operate either by modifying a union's rules as they operate in practice, or by compensating for the absence of formal rules'.[1]

> 1. *Heatons Transport (St. Helens) Ltd.* v. *TGWU* [1972] ICR 308 (HL).

425. For most of this century, the primary means of regulating trade union rules has been by judge-made common law. In 1971, as part of its general policy of legal regulation, the Industrial Relations Act imposed detailed requirements as to the matters to be specified in trade union rules, a legislative package with which the trade unions refused to co-operate. The mandatory requirements were repealed by the Trade Union and Labour Relations Acts 1974 and 1976, except for detailed rules relating to union accounts and members' superannuation schemes. The return to 'voluntarism' so far as internal trade union affairs were concerned reflected the belief that the needs of the many types of union in Britain were not capable of fitting into a single legislative model. The reform of union rule books advocated by the Donovan Commission was left to voluntary action by the unions themselves. Many unions have improved the scope and precision of their rule books, but the differences between rule books are still enormous. No two unions have the same system of government.

426. The legislation since 1980 has made several significant inroads into the voluntary approach, without sweeping away the framework of the 1974–1976 Acts. Trade unions are required to hold elections in the prescribed form for certain trade union posts (below, para. 431), and to ballot their members before taking industrial action (below, para. 493) and to retain the political fund (above, para. 411). In addition, where a closed shop is in operation, a trade union may not unreasonably expel or exclude a member or applicant for membership (above, para. 393). The rules relating to union accounts and members' superannuation schemes remain in force, together with special legislative rules protecting workers from discrimination by trade unions in respect of their colour, race, nationality, ethnic or national origins,[1] or their sex or marital status,[2] or by reason of their non-contribution to the union's political fund.[3]

1. Race Relations Act 1976, s. 11; EEC Reg. 1612/68, art. 8.
2. Sex Discrimination Act 1975, s. 12.
3. Trade Union Act 1913, s. 3.

427. In parallel with the statutory provisions, the judges have developed a set of principles regulating the relationship between individual members and the trade union. This common law control of internal union activities is exercised through the notion that when a worker joins a union he or she becomes a party to a contract of association. This contract is subject to the same general principles as apply to other contracts, with some modifications The rules are not to be construed literally or like a statute, but so as to give them a reasonable interpretation which accords with the court's view of what they must have been intended to mean, bearing in mind their authorship, their purpose and the readership to which they are addressed.[1]

1. *Heatons Transport (St. Helens) Ltd.* v. *TGWU* [1972] ICR 398 (HL); *British Actors Equity Association* v. *Goring* [1977] ICR 393 (HL); *Porter* v. *National Union of Journalists* [1980] IRLR 404 (HL).

428. The first of these principles is that the rules must be construed, in cases of ambiguity, against those who made them (*contra proferentem*). In recent years, the analogy has been drawn between union rules and a legislative code drawn up by some members to be imposed on all members, and this has enabled the courts to treat the actions of the organs and officers of a union like those of a governmental agency. Doctrines of administrative law have, in this way, infiltrated into the former contractual analysis of union rules. For example, the courts have insisted that, like administrative authorities, the powers exercised by union authorities must arise under the express or implied rules, that procedural requirements in the rules must be strictly observed, and that the so-called rules of natural justice must be followed when disciplinary action is taken. (Natural justice is similar in concept to the concept of 'due process'. In essence, it means that a person accused of a serious offence must be given a fair hearing before an unbiased body.) Moreover, the administrative law analogy has led the courts to require discretions conferred on officials and committees to be exercised for proper purposes.

429. The second principle applied to contracts of union membership is that rules which are contrary to public policy, as interpreted by the judges, will be struck out. The most jealously guarded of the heads of public policy is that unions cannot oust the jurisdiction of the courts as the final arbiters on questions of law. The court have said that even where there is an express requirement in union rules that internal remedies must be exhausted before a member can take his grievance to the court, the court is not bound by such a requirement. In deciding whether or not to intervene the court will consider the nature of the issue. If it is a question of legal interpretation of the rules, the court is likely to intervene even before internal appeals procedures laid down in the union rules have been exhausted.

430. These principles were particularly strictly applied in the miners' strike of 1984–1985, when several trade union members sued the union for breach of the rules in declaring a strike without balloting the members as required by the rules. In several cases, trade union officials were held to by acting *ultra vires* (*i.e.* beyond their powers), with the result that actions taken in pursuance of the strike, such as the expulsion of members who refused to strike, or the use of union funds for strikers' families, were declared to be unlawful. The court granted injunctions (including mandatory injunctions) requiring the union to desist from the unlawful action. The refusal to comply with such injunctions in turn led to contempt proceedings and sequestration of the union's assets.[1] These cases have left a number of questions unanswered. For example, it is unclear to what extent the *ultra vires* doctrine in its company or administrative law sense applies to trade unions, and how *ultra vires* relates to breach of trade union rules.

1. *Taylor* v. *National Union of Mineworkers (Derbyshire Area)* [1984] IRLR 440; *Taylor* v. *NUM* (1985) IRLR 99; *Hopkins* v. *NUS* [1985] ICR 268; *Thomas* v. *NUM* [1985] IRLR 136 (Ch.D.). See above, para. 423.

§11. TRADE UNION ELECTIONS

431. As we have seen, trade unions have, for most of this century, been left to determine their own methods of appointing their officials. There is therefore a wide variety of methods, ranging from direct periodic elections, to life-time appointments to indirect elections via delegates. The Trade Union Act 1984, however, introduced a statutory scheme for electing certain union officials, despite trade union opposition to what was considered an unwarranted incursion into internal affairs.

432. The Act, which came into effect on 1 October 1985, requires the trade union to hold periodic elections for voting members of the 'principal executive body', defined as the principal body of the union exercising executive functions. There is no need to elect other officials, such as shop stewards, branch officials or general secretaries who do not have a vote on the principal executive body, even though such officials may play a significant role in union affairs. No voting member of the principal executive body may hold his or her position for more than five years without being re-elected.

433. The Act imposes a particular model of democracy on trade unions. First, elections must be *direct*, in that each relevant member must vote directly for the official, rather than electing a delegate who then has the power to cast a block vote for a particular candidate. All members must have an equal vote, but the trade union may define particular constituencies, provided no member is deprived of a vote in all relevant elections. Secondly, voting must be by *secret* ballot, rather than by show of hands, a method which before the Act was used by many unions. Thirdly, the primary method of voting is a *full postal* method, with the trade union being required to send ballot forms and a list of candidates to voters at their home addresses, and votes being returned by post. This slow and costly method (unions are now required to keep an up-to-date register of members) was imposed in preference to voting at workplace or branch meetings on the assumption that voters may be subject to pressure at such meetings. Unions who have traditionally conducted elections at branch or workplace meetings argue in response that it is important to hear the debate before casting a vote. The government has made a small concession to the difficulties faced by unions in keeping track of all members by permitting ballot papers to be distributed at the workplace immediately before, after or during working hours. Members may then be permitted to return their votes at the workplace or by post or given the option between these two ways of returning the ballots. This alternative is only allowed where a trade union is satisfied that there are no reasonable grounds to believe that the other conditions of the Act will not be satisfied by the workplace ballot. In particular, the voters must not be subject to interference from or constraint imposed by the union, its members or its officials. Government funds are available to meet the cost of ballots. The TUC at present opposes the use by its affiliates of such money, but Government funds have been accepted by some unions, such as the Amalgamated Union of Engineering Workers, which has traditionally conducted postal ballots. TUC policy on this issue is currently under review.

434. The Act does not impose criminal sanctions for failure to conform to its provisions, nor does it set up an independent supervisory agency. Instead enforcement is left to individual members of the union. Applications may be made either to the Certification Officer or the High Court for a declaration that the statutory provisions have not been complied with. The EAT has no jurisdiction. If application is made to the High Court, a declaration may be accompanied by an 'enforcement order', requiring the union to remedy the defect, unless it is considered inappropriate. Where a new election is ordered, the union is not permitted to use the workplace alternative, but must send out ballot forms to voters' homes and receive returns by post.

435. A recent study showed that about 61 per cent of trade unions who are affiliated to the TUC already elect their executives by votes of the whole membership.[1] However, very few use the precise method adopted by the statute, and many unions are now making extensive rule changes in order to comply with the legislation. Moreover, views differ as to whether periodic direct elections do in fact promote internal democracy, or whether they lead to factionalism, more militant bargaining positions, or disruptive policy changes.

1. R. Undy and R. Martin, *Ballots and Trade Union Democracy*, Oxford, 1984, pp. 105–106.

§12. EMPLOYERS' ASSOCIATIONS

436. The legal definition of an 'employers' association' is identical to the definition of a 'trade union' except that the organisation must consist 'wholly or mainly of employers or individual proprietors of one or more description'.[1] The legal status of employers' associations differs from that of trade unions (other than special register bodies), however, because such an association may be either a body corporate or an unincorporated association. If it is unincorporated it possesses the same quasi-corporate attribute as a trade union (above, para. 419). An employers' association may have its name listed by the Certification Officer (in order to establish that it fulfils the statutory definition). Whether or not listed, an employers' association is under the same duties as a trade union in respect of annual returns and accounting records. An employers' association, like a trade union, is no longer immune from actions in tort (above, para. 420), but there are no special rules regarding the vicarious liability of employers' associations.

1. TULRA 1974, s. 28(2).

437. No general statistics are available regarding the number, size and membership of employers' associations, although the Certification Officer reported that there were 157 such associations listed on 31 December 1983 and a further 218 submitted annual returns. This represents a sharp reduction from 1968 when the Department of Employment suggested that there were 1,350 employers' organisations. The reduction is largely due to the winding-up of a number of small local organisations and the expansion of some nationally-based bodies like the Engineering Employers' Federation, the National Federation of Building Trade Employers and the British Printing Industries Federation. There has been particular growth in the private service sector. Some of the larger corporations prefer to remain non-federated, such as Ford, Imperial Chemical Industries (ICI) and the General Electric Company (GEC). It has been estimated that 70 to 75 per cent of employers in most industries among establishments with 50 or more employees belong to organisations.[1] The organisations engage in a variety of functions, depending on the industry, ranging from collective bargaining over pay and conditions, to the operation of disputes procedures, advisory services, and representation of members before tribunals and other bodies.

1. The statistics are taken from K. Sisson, Ch. 5 in *Industrial Relations in Britain*, Oxford, 1983, pp. 122–125; and see generally K. Sisson, *The Management of Collective Bargaining: an International Comparison*, Oxford, 1984.

438. The main national organisation is the Confederation of British Industry (CBI) which was formed in 1965 by the merger of three earlier bodies. It claims to have 4,500 individual member companies, with 11,000 to 12,000 subsidiaries, and more than 200,000 employers' and trade organisations which in turn represent 300,000 companies. Most of the public corporations are among the members. The number of persons employed by members and affiliates of the CBI is around 12 million. The CBI does not, however, engage in collective bargaining on its own account.

Chapter III. Workers' Participation in the Enterprise

§1. The Concept of 'Workers' Participation'

439. Corporate enterprises in the private sector are, in law, owned and controlled by their shareholders. The result of the 'managerial revolution' has been to concentrate power in the hands of boards of directors of companies, particularly the hands of executive directors. Major decisions are taken by the directors, and as enterprises have become larger and more complex, the effective decisions have been taken by directors of parent or holding companies, sometimes overseas, remote from the working environment. An amendment to the Companies Act in 1980 required directors to have regard to the interests of employees as well as those of their shareholders when performing their duties,[1] but the employees as such cannot enforce this duty because it is owed to the company alone. It is unlikely that the company (acting through the board of directors or a majority of shareholders in general meeting) would seek to initiate legal action, and an employee or trade union with a minority shareholding would face almost insuperable barriers in proving that the directors had not acted '*bona fide* in the interests of the company'. A minor stimulus to directors was given by section 1 of the Employment Act 1982, introduced by Liberal and Social Democratic peers. This requires directors of companies with more than 250 employees to state in their annual reports what they have done over the year to promote employee involvement arrangements. A survey by the Department of Employment[2] of the first full year of operation (1984) showed that not all large companies were fulfilling this requirement. Among those who were, a wide variety of differing practices was found, headed by share schemes, incentive and bonus arrangements, and magazines, newspapers and newsletters for employees. The next most frequently identified practices were formal and informal management line communications or meetings; employee reports and accounts; and the use of consultative councils or joint committees. It is striking that this legal provision envisages forms of dealing with emloyees which do *not* involve trade union channels and collective bargaining.

1. Companies Act 1980, s. 46(1), now Companies Act 1985, s. 309.
2. Department of Employment, Press Notice, 10 June 1985.

440. The notion that workers' representatives should be involved to a greater extent in the decision-making process has come to be described either as *workers' participation* or *industrial democracy*. The two essential characteristics of developments in this direction in Britain are, first that trade unions have traditionally regarded *collective bargaining* as the primary way to extend collective control by workers of their work situation, and, secondly, that participation has developed without institutional devices of the kind found in some other European countries, such as works councils. Before 1974, there had been no significant attempt to establish forms of worker participation additional to collective bargaining in the private sector. There were a few schemes of 'profit-sharing' or shareholding by workers, a few 'workers' cooperatives' and the 'partnership system' of a large retail organisation. But the participation of workers in the enterprise had grown primarily through the shop steward system and collective bargaining (see Ch. IV, below). A major survey of workplace industrial relations (including public and private services, nationalised industries and private manufacturing in establishments of 25 or more employees) conducted in 1980, showed that there had been a substantial growth of joint consultative committees and works committees during the 1970s.[1] Thirty-seven per cent of workplaces had such committees, one-fifth having been established in the previous three years and two-fifths within the previous five. Over one-half of employees were in workplaces that had both a joint consultative committee and trade union recognition. The survey indicated that joint consultation was generally regarded as an adjunct to collective bargaining: unions played a major part in the appointment of consultative committees, and substantive matters were most likely to be discussed in consultative committees where these were also the subject of workplace negotiations There was considerable overlap between matters which were the subject of joint consultation and those that were the subject of negotiation. However, in a minority of workplaces, joint consultation was being established in the absence of, or perhaps as an alternative to trade union representation and collective bargaining. In a very small minority of, mainly small private sector, establishments non-union works committees were established by employers who were resistant to trade unions. The authors of the workplace survey concluded that 'there have been substantial developments on a voluntary basis to promote worker involvement, in the absence of any general legislative framework to promote worker involvement in decision-making'.[2]

1. W. W. Daniel and Neil Milward, *Workplace Industrial Relations in Britain.* The DE/PSI/ SSRC Survey, London, 1983, pp. 129–141.
2. *Ibid.*, p. 289.

441. These forms of participation, as an adjunct to collective bargaining, suffer from the weakness that they are generally confined to the level of the plant or establishment, and so are unable to influence decision-making at the *corporate* level. According to a recent survey,[1] almost three-quarters of manufacturing establishments of 50 or more employees are part of a multi-plant enterprise; the larger an establishment is, the less likely it is to be single and independent. Since the 1950s, there has been a striking growth of giant corporations or enterprises, much of it due to mergers and takeovers. The Bullock Report[2] noted that the degree of concentration is greater in British industry than it is elsewhere in Europe or in North America. For example, in shipbuilding and marine engineering, in 1978 the five largest enterprises had three-quarters of the employees in the industry; in electrical engineering six enterprises, each with over 20,000 employees, employed over 37 per cent of the employees in the industry; in vehicles, seven enterprises, each with over 20,000 employees, employed 57 per cent of the employees in the industry. Large enterprises are also prevalent in food, drink and tobacco and in the service sector.[3] Institutional shareholding – notably by a small number of financial institutions and pension funds – has become the dominant source of control, and this is likely to continue to grow. Foreign ownership has also increased: in 1979, 23 per cent of the largest companies in Britain were owned by foreign interests and these employed just over one million workers in their British establishments.[4] The growth of multidivisional forms of organisations in large enterprises has enhanced the role of relatively few senior managers in each enterprise in developing corporate strategy and controlling subsidiary companies, particularly through budgetary policy. Corporate decisions by these managers about matters such as investment policy, product development, the closure and relocation of plants clearly lie beyond the scope of establishment-level negotiations, which is the predominant form of bargaining in British industry. Where corporate bargaining does take place, for a minority of establishments, the role of shop stewards is restricted and the possibilities of effective collective action are reduced.[5] So whether bargaining takes place at establishment or corporate level, strategic decisions by managers are unlikely to be much influenced by workers' views.

1. W. W. Brown (ed.), *The Changing Contours of British Industrial Relations*, London, 1981, p. 68.
2. Report of the Committee of Inquiry on Industrial Democracy (Chairman: Lord Bullock). Cmnd. 6706, London, 1977, p. 4.
3. J. Purcell and K. Sisson in *Industrial Relations in Britain* (ed. G. S. Bain), Oxford, 1983, pp. 97–98.
4. *Ibid*.
5. Brown *op. cit.*, pp. 68–69; Purcell and Sisson, *op. cit.*, pp. 108–112.

§2. The Rise and Decline of the Movement for Industrial Democracy

442. Three major developments in the 1970s seemed to herald a change in this situation. First,there was the adoption of new forms of industrial action by work groups threatened with the closure of their establishments or other major managerial decisions. These included 'work-ins' of the kind which occurred at Upper Clyde Shipbuilders in 1971–1972 and sit-ins (passive factory occupations). The significance of these forms of action was that they indicated the failure of collective bargaining to cope with the ultimate power of management to introduce major changes, to close down or to shift activities to other areas. The second development resulted from Britain's accession to the EEC from 1 January 1973. The EEC Commission's draft proposals for a fifth directive on company law, proposing employee representation on the supervisory boards of all companies in the EEC with over 500 employees, and the amended proposals for a European Company Statute, which would require 'European Companies' (a new type of legal entity) to have certain types of worker participation, would inevitably involve certain changes in British company law. The third major development was a change of policy on the part of the TUC which, in 1974,[1] came to see board level representation as a right that should be made available to organised workers by legislation.

1. TUC, *Industrial Democracy*, London, 1974, revised 1976.

443. As a result of these developments, and as a part of the 'social contract' with the TUC, the Labour Government appointed a committee of inquiry under the Chairmanship of Lord Bullock. This Committee reported in January 1977.[1] The members of the Committee were divided. The main recommendation of the majority was that there should be equal representation of employees and shareholders on company boards. This they believed should be achieved by reconstituting boards to consist of three elements – an equal number of employee and shareholder representatives plus a third group of co-opted directors (the so-called 2X & Y formula where X represents the number of employee representatives and also the number of employer representatives and Y represents the co-opted directors). The third group would be chosen with the agreement of a majority of each of the other two groups, they would be an uneven number greater than one, and would form less than one-third of the board.

1. Cmnd. 6706, January 1977.

444. The two most significant aspects of the proposal by the majority of the Committee were that they proposed introducing the 2X & Y formula for the present unitary company Boards, and rejected the West German two-tier Board as imposing on companies an undesirable measure of inflexibility; and, secondly, that this form of employee representation was to be based entirely on trade union machinery, in particular the shop steward organisation and its equivalent. The majority rejected representation based on works councils or consultative machinery separate from collective bargaining. According to their proposals, before a company could be required to accept employee representatives on its board, a secret ballot of all full-time employees would be held. A simple majority representing at least one-third of the eligible employees favouring representation would be sufficient. If the vote was favourable, the recognised trade unions would have the responsibility of devising an appropriate method of selecting the employee representatives.

445. A minority report, drawn up by the employers' representatives on the Bullock Committee, expressed the fear that the majority's proposals would put companies under trade union control. Their view was that, if some form of employee participation were to be introduced, this should be through a system of supervisory and not unitary boards, employee representation should always constitute less than one-half of the supervisory board, at least one representative of each category of employees (including managerial employees) should be included, issues of board level representation should not be voted upon until a 'substructure' of an Employee Council had operated effectively for a specified number of years, and all employees should be involved in elections.

446. In May 1978[1] the then Labour Government published proposals substantially modifying the majority report of the Bullock Committee. If implemented these proposals could have led to the development of one-third board-level representation for workers on a supervisory board through the single channel of a company-wide shop stewards' committee (the Joint

Representation Committee). The company would also have been placed under a statutory duty to discuss with the Joint Representation Committee corporate strategy issues, such as investment plans, mergers and takeovers, expansion and contraction of undertakings and major organisational changes. However, the Conservative Government, elected in May 1979, is strongly opposed to legislative attempts to increase workers' participation, and has supported only cosmetic measures (such as those mentioned in para. 439, above) to encourage voluntary measures at establishment and company level. This is in line with the general approach of the CBI which favoured the 'organic' growth of employee involvement. Several companies responded to the Bullock Report by setting up consultative committees separate from collective bargaining machinery at plant and company level.[2] At the board level, a two-year experiment under which the (public sector) Post Office Board was composed of equal numbers of trade union-nominated members and management members wth a small group of independent (consumer) members, was ended on 31 December 1979, and not renewed.[3]

1. Cmnd. 6706 (1978). There is a vast literature on the subject. Special mention may be made of Sir Otto Kahn-Freund, 'Industrial Democracy' (1977) 6 *Industrial Law Journal* 65; Paul Davies and Lord Wedderburn of Charlton, 'The Land of Industrial Democracy' (1977) 6 *Industrial Law Journal* 197, and John Elliott, *Conflict or Co-operation? The Growth of Industrial Democracy*, London 1978.
2. W. R. Hawes and C. C. P. Brookes, *Employment Gazette* vol. 88 (1980), p. 353.
3. For a study see E. Batstone, A. Ferner and M. Terry, *Unions on the Board: An Experiment in Industrial Democracy*, Oxford 1983.

447. The opposition of the Conservative Government to legislation on workers' participation is also shown by their coolness towards the draft of the directive on company law (above, para. 442) and the Vredeling draft directive of the EEC[1] on procedures for informing and consulting employees of undertakings with complex structures. The latter directive, if implemented, would require information to be disclosed to employee representatives on the general business situation of the group and management's future plans. This would go beyond the requirements of present British law (see para. 461, below). Consultation would be obligatory where management 'of a parent undertaking proposes to take a decision concerning the whole or a major part of the parent undertaking or of a subsidiary in the Community which is liable to have serious consequences for the interests of the employees of its subsidiaries in the Community' (art. 4). This too goes beyond the requirements of present British law. The general conclusion that may be drawn is that schemes which involve a genuinely independent voice for employees in decision-making are likely to occur only when the general political and economic climate is favourable to the extension of workers' rights. That has not been the case in Britain since 1979.

1. *Official Journal* of the European Communities, C217, 12 August 1983; see Ch. IV below on the effect of other EEC consultation measures.

§3. Safety Representatives and Safety Committees

448. There has, however, been one form of institutionalised participation which has survived the cold climate of the 1980s. Before 1975 safety and health issues were generally not regarded as matters of active 'worker participation'. However, the Health and Safety at Work etc. Act 1974, embodying the proposals of the Committee of Inquiry under the Chairmanship of Lord Robens,[1] empowered the Secretary of State to make regulations for the election by employees of safety representatives from amongst the employees to represent employees in consultation with employers. The underlying philosophy was that employees and employers have a common interest in a self-regulating system of industrial accident prevention. The Employment Protection Act 1975 amended the 1974 Act by limiting to recognised trade unions the power to appoint safety representatives, so clearly embodying the philosophy of collective barganing, namely that health and safety should be a matter for *negotiation* between trade union representatives and management. The regulations (in force since 1 October 1978) empower a recognised trade union to appoint safety representatives from among employees in all cases where one or more employees are employed by an employer by whom it is recognised. The employer must be notified in writing of their appointment before they are entitled to exercise their statutory functions, and to make inspections of the workplace and to be provided with documents and information. Safety representatives are entitled to time off with pay during working hours to perform their statutory functions and to undergo reasonable training. If at least two safety representatives request the employer in writing to establish a safety committee he must do so within three months, after consulting with those representatives and with representatives of recognised trade unions whose members work in any workplace in respect of which the committee is to function. A survey conducted in 1980 indicated that 37 per cent of establishments had such a committee, two-thirds of these having been established since 1975.[2] The Health and Safety Commission has issued a Code of Practice giving guidance on the establishment and duties of representatives and committees. A breach of the Code is relevant in any proceedings. A contravention of the regulations may result in the issuing of an improvement notice by the Health and Safety Executive, or criminal proceedings giving rise on conviction to a fine, or possibly to an action for civil remedies. In practice it is likely that disputes will usually be resolved through voluntary procedures.

1. Cmnd. 5034 (1972).
2. W. W. Daniel and N. Milward, *op. cit.*, p. 142.

Chapter IV. Collective Bargaining

§1. LEVELS AND EXTENT OF BARGAINING

449. The most striking feature of collective bargaining[1] in Britain is its diversity and the multiplicity of levels at which it takes place. There are national or industry-wide negotiations between employer's associations and trade unions; multi-employer bargaining at regional or district levels; corporate bargaining between a single employer and the recognised trade union or unions, sometimes at group level and sometimes at divisional level; workplace or plant bargaining; and also negotiations at the level of a particular shop or department. There are marked differences from establishment to establishment, and also between the public and private sectors over both the extent to which pay is directly influenced by collective bargaining, and also the relative levels of bargaining which have the most influence. This makes it difficult to present any clear or comprehensive description, and only a few trends which have been of particular importance to legal and other institutional arrangements can be highlighted.

1. For a definition see Introduction, paras. 40 and 41, above.

450. Industry-wide bargaining was mainly a development of the period after the First World War. This was due to several factors including the continuation of arrangements made during the war, when central decisions about pay were taken by Government, and the advantages seen by employers in industry-wide pay cuts in the deflationary post-war period. An impetus to this development was given by the recommendations of the Committee, under the Chairmanship of J. H. Whitley in 1919, that industry-wide negotiating agreements should be established on a voluntary basis in all major industries. By 1965, there were about 500 separate industry-wide negotiating agreements covering 14 million of the 16 million manual workers in Britain and 4 million of the 7 million non-manual workers.[1]

1. Ministry of Labour, Memorandum of Evidence to the Royal Commission on Trade Unions and Employers' Associations (1965) p. 19.

451. No single description is possible of the multiplicity of industry-wide negotiating bodies. The typical form, however, is that there is a permanent body known as a joint industrial council, or a conciliation board, or a joint committee, on which employers and trade unions are represented by an equal number of members, occasionally with an independent chairman presiding. Just as the establishment and constitution of such a body are voluntary, so too the demarcation of an industry for bargaining purposes tends to be by agreement. Multi-unionism is accommodated within this structure by agreement between appropriate unions as to membership of the 'workers side'. Sometimes each side will have its own secretariat and will operate on a permanent basis. (The dynamic approach to bargaining which this reflects is discussed in para. 43, above, and the legal effect on the contract of employment of the resolutions and awards of such bodies in para. 149, above.) In central and local government and the National Health Service the Whitley model is still of primary importance in pay determination, and in the public corporations responsible for the nationalised industries, such as coal, steel, gas and electricity, transport and communications, corporate bargaining tends to be indistinguishable from national or industry bargaining. The 1980 workplace industrial relations survey[1] of establishments with 25 or more employees found that national/industry bargaining directly influenced the pay levels of 64 per cent of manual and 62 per cent of non-manual employees. In the public sector formal collective bargaining over rates of pay tends to be confined to the national level; the survey found that this level of bargaining directly influenced the pay of 77 per cent of manual workers (84 per cent in public administration), with the pattern for non-manual workers being similar. In the private sector, on the other hand, workplace bargaining (below) is much more important, particularly for manual workers: the survey found that national/industry bargaining directly influenced the pay of 54 per cent of manual workers; non-manual pay is less likely than manual pay to be determined by collective bargaining in the private sector and where it is jointly regulated negotiations are more likely to be centralised at corporate level.[2] Examples of national/industry bargaining are to be found in the construction industry, textiles, leather, clothing, footwear, furniture, paper and printing.

1. W. W. Daniel and Neil Millward, *Workplace Industrial Relations in Britain*, The DE/PSI/SSRC Survey London 1983, pp. 184–189.
2. *Ibid.*, p. 191.

452. Multi-employer bargaining at *regional or district levels* was historically the level of negotiations which was most important before the First World War. . Employers could be persuaded to bargain over wage rates at this level, in order to prevent wage-cutting competition by other employers in the same district, while retaining a high degree of managerial control within the establishment. In modern times, however, this level is of relatively small importance. The 1980 workplace industrial relations survey found that regional/district negotiation resulted in pay increases for only 9 per cent of manual and 6 per cent of non-manual workers,[1] the percentage being higher in the public than the private sector. Examples of regional bargaining may be found in road haulage and some parts of the textile industry.

1. Daniel and Millward, *op. cit.*, p. 185.

453. Single-employer bargaining takes place at both *corporate* and *workplace* levels. The 1980 workplace industrial relations survey found that the company level was responsible for pay increases for 31 per cent of manual and 34 per cent of non-manual workers, compared to 26 per cent of manual and 15 per cent of non-manual workers affected by plant/establishment bargaining.[1] However, there are major variations between the public sector, where establishment-level negotiations are rare, and the private sector, and also considerable differences between different industries and services within the private sector. In manufacturing industry, the 1977–1978 Warwick survey of establishments of 50 or more workers found that for two-thirds of manual and three-quarters of non-manual employees the formal structure of bargaining was one of single-employer agreements covering one or more factories within a company; multi-employer agreements covered only a quarter of the manual and a tenth of the non-manual manufacturing workforce.[2] The bulk of single-employer arrangements were at the workplace or establishment level. Examples of corporate bargaining may be found in banking, insurance, transport, distribution, food, drink and tobacco industries, and also among the motor assembly 'giants' (British Leyland, Ford, Vauxhall and Talbot) and in the largest chemicals enterprise, ICI. Workplace bargaining is most common in the metalworking industries, even in multi-establishment enterprises such as General Electric (GEC). One of the most important factors determining the level of bargaining appears to be the size of the workforce. The 1980 survey revealed that the larger the establishment the greater the importance attached to plant bargaining; at the same time the larger the enterprise, the greater the importance was attached to corporate bargaining.[3]

1. Daniel and Millward, *op. cit.*, p. 179.
2. W. W. Brown (ed.), *The Changing Contours of British Industrial Relations*, Oxford 1981, pp. 7–16.
3. Daniel and Millward, *op. cit.*, p. 189.

454. The patterns of bargaining over pay, sketched out here, indicate that there have been important changes since the Donovan Commission reported in 1968 on the conflict which they found in the private sector between the formal industry-wide system of collective bargaining and the relatively informal system of workplace bargaining. The Commission said that workplace bargaining had three main characteristics: it was largely informal because of the predominance of unwritten arrangements and custom and practice; it was largely fragmented because individual shop stewards bargained for small work groups; and it was largely autonomous because it fell outside the control of employers' associations and full-time trade union officials. The Commission diagnosed the 'central defect' of British industrial relations as 'the disorder in factory and workshop relations'.[1] This defect was largely responsible for the gap between multi-employer collective agreements and actual earnings, a source of inflation under the pressure of full employment, and the relatively high incidence of unofficial (wildcat) strikes. Their solution was to formalise the informal system, by 'confining industry-wide agreements to matters which they are capable of regulating, providing guidelines for satisfactory company and factory agreements, and where appropriate granting the agreements which follow these guidelines exemption from clauses of the industry-wide agreements'.[2]

1. Report of the Royal Commission on Trade Unions and Employers' Associations, Cmnd. 3623, p. 12.
2. *Ibid.*, p. 46.

455. Since the late 1960s, there have been a number of major changes. In the words of Sisson and Brown,[1] 'Britain has developed a dual structure of pay bargaining which is in some respects similar to that in North America. In industries with a large number of small establishments, and with relatively low capital requirements and ease of entry, multi-employer bargaining continues to be of primary importance . . . Elsewhere, and more generally, among the larger establishments, single employer pay bargaining has now become a formal system'. The level of bargaining depends, above all, on the strategies of management. Multi-employer bargaining prevents wage-cutting competition in industries with a large number of small establishments and it reduces the influence of trade unions in the workplace. Corporate bargaining makes it possible to standardise terms of employment in multi-establishment enterprises, and by raising the level of decision-making it tends to restrict the influence of shop stewards (below) whose main power-base is the shop floor. Workplace bargaining, on the other hand, tends to narrow the range of subjects of bargaining, to reduce inter-plant solidarity, and to leave strategic company policy largely uninfluenced by workers' representatives.

1. K. Sisson and W. Brown in *Industrial Relations in Britain* (ed. G. S. Bain) Oxford 1983, pp. 147–148.

456. Apart from pay and related matters such as hours and holidays, collective bargaining also takes place over a wide variety of other issues. The 1980 workplace industrial relations survey asked managers in workplaces whose unions were recognised whether they negotiated with representatives of manual workers, and nearly two-thirds of these respondents reported that they did so over physical working conditions and redeployment of labour within the establishment; in nearly one-half of these cases, issues concerning manning levels, redundancy and methods of recruitment were negotiated at the workplace.[1] 'Custom and practice' at workplace level, however, remains largely uncodified and matters such as discipline are rarely the subject of formal agreements. There are great variations from industry to industry. Sisson and Brown[2] comment that 'defining existing practices is often open to a great deal of argument. In these and other cases, then, one or other of the parties may refuse to enter into either a formal or an informal agreement or to recognise custom and practice. Usually, one of the parties seeks to impose a settlement on the other; it is left to the other party to react'. Managements have been reluctant to reach precise agreements on these matters for a variety of reasons including the difficulty of withdrawing concessions, the danger of 'leapfrogging' to further formal concessions and the reduction of flexibility of local management. Formalization also tends to be opposed by shop stewards who believe it would restrict the scope of bargaining and limit their freedom of action, for example, to oppose managerial decisions over discipline and redundancy.[3] In respect of non-pay matters, therefore, not a great deal has changed in collective bargaining since the Donovan Report.

1. Daniel and Millward, *op. cit.*, pp. 197–199
2. Sisson and Brown, *op. cit.*, p. 151.
3. See Part I, paras. 274, regarding disciplinary and redundancy procedures.

§2. THE ROLE OF SHOP STEWARDS

457. Workplace bargaining is largely the responsibility of *shop stewards*. It is not easy to explain the essential character of the British shop steward. He is not the same, for example, as the French *délégue du personnel* or the German works council member. At one time it was unusual to describe him or her as an 'official' of the union. But since 1971, the legal definition of an 'official'[1] has included a person, elected or appointed as a representative of union members, who is an employee of the same employer as the members whom he represents. This includes a shop steward, who may go under other names such as (in the printing industry) 'father/mother of the chapel'. The steward is both an employee of the enterprise and also a representative of those other employees who hold union membership. He or she is usually elected by union members at the place of work, and is not appointed by the branch or executive committee of the union. However, in some unions the election must be ratified by a higher union authority than the members at the workplace. The courts have occasionally intervened to protect an elected shop steward whose credentials have not been issued by the union for reasons that are palpably bad, such as that the steward refuses to give an undertaking to follow all instructions of the union.[2] This highlights the 'dual authority' of the steward.[3] He or she is at one and the same time the representative of members at the workplace, which is the basis of the steward's power, and also the representative of the external union.

1. Now embodied in TULRA 1974, s. 30(1).
2. *E.g. Shotton* v. *Hammond, The Times*, 2 December 1976.
3. In *Heaton's Transport Ltd.* v. *TGWU* [1972] ICR 308, HL this analysis was used to impose vicarious liability on the union for the acts of stewards: see further para. 421, above.

458. In most places of work there is likely to be more than one shop steward (the 'shop' is defined by custom and may cover one or more departments in a plant) and a shop stewards' committee with a 'chief steward' or 'convenor' (sometimes full-time) may then exist. Because of the structure of British trade unions (see Ch. II, above) several unions are likely to have to work together in one office or factory. In these cases the stewards' committee will be multi-union. The 1980 workplace industrial relations survey found such committees for manual workers in the case of 32 per cent of establishments and 17 per cent for non-manual workers;[1] the larger the establishment, and the greater the number of unions recognised, the more likely it is that there will be a joint committee. This has the important consequence that the committees are not easily made responsible to union authority outside the workplace. The shop steward organisation at the workplace is also a far more important link between the member and the union than the trade union branch. In many unions the branch consists of small groups of members from a number of different factories and offices. The branch is therefore separate from the real business of the union at the workplace and it is left to the shop steward organisation to conduct collective bargaining.

1. Daniel and Millward, *op. cit.*, pp. 97–100.

459. Shop steward organisations grew considerably in the 1960s and 1970s. In 1961 their number was estimated at 90,000;[1] by 1978 there were thought to be more than 250,000.[2] In manufacturing industry alone the 1978 Warwick survey suggested a total of 119,000 manual shop stewards (each representing an average of 31 workers) and 37,000 non-manual stewards (each representing on average 22 workers).[3] There was also a substantial growth in private services and in the public sector. One of the most important developments was the growth in the number of full-time stewards. The number in manufacturing industry probably quadrupled between 1966 and 1976[4] so that they far outnumbered full-time officials employed by the union. This development was accompanied by the growing formalisation of shop steward bargaining, partly as a result of legislative measures such as the encouragement of the closed shop by legislation of the Labour Government (1974–1979) and the establishment of health and safety committees and the election of shop stewards as safety representatives (see para. 448, above), as well as encouragement by managers who found stewards 'more of a lubricant than an irritant'[5] in the conduct of workplace relations. In the 1980s, the economic recession and the policies of the Conservative Government have put shop steward organisation under great pressure. In some instances, such as British Leyland in 1981–1982, 'tough' managements have moved from plant to corporate bargaining and severely undermined the shop steward movement. In others, however, it appears that the number of stewards has declined less rapidly than jobs in their plants; one recent survey covering the period 1979–1984 found that in maintenance engineering 20 per cent of establishments still have two or more full-time stewards, and in production chemicals, 24 per cent.[6] The survey also indicates that the trend towards decentralisation of pay bargaining has continued.

1. H. Clegg, A. J. Killick, R. Andrews, *Trade Union Officers*, Oxford 1961, p. 153.
2. H. Clegg, *The Changing System of Industrial Relations in Great Britain*, Oxford 1979, pp. 51–53.
3. Brown, *op. cit.*, p. 62.
4. *Ibid.*, p. 66.
5. W. E. J. McCarthy and S. R. Parker, *Shop Stewards and Workshop Relations*, Royal Commission Research Paper No. 10, London 1968, p. 15.
6. E. Batstone, S. Gourlay, H. Levie, R. Moore, *Union Structure and Strategy in the Face of Technical Change*, Oxford (forthcoming 1986); *Financial Times* 23 October 1985.

§3. LEGAL SUPPORT FOR COLLECTIVE BARGAINING

460. In the Introduction (paras. 52–54, 60–67) an outline was given of the relatively few legal supports for the essentially voluntarist system of collective bargaining, and of the measures taken by the Conservative Government since 1979 to dismantle even those few statutory props for joint regulation. The repealed measures include: (1) the right to recognition for collective bargaining, first introduced in 1971, and renewed in 1975, removed by the Employment Act 1980; (2) the procedure for the extension of collective agreements, originating in war-time legislation, renewed and extended in Schedule 11 of the Employment Protection Act 1975, also removed by the Employment Act 1980;

(3) the Fair Wages Resolution of the House of Commons of 1946, renewing and extending earlier Resolutions since 1891, obliging government contractors to observe terms and conditions not less favourable than those established by collective bargaining, rescinded in 1983; (4) the Road Haulage Wages Act 1938, which established tripartite machinery to fix minimum wages in that industry, repealed by the Employment Act 1980. All that remain are (1) the Wages Councils (discussed in Part I, paras. 205–212, above), whose coverage is to be severely restricted in 1986; (2) the individual employment rights to protect those belonging to unions or participating in trade union activities at the 'appropriate time' (discussed in Ch. I, paras. 376–380, above); (3) specific duties to consult workers' representatives over health and safety matters (Ch. III, para. 448, above), proposed redundancies (Part I, paras. 325–327) and over proposed transfers of undertakings (Part I, para. 287); and (4) a duty to disclose information for bargaining purposes to recognised trade unions.

461. The only one of these items not so far discussed is the *duty to disclose information.* The Industrial Relations Act 1971 contained provisions to oblige employers to disclose information to registered trade unions and to employees in the larger enterprises. These provisions were not brought into operation before the Act was repealed. The Employment Protection Act 1975, ss. 17–21 obliges the employer to disclose information to an independent trade union which he has already recognised for collective bargaining. The information must be such that without it the union would be impeded in collective bargaining to a 'material extent' and such that the employer should disclose it in accordance with good industrial relations practice. ACAS has issued a Code containing practical guidance, which suggests that subjects which are not listed in section 29(1) of the Trade Union and Labour Relations Act 1974 as subjects of collective bargaining (below para. 466) can nevertheless be relevant so far as disclosure of information is concerned, such as the employer's investment plans, return for capital invested, sales and the state of the order book.

462. The enforcement procedure is complex. An independent trade union may complain to the Central Arbitration Committee (CAC) which must refer the matter to ACAS for conciliation. If this fails, the CAC must make a declaration whether it finds the complaint well-founded and stating its reasons. The employer then has an opportunity to comply, and if he does not do so, a further complaint may be presented to the CAC. The CAC again makes a declaration whether the complaint is well-founded, giving its reasons, and it may also determine a claim by the union regarding the terms and conditions of employment which should be observed by the employer. The award takes effect as a term of the contracts of employment of the individual employees affected. There are a number of statutory limitations on the duty to make disclosure in section 19 of the Act. These include information disclosed to the employer in confidence, and information the disclosure of which would 'cause substantial injury to the employer's undertaking, for reasons other than its effect on collective bargaining'.

463. In view of the circumscribed nature of the duty to disclose it is not surprising that little use has been made of this right. Between 1977 and 1984, only 54 awards were made by the CAC. An analysis of awards up to the middle of 1980 by Gospel and Willman[1] indicated that the subjects on which disclosure was sought were limited, such as job evaluation schemes, grading and pay scales. The union success rate when information was requested on other subjects such as profits, closures and redundancy was negligible.

    1. H. Gospel and P. Willman (1981) 10 *Industrial Law Journal* 10.

464. In all these cases of a statutory duty to consult or to provide information, the legal obligations are triggered only if the employer has already decided to recognise a trade union or unions. The 1980 workplace industrial relations survey found that over one-half of establishments with 25 or more workers recognised trade unions for manual workers, but in the private sector there was a marked tendency for recognition of non-manual unions to be less common.[1] With the repeal in 1980 of the recognition provisions of the Employment Protection Act 1975, there is no legal procedure, outside some of the public corporations, by which unions can obtain recognition, and in the economic and political climate of the 1980s there has been an attrition of union recognition agreements. The result has been to limit the effectiveness of the remaining statutory consultation and information provisions. In summary, it can be said that the only duties which remain are those imposed by virtue of the United Kingdom's membership of the EEC (redundancies and transfer of undertakings) or which have proved to be of little practical importance (disclosure of information) and that these duties themselves can be evaded simply by the de-recognition of unions, a tactic made possible by the lack of enforceability of collective agreements (below).

§4. Collective Agreements

465. The view that a collective agreement 'is an industrial peace treaty and at the same time a source of rules for terms and conditions of employment, for the distribution of work and for the stability of jobs'[1] is now widely accepted in Britain, largely due to the influence of Otto Kahn-Freund (see para. 36, above). This dual social function is not, however, directly reflected in the legal characteristics of collective agreements in Britain. The agreement is usually not a legally enforceable contract between the trade union and employer or employers' association. Nor is it a universally binding legal code. As we have seen, the main legal effect of the collective agreement is as an express or implied or customary term of individual contracts of employment (above, para. 149). To the extent that a collective agreement is so incorporated in individual contracts it may be said to have a legislative function, but only if the individual parties expressly or impliedly agree to this. In this section, the effect of the agreement between the collective parties is examined.

    1. O. Kahn-Freund, *Labour and the Law*, 3rd ed., p. 154.

466. The law governing the status of collective agreements between the parties now falls into three parts. First, those which fall within the definition of a 'collective agreement' in section 30(1) of the Trade Union and Labour Relations Act 1974, and made before 1 December 1971 and after 31 July 1974, are conclusively presumed not to have been intended by the parties to be a legally enforceable contract unless the agreement (a) is in writing, and (b) contains a provision which (however expressed) states that the parties intend the agreement to be a legally enforceable contract.[1] It does not inevitably follow that an agreement with such a provision is a contract, because it may still be expressed in language which is too uncertain to be interpreted, or it may be void as in restraint of trade or for some other reason not a contract.[2] In order to fall within the definition of a 'collective agreement' for this purpose, the agreement or 'arrangement' must be made between one or more trade unions and one or more employers or employers' associations. It must relate to one or more of the following matters:

'(a) terms and conditions of employment, or the physical conditions in which any workers are required to work;

(b) engagement or non-engagement, or termination or suspension of employment or the duties of employment, of one or more workers;

(c) allocation of work or the duties of employment as between workers or groups of workers;

(d) matters of discipline;

(e) the membership or non-membership of a trade union on the part of a worker;

(f) facilities for officials of trade unions;

(g) machinery for negotiation or consultation, and other procedures, relating to any of the foregoing matters, including the recognition by employers or employers' associations of the right of a trade union to represent workers in any such negotiations or consultation or in the carrying out of such procedures.'[3]

1. TULRA 1974, s. 18(1).
2. An agreement which is not legally enforceable is not a contract at all: *Monterosso Shipping Co. Ltd.* v. *ITF* [1982] ICR 675, CA
3. TULRA 1974, s. 29(1).

467. Secondly, there are those collective agreements which were made during the period when the Industrial Relations Act 1971 was in force (*i.e.* 1 December 1971 and 31 July 1974). These are conclusively presumed to be intended to be enforceable as contracts unless containing an express clause to the contrary. Most agreements made during that period in fact contained such a clause, stating that the agreement was not intended to be a legally enforceable contract.

468. Thirdly, there are those agreements which are not 'collective agreements' as defined above. For example, an agreement about investment plans or an occupational pension scheme which is not to operate as a term and condition of employment would not be a 'collective agreement' within the legal definition. These agreements are governed by the common law. There is considerable uncertainty about the legal status of such agreements. One view is that they are not contracts because the parties do not 'intend to create legal relations'.[1] Another view is that no general answer can be given to the question of legal enforceability. Some are contracts (*e.g.* some agreements in the mining industry and boot and shoe trade are expressed in a form that makes it clear that they are contracts). Others are too vague or uncertain to be capable of taking effects as contracts, but may still have a quasi-legislative function.[2]

1. This is the view of O. Kahn-Freund in *The System of Industrial Relations in Great Britain* (ed. A. Flanders and H. A. Clegg) Oxford 1954, pp. 56–58, and was applied to the facts of *Ford Motor Co. Ltd.* v. *AEF* [1969] 2 QB 303.
2. This is the view of Paul O'Higgins, *Industrial Relations Review and Report* No. 12 (July 1971), pp. 3–5, and in his contribution to T. Mayer-Maly (ed.) *Kollektivverträge in Europa*, Munich and Salzburg, 1972, a view shared by the present authors.

469. A final point which must be noted about collective agreements in Britain is that the parties are free to include any matter they please in the agreement. The content of the agreement will be entirely within the discretion of the parties with a few exceptions such as the prohibition on racial and sex discrimination. The scope and comprehensiveness of collective agreements varies from industry to industry. (For other features, see above paras. 449–456.)

Chapter V. Industrial Action

§1. PATTERNS OF INDUSTRIAL ACTION

470. The pattern of industrial action in the United Kingdom since 1960 shows wide fluctuations, as can be seen from Table 1.[1] The number of strikes peaked in 1970 and then fluctuated during the 1970s, until the dramatic fall in the years 1980–1983. The number of working days lost fluctuated even more dramatically, partly because one long dispute has a substantial effect on the numbers. A mark of the success of the Labour Government's 'social contract' with the unions in 1975–1976 was the decrease in the number of working days lost, whereas the peak in 1979 reflects the 'winter of discontent' which was a major cause of the Labour Party's defeat in the election of that year. After a steep decline in the early 1980s, the number of working days lost surged to 27.1 million in 1984. This was almost entirely due to the strike in the mining industry, which accounted for 22.3 million of the total number of working days lost.

> 1. Table and all figures in this section are taken from *Employment Gazette*, vol. 93, August 1985, pp. 295–301.

471. The reasons for such fluctuations are complex, but an important factor has always been the level of unemployment.[1] Thus, the high levels of industrial action in the 1960s and 1970s were closely associated with a low incidence of unemployment and the rise of shopfloor bargaining. The most prominent characteristic of industrial action in the 1960s, in the manufacturing industries at least, was the high incidence of small unofficial strikes (*i.e.* strikes not ratified by the union executive). The lower levels of industrial action since 1980 reflects in part the steep incline in unemployment rates. Recent years have seen the re-emergence of the large official strike, particularly in the public sector, involving hitherto strike-free groups such as civil servants, teachers, health service and local authority workers. Thus a dispute in the nationalised steel industry accounted for 74 per cent of working days lost in 1980; in 1981 one dispute by civil servants contributed 0.9 million days lost; strikes in the National Health Service and by railway workers accounted for 43 per cent of the 5.3 million days lost in 1982; and the miners' strike of 1984 contributed 83 per cent of the total days lost. It is important to note that figures on strike activity are only partial indicators of industrial action, since increasing use is being made of action short of strikes. A recent survey revealed that less than half of the establishments affected by any type of industrial action were affected by a strike which would have come within the definition used for official records. This is particularly so in local and national government.[2]

> 1. P. F. Edwards in *Industrial Relations in Britain* (ed. G. S. Bain), London 1983, pp. 209–234.
> 2. W. W. Daniel and N. Millward, *Workplace Industrial Relations in Britain*, London 1983, p. 292.

472. The latest available data on international disputes statistics[1] indicate that in the ten year period 1974–1983 the United Kingdom occupied a broadly

TABLE 1. *United Kingdom: Stoppages in years 1964–1984*

Year	Stoppages		Workers* involved in stoppages (thousands)			Working days lost in stoppages (thousands)		
	Beginning in year	In progress in year	*Beginning in year* Directly	Indirectly	In progress in year	*Beginning in year* (a)	(b)	In progress in year
1964	2,524	2,535	700†	172	883†	2,011	2,030	2,277
1965	2,354	2,365	673	195	876	2,906	2,932	2,925
1966	1,937	1,951	414†	116	544†	2,372	2,395	2,396
1967	2,116	2,133	551†	180	734†	2,765	2,783	2,787
1968	2,378	2,390	2,073†	182	2,258†	4,672	4,719	4,690
1969	3,116	3,146	1,426	228†	1,665†	6,799	6,925	6,846
1970	3,906	3,943	1,460	333	1,801†	10,854	10,908	10,980
1971	2,228	2,263	863†	308†	1,178†	13,497	13,589	13,551
1972	2,497	2,530	1,448†	274†	1,734†	23,816	23,923	23,909
1973	2,873	2,902	1,103	410	1,528	7,089	7,145	7,197
1974	2,922	2,946	1,161	461	1,626	14,694	14,845	14,750
1975	2,282	2,332	570	219	809	5,861	5,914	6,012
1976	2,016	2,034	444†	222†	668†	3,230	3,509	3,284
1977	2,703	2,737	785	370	1,166	9,864	10,378	10,142
1978	2,471	2,498	725†	276†	1,041†	8,890	9,391	9,405
1979	2,080	2,125	4,121	463	4,608	28,974	29,051	29,474
1980	1,330	1,348	702†	128†	834†	11,887	11,965	11,964
1981	1,338	1,344	1,326	173	1,513	4,188	4,244	4,266
1982	1,528	1,538	1,974†	127†	2,103†	5,258	5,276	5,313
1983	1,352	1,364	500†	71†	574†	3,736	3,981	3,754
1984	1,206	1,221	1,272	119	1,464	26,890	31,051	27,135

(a) The figures in this column include only days lost in the year in which the stoppages began.

(b) The figures in this column include days lost from stoppages which continued into the first two months of the following year.

* Workers involved in more than one stoppage in any year are counted more than once in a year's total. Workers involved in a stoppage beginning in the year and continuing into the first two months of the following year are counted in both years in the column showing the number of workers involved in stoppages in progress.

† Figures exclude workers becoming involved after the end of the year in which the stoppage began.

middle-ranking position compared with other OECD countries in the incidence of working days lost per employee. Over this period, the UK had a lower incidence of working days lost than Italy, Greece, Spain, Canada, Ireland and Australia, but higher than the Netherlands, Germany, Norway, Sweden and Japan. Considerable care has to be taken in making comparisons of this kind, however, because of the different coverage of each country's statistics.

1. *Employment Gazette*, vol. 93, April 1985, p. 149.

§2. The Freedom to Strike

473. The law regulating strike action in Britain is extremely complex, and can only be understood in the context of a century of overlapping and conflicting judicial and legislative developments. Although the 'right to strike' was described by a leading British judge in 1942 as being 'an essential element in the principle of collective bargaining',[1] there is no legally guaranteed 'right' of the individual citizen to withdraw his or her labour in combination with others; nor do trade unions have such positive rights. Nor is there a generally applicable legal definition of a 'strike' or 'lock-out' in British legislation: indeed, 'strike' is only defined for the purposes of two specific statutory provisions.[2] Instead, industrial action is regulated by a series of common law wrongs, chiefly in tort and contract, limited and circumscribed by statutory immunities for action 'in contemplation or furtherance of a trade dispute'. The criminal law ceased to be a central regulating force in 1875, but it retains an important role in respect of ordinary criminal actions such as criminal damage or breach of the peace which may take place in the course of industrial action, particularly picketing. This chapter examines the common law liabilities, the scope of the statutory immunities and the law governing picketing.

1. *Crofter Hand Woven Harris Tweed Co.* v. *Veitch* [1942] AC 435 at p. 463.
2. EPCA 1978, Sched. 13 (continuity of employment); Trade Union Act 1984, s. 11 (ballot provisions).

474. It is useful to approch the question of whether industrial action is lawful in three stages:
(1) Does the act in question give rise to civil liability at common law?
(2) Is this liability removed by the immunities afforded by section 13 of the Trade Union and Labour Relations Act 1974?
(3) Are these immunities in turn withdrawn because (a) the act amounts to unlawful 'secondary action' by virtue of section 17 of the Employment Act 1980; or (b) where the defendant is a trade union, the balloting provisions in Part II of the Trade Union Act 1984 have not been complied with?
It is crucial to note that the withdrawal of the relevant immunity gives rise to civil liability if the original act is tortious. Neither of the provisions in (3) above give rise to liability independently of the commission of a tort.

§3. Civil Liability

A. Contract and no-strike agreements

475. An individual who takes part in industrial action almost certainly breaks his or her contract of employment. This is so even if strike notice has been given to the employer, since such notice is not generally construed as equivalent to notice to terminate the contract. At common law, this breach will usually be construed as a repudiation by the employee of the fundamental obligation to work, so entitling the employer to summarily dismiss him or her.[1] Although an attempt was made in one case to avoid this result by creating a legal right to suspend the contract by giving strike notice corresponding in length to the notice required to terminate the employee's contract,[2] this has subsequently been rejected.[3] The employer's remedies against an employee for breach of contract are, however, of limited value in this context. The courts will not grant specific performance of the employment contract, and the measure of damages has been held in the case of a non-production worker to be limited to the cost of finding a replacement for the absent workers.[4] Thus the action in tort (below) has been a more fertile source of legal action in this context.

1. *Simmons* v. *Hoover Ltd.* [1977] ICR 61 (EAT).
2. *Morgan* v. *Fry* [1968] 2 QB 710, CA *per* Lord Denning MR at p. 730.
3. *Simmons* v. *Hoover Ltd.* [1977] ICR 61 at pp. 70–77.
4. *National Coal Board* v. *Galley* [1958] 1 WLR 16.

476. It will be recalled that collective agreements are not legally binding unless the contrary is stated in writing.[1] Thus no action lies for breach of a peace (or 'no-strike') obligation in such an agreement unless the parties to the collective agreement expressly agree that this is to be the case and this is unusual. There have, however, been a few recent examples of binding 'no-strike' agreements between the Electrical, Electronic, Telecommunications and Plumbing Trades Union (EETPU) and a number of high-technology, principally Japanese-owned companies, and such an agreement has been proposed by News International for its new printing plant in East London. A 'no-strike' clause in the collective agreement will be incorporated in individual contracts of employment only if five conditions are satisfied. These are laid down by the Trade Union and Labour Relations Act 1974, s. 18(4) as follows: (a) the collective agreement must be in writing; (b) it must contain a provision expressly stating that such terms shall or may be incorporated into the individual contracts; (c) it must be reasonably accessible at the workplace and available during working hours; (d) each trade union party to the collective agreement must be independent; and (e) the relevant individual contract must expressly or impliedly incorporate such terms into the contract. This fifth condition is particularly important because it means that the 'translation' problem (see above, Part I, para. 153) must, in each case, be answered affirmatively before the term may be incorporated. The employer cannot contract-out of these provisions either with the union or the individual worker.

The provisions apply to any terms of a collective agreement which prohibit or restrict the right of workers to engage in a strike or other industrial action or have the effect of prohibiting or restricting that right.

1. TULRA 1974, s. 18(1), see above, para. 466.

B. Loss of Statuory Rights

477. It should be noted that in general an employee may not complain of unfair dismissal if he or she is dismissed while participating in a strike or any other industrial action, provided the employer dismisses all relevant employees.[1] A claim does, however, lie if an employee is dismissed while taking industrial action and some or all the other participants are not dismissed or are allowed to return to work within three months of the dismissal. In such a case, the tribunal determines the merits of the dismissal in the ordinary way (above, Part I, para. 305). There is no claim if some of the relevant employees are reinstated after three months. Nor are employees entitled to redundancy payments if dismissed while undertaking any industrial action which puts them in breach of their contracts of employment, unless redundancy notice was given before the industrial action began.[2] Similarly, an employee is not entitled to a guarantee payment if the failure to provide work is due to a strike, lockout or other industrial action involving any employee of his employer or an associated employer.[3]

1. EPCA 1978, s. 62, as amended by EA 1982.
2. EPCA 1978, s. 82(2), s. 92; *Simmons* v. *Hoover* [1977] ICR 61 (EAT).
3. EPCA 1978, s. 13(3).

C. Tort

478. There are five main torts which have been developed by the judiciary with specific relevance to industrial action. Since each of these effectively removes the freedom of workers to withdraw their labour collectively, Parliament, in pursuit of the policy of tolerating collective bargaining, has responded periodically by creating negative 'immunities' for those who commit certain specified torts 'in contemplation or furtherance of a trade dispute'. In situations in which the immunity does not apply, civil liability remains. In particular there is the possibility of an injunction being obtained against the organisers of industrial action, including (since 1982) the trade union itself (see para. 420, above). Each of the main torts will be considered, followed by a description of the scope of the immunities, and the use of injunctions in disputes.

479. (i) Civil conspiracy to injure. Conspiracy ceased to be of importance in trade disputes as a criminal offence after 1875 in situations where the act would not have been punishable if done by an individual,[1] and the common law crime of conspiracy was abolished (with a few exceptions not relevant here) in 1977.[2] However, civil conspiracy to injure (or 'simple' conspiracy) was developed as a major weapon against union organisers between 1901 and 1906. This tort consists of a combination of two or more persons whose predominant purpose is it to inflict damage on the plaintiff rather than to serve their own *bona fide* and legitimate interests. In the early cases trade union objectives, such as the closed shop, were not regarded as legitimate,[3] and this is why the Trade Disputes Act 1906 enacted an immunity in respect of 'simple' conspiracy in 'trade disputes' (para. 485, below). However, by 1942 the House of Lords had come to recognise the legitimacy of at least some trade union objectives,[4] and later others, such as opposition to a colour bar, were also held to excuse combinations.[5] Accordingly, this tort ceased to have much practical relevance.[6] In 1981, the House of Lords recognised that the tort is 'highly anomalous' but felt that it was too well-established to be discarded.[7]

1. Conspiracy and Protection of Property Act 1875, s. 3.
2. Criminal Law Act 1977, s. 5. This Act created a new offence of conspiracy to commit an offence, but an agreement to commit a summary offence not punishable by imprisonment in contemplation or furtherance of a trade dispute is excluded from the scope of this offence. This overcomes the main criticism of the *Shrewsbury pickets* case (*R* v. *Jones* [1974] ICR 310) decided under the old law, in which sentences of up to 3 years' imprisonment were imposed on the organisers of 'flying pickets' for conspiracy to intimidate, a substantive offence with a maximum penalty of a fine of £20 or up to 3 months' imprisonment.
3. *Quinn* v. *Leathem* [1901] AC 495, HL.
4. *Crofter Hand Woven Harris Tweed Co.* v. *Veitch* [1942] AC 435, HL.
5. *Scala Ballroom (Wolverhampton) Ltd.* v. *Ratcliffe* [1958] 3 All ER 220, CA.
6. But see *Huntley* v. *Thornton* [1957] 1 All ER 235, where district officers of a union were held liable for victimising an individual who had failed to participate in an unofficial strike.
7. *Lonrho Ltd.* v. *Shell Petroleum Co. Ltd.* [1982] AC 173, 188–189.

480. (ii) Civil conspiracy to commit an unlawful act or use unlawful means. Where an act is itself a tort, then a combination by two or more persons to do that act is a tortious conspiracy. The scope of this tort is uncertain, but in 1981 the House of Lords placed an important restriction upon it by suggesting that it must be shown in this form, as in conspiracy to injure, that the combiners' predominant purpose was to injure the plaintiff.[1] Where this can be shown, the allegation of conspiracy makes it possible to impose liability on a person who cannot himself commit the tort in question: for example, a union official who supports employees who threaten to break their contracts of employment.[2] The allegation may also make it easier to obtain exemplary and aggravated damages. What is unclear about this tort is whether it extends beyond combinations to commit a tort.[3] An unresolved issue is whether there can be an actionable conspiracy to break contracts, for example by two or more workers walking off the job.[4] As will be seen below, there is no immunity in respect of such a combination.

1. *Lonrho Ltd* v. *Shell Petroleum Co. Ltd.* [1982] AC 173,HL.
2. As in *Rookes* v. *Barnard* [1964] AC 1129, HL.
3. In the *Lonrho* case, the House of Lords held that there cannot be liability to commit criminal acts which did not also constitute torts; see too *RCA Corpn.* v. *Pollard* [1983] Ch. 135.
4. A point left open in *Rookes* v. *Barnard* (above).

481. (iii) Inducing a breach or interfering with performance of a contract. If

A intentionally induces B to breach a contract between B and C, A may be liable in tort to C.[1] This tort may take place *directly*, for example where A persuades B not to fulfil the contract or *indirectly*, as where A persuades B's employees to prevent B from fulfilling the contract.[2] *Direct* inducement gives rise to liability in tort even if the act of inducement is itself *lawful*, whereas *indirect* inducement (or procurement) is tortious only if *unlawful* means are used. As we have seen, in most cases, employees who take part in industrial action are in breach of contract. Thus the organisers of such action will generally be liable for directly inducing breach of the contract of employment. Moreover, if the employer is thereby disabled from fulfilling commercial contracts, the organisers may be liable for indirectly procuring breach of the commercial contracts, provided unlawful means are used. This last criterion will be fulfilled in most cases, since the means of procuring the breach of commercial contracts will be the unlawful act of inducing breach of the employment contracts of individual workers. Thus, apart from the statutory immunities, the effect of this tort is to undermine the freedom to organise industrial action. This is further compounded by the more recent extension of the tort to include interference with a contract short of breach, for example, preventing performance in cases where a contract contains a *force majeure* clause, exempting a party in breach from liability to pay damages.[3] So it seems that there can be liability for direct or indirect interference even without any actual *breach* of contract.

1. *Lumley* v. *Gye* (1853) 2 E&B 216; *South Wales Miners' Federation* v. *Glamorgan Coal Company Ltd.* [1905] AC 239.
2. *D. C. Thomson* v. *Deakin* [1952] Ch. 646.
3. *Torquay Hotel Co. Ltd.* v. *Cousins* [1969] 2 Ch. 106, CA *per* Lord Denning, approved in *Merkur Island Shipping Co. Ltd.* v. *Laughton* [1983] 2 AC 570, HL, which applies this as well to *indirect* interference.

482. (iv) Intimidation. This tort was developed by the House of Lords in 1964 to deal with a situation in which two shop stewards and a full-time union official threatened an employer with a strike, so causing the employer lawfully to terminate the contract of employment of a non-unionist who brought an action for damages against them.[1] It had been conceded, unusually, that a 'no-strike' clause in a collective agreement was incorporated as a term in the shop stewards' contracts of employment. It was the threat to break their own contracts which constituted the tort of intimidation. Generalising, it appears that the tort is committed where A threatens B that he will use means which are unlawful as against B with the intention of causing B to do or refrain from doing something he is at liberty to do, so causing damage either to himself (two-party intimidation) or to C (three-party intimidation). There was some attempt after 1964 to cut down the tort to threats of breach of contract which were not minor ones (*e.g.* an incorporated no-strike clause),[2] but its potential as a weapon in the hands of employers or third parties against *threats* of strike action, an everyday part of the collective bargaining process, are obvious. In 1982 the House of Lords developed a related doctrine of 'economic duress' to enable the owners of a ship flying a 'flag of convenience' to recover from the

International Transport Workers' Federation payments which they had agreed, under threat of blacking, to make of back pay to the crew and a contribution to the ITF's welfare fund.[3] Although 'economic duress' is not a tort *per se*, it seems that facts which constitute intimidation may also amount to economic duress. Duress may be even wider than intimidation covering a threat of coercive lawful action, or an *implied* threat not to perform a contract.

1. *Rookes* v. *Barnard* [1964] AC 1127, HL.
2. *Morgan* v. *Fry* [1968] 2 QB 710 *per* Russell LJ.
3. *Universe Tankships Inc. of Monrovia* v. *ITF* [1983] 1 AC 366.

483. *(v) Interference with trade by unlawful means.* This tort is committed where A intentionally uses unlawful means with the purpose and effect of causing damage to B in his trade or business. This category of interference by unlawful means is a 'genus' tort wide enough to cover (iii) indirect interference with contract and (iv) intimidation above, but it is of wider and more uncertain scope. One of the main uncertainties is the meaning given to 'unlawful means' for purposes of this tort. It seems that breach of a criminal statute would be sufficient only if the breach in itself could give rise to liability in tort.[1] For example, breach of local byelaws regarding demonstrations would be insufficient.[2] The torts of nuisance (*e.g.* blocking the entrance to the employer's site) or defamation (*e.g.* by words on placards) would be unlawful means. A threat to induce employees to breach their contracts of employment by going on strike would be unlawful means.[3] It is uncertain whether a breach of contract *per se* (*e.g.* workers putting down their tools) would be sufficient.[4] In one case it was suggested that interference with the freedom of the press was unlawful means,[5] and in another that inducing an education authority to break its statutory duty to provide education was sufficient for the purposes of this tort.[6] The scope for judicial extension of liability under this 'genus' tort is almost endless.

1. *Lonrho Ltd.* v. *Shell Petroleum Co. Ltd.* [1982] AC 173, HL.
2. *Cf. Camellia Tanker Ltd.* v. *ITF* [1976] ICR 274.
3. *Hadmor Productions Ltd.* v. *Hamilton* [1983] 1 AC 191.
4. *Rookes* v. *Barnard* [1964] AC 1129, HL.
5. *Associated Newspapers Ltd.* v. *Wade* [1979] ICR 664 *per* Lord Denning MR.
6. *Meade* v. *Haringey London Borough Council* [1979] ICR 494 *per* Lord Denning and Eveleigh LJ.

§4. The 'Trade Disputes' Immunity

484. The legislature has responded to the judicial extensions of liability in tort described above by periodically enacting specific immunities from liability in tort for those who act in contemplation or furtherance of a trade dispute. The earliest was the 1906 Trade Disputes Act which gave immunity from action for civil conspiracy to injure and inducing breach of the contract of employment. This was supplemented in 1965, in the wake of the decision in *Rookes* v. *Barnard*[1] establishing the tort of intimidation (above, para. 482). The immunities were repealed during the currency of the 1971 Industrial Relations Act, and then reinstated and strengthened in the Trade Union and Labour Relations Act 1974 as amended in 1976. Since 1980, successive enactments have severely limited the applicability of the immunities.

1. [1964] AC 1129, HL.

485. The immunities are now contained in what remains of section 13 of the Trade Union and Labour Relations Act 1974 which reads:

'(1) An act done by a person in contemplation or furtherance of a trade dispute shall not be actionable in tort on the ground only (a) that it induces another person to break a contract or interferes or induces any other person to interfere with its performance or (b) that it consists in his threatening that a contract (whether one to which he is a party or not) will be broken or its performance interfered with, or that he will induce another person to break a contract or interfere with its performance.

....

(4) An agreement by two or more persons to do or procure the doing of any act in contemplation or furtherance of a trade dispute shall not be actionable in tort if the act is one to which, if done without such agreement or combination, would not be actionable in tort.'

It will be noted that the immunity does not extend to torts such as defamation or nuisance or breach of statutory duty.[1] One important question is whether an act which is immune by virtue of section 13 may nevertheless constitute 'unlawful means' for torts such as interfering with business by unlawful means. Prior to 1980, section 13(3) of the Trade Union and Labour Relations Act 1974 specifically provided 'for the avoidance of doubt' that acts which were not actionable by virtue of sections 13(1) or 13(2) of the 1974 Act were not to be regarded as unlawful means. It appears that this remains the law despite the repeal of this section by section 17 of the Employment Act 1982.[2]

1. *Mersey Dock and Harbour Co.* v. *Verrinder* [1982] IRLR 152.
2. *Hadmor Productions Ltd.* v. *Hamilton* [1982] ICR 114, HL.

486. The scope of the freedom to organise industrial action is thus delimited by what Wedderburn dubbed the 'golden formula'.[1] 'Trade dispute' is defined by section 29 of theTrade Union and Labour Relations Act 1974, substantially amended by the Employment Act 1982. It is defined by reference to (i) the parties; (ii) the subject matter. In addition, section 13 of the Trade Union and Labour Relations Act 1974 requires that the action be in 'contemplation or furtherance' of the trade dispute. The elements of this formula are examined below.

(1) *The parties.* The 'golden formula' only includes disputes 'between workers and their employer'. It thus excludes industrial action in protest against government action, except where the government is the employer, or has a statutory power to control the settlement of the matters at issue, or is represented on the bargaining committee which is considering the issues.[2] However, in modern industrial society, governments are so closely involved in the economy that the line is often difficult to draw. As Kahn-Freund put it in 1954: 'The level of wages depends today only partly and perhaps only to a minor extent on decisions of private employers. In all sorts of ways it depends

on governmental policies . . . How then can anyone . . . determine how far any strike is intended primarily to induce the employers to pay wages of a certain amount or the government to change its policy?'[3] Since 1982 the formula has ·excluded disputes between workers and other workers, such as demarcation or inter-union disputes. Also excluded are cases where the employer's own workers are not in dispute, for example, where an employer is picketed or blacked for employing non-union labour or low-paid foreign workers, where the latter themselves are not parties to the dispute.[4] It should be noted that this does not exclude all action taken by one group of workers in support of another group ('secondary' action). Provided that there is a dispute between workers and their own employer, other workers may take action against that employer (subject to separate restrictions against secondary action, below para. 490).

1. K. W. Wedderburn, *The Worker and the Law*, Harmondsworth 1965, p. 222.
2. TULRA 1974, s. 29(2).
3. O. Kahn-Freund 'Legal Framework' in A. Flanders and H. A. Clegg (eds.), *The System of Industrial Relations in Great Britain*, Oxford 1954, p. 127.
4. *Midland Cold Storage* v. *Turner* [1972] ICR 230; *Star Sea Transport Corporation of Monrovia* v. *Slater* [1978] IRLR 507; *NWL* v. *Woods* [1979] 1 WLR 1294, HL.

487. (2) *The subject matter.* Section 29(1) of the Trade Union and Labour Relations Act 1974 provides that the dispute should relate wholly or mainly to one of the subjects listed in that section. The phrase 'wholly or mainly' was inserted by the Employment Act 1982 in substitution for the phrase 'connected with'. The new phrase has been interpreted to mean 'predominantly about', and will exclude disputes which, although connected with workers' fears for their jobs or their terms and conditions, are 'predominantly about' a subject not listed in section 29(1), which is set out above, para. 466.

1. *Mercury Communications Ltd* v. *Scott-Garner* [1984] ICR 74, CA.

488. Disputes which relate wholly or mainly to political or non-industrial subject-matter are thus excluded. For example, industrial action taken by a trade union in protest against apartheid in South Africa was held to be excluded from the definition.[1] Again, the line between a dispute about workers' terms and conditions and a political dispute is not always easy to draw. Thus a day of action taken by a trade union in protest against Government economic policies[2] or industrial action taken by a trade union opposed to the Government's plans to privatize their employer[3] have been held to fall outside the definition of a trade dispute. Since 1982, disputes concerning matters occurring outside the United Kingdom are only protected if the workers taking industrial action are likely to be affected in respect of one or more of the matters specified in section 29(1) of the Trade Union and Labour Relations Act 1974 (above, para. 466) by the outcome of that dispute.[4]

1. *BBC* v. *Hearn* [1977] ICR 685, AC.
2. *Express Newspapers Ltd.* v. *McShane* [1980] IRLR 247.
3. *Mercury Communications Ltd.* v. *Scott-Garner* [1984] ICR 74, CA.
4. TULRA 1974, s. 28(3) as amended by EA 1982, s. 18. See para. 106 above.

489. (3) *'Contemplation or furtherance'.* Since 1906, the test of whether an act was done 'in contemplation or furtherance' of a trade dispute has generally been regarded as a subjective one turning upon the *bona fide* purpose of the person doing the act. However, dislike of the consequences of the widening of the statutory immunities by the Trade Union and Labour Relations Acts 1974–1976 led the Court of Appeal, between 1977 and 1979, to seek to add an objective element to this test in a variety of forms such as whether the act was too remote from the dispute to be protected, whether the act would help one side or another in a 'practical' way and whether the act was reasonably capable or had a reasonable prospect of achieving the honestly held objective of the person acting. These limitations were overruled by the House of Lords in a trilogy of cases[1] and the traditional subjective test was reasserted. Although the 'trade dispute' itself must exist or be imminent as an objective fact, 'contemplation' and 'furtherance' refer to states of mind and so long as the person acting honestly thought at the time that he or she might help one of the parties to a trade dispute to achieve their objectives and did it for that reason, he or she is protected. This subjective test is not altered by the Employment Acts of 1980 and 1982. Instead, its wider implications for the lawfulness of 'seondary' or 'tertiary' picketing or boycotts were limited by specific restrictions on such action. These limitations are dealt with below.

1. *NWL* v. *Woods* [1979] ICR 897; *Express Newspapers Ltd.* v. *McShane* [1980] ICR 42; *Duport Steels Ltd.* v. *Sirs* [1980] ICR 161.

§5. RESTRICTIONS ON THE TRADE DISPUTES IMMUNITY

A. Secondary action

490. A central policy of the legislation since 1980 has been to restrict industrial disputes from extending beyond the establishment concerned. There is a long tradition in Britain of 'secondary action', or action taken by workers not employed by the employer in dispute (the 'primary' employer) in support of those who are directly affected. For example, workers not employed by the primary employer may refuse to deliver raw materials to or to handle goods produced by that employer. The aim of such action is to increase the pressure on the primary employer or, where that employer is being supported by the government, to disrupt economic life more generally in order to force government concessions. The extent to which such action enjoys immunity from liability in tort is determined by the complex and obscure provisions of section 17 of the Employment Act 1980. The aim of this section is to withdraw immunity from certain types of secondary action, namely action against 'secondary' employers who are not 'first customers or first suppliers' of the primary employer. The Act utilises a specific, technical definition of secondary action, applying to situations in which organisers of industrial action induce employees of an employer who is not party to the dispute to breach their contracts of employment and this in turn leads to the breach by that employer of a commercial contract. (The section applies equally to interference, inducement to interfere, and threats to breach or interfere or to induce breach or interference.) However, not all secondary action thus defined leads to loss of immunity. Immunity is preserved where the secondary action leads to breach of a commercial contract with the primary employer, where the secondary employer is a 'first customer or first supplier' of the primary employer. The conditions for retention of immunity for secondary action are:[1]

(1) There is a contract subsisting between the employer who is a party to the trade dispute and the employer of the employees taking the secondary action;

(2) The purpose or principal purpose of the secondary action is to prevent or disrupt the supply of goods or services between the parties to the contract in (1), *i.e.* the primary and secondary employers;

(3) The prevention of disruption in (2) is brought about 'directly', *i.e.* by some means other than by preventing or disrupting the supply of goods or services by or to any person other than a party to the contract in (1);

(4) The secondary action is likely (objectively) to achieve the purpose in (2).

    1. See *Merkur Island Shipping Corporation* v. *Laughton* [1983] ICR 490, HL.

    491. For example, assume that A is in dispute with A's employees and A has a contract for the purchase of goods from B. B's employees refuse to deliver the goods to A, in breach of their contracts of employment, with the intended and likely result that B is unable to fulfil the contract with A. B is a 'first supplier', *i.e.* (1) to (4) above are fulfilled. Thus the organisers of the action among B's employees retain their immunity under section 13 of the Trade Union and Labour Relations Act 1974. However, assume that B has contracted with a road haulage company C to deliver the goods to A, and C's employees refuse to do so in breach of their contracts of employment, with the intended and likely result that C is in breach of the contract of carriage with B. Then (1) above is not fulfilled, since C has no subsisting contract with the employer in dispute, A. Thus the organisers of the action among C's employees lose their immunity under section 13. 'It is a very winding path that leads to this conclusion but the maze through which it winds has only one centre, which, when one reaches it is unmistakable'[1] (see Chart, below).

    1. *Merkur Island Shipping Corporation* v. *Laughton* [1983] ICR 490, HL at 509, *per* Lord Diplock.

    492. However, because the restrictions in section 17 of the Employment Act 1980 depend on the contractual nexus of the parties affected, this provision yields arbitrary results. For example, in a dispute with a ship-owner, a trade union may lose its immunity because it has conducted secondary action which, unbeknown to the union organisers, disrupts the commercial contracts of the charterer of the ship rather than those of the shipowner.[1] Similarly, a trade union may lose its immunity by taking action which, because of the operation and organisation of the employer, happens to disrupt the commercial contracts of an associated company of the company in dispute. The fact that two separate legal entities are involved is decisive even if the shareholders and directors of both companies are identical.[2] It should be noted that a union may retain its immunity under section 17 if it takes action against an associated employer, but only if the primary employer has diverted production to the associated employer.

1. *Marina Shipping Ltd.* v. *Laughton* [1982] QB 1127; *Merkur Island Shipping Corporation* v. *Laughton* [1983] ICR 490, HL.
2. *Dimbleby & Sons Ltd.* v. *NUJ* [1984] 1 All ER 751.

CHART

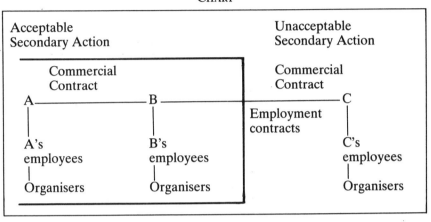

B. Union-only practices

492 bis. A second element of the restrictive strategy of the present government is to discourage 'union-only' or 'recognition-only' practices, whereby union members attempt to spread unionism by insisting that their employers require suppliers to employ union labour, or to recognise, negotiate with or consult union officials (see para. 396). By section 14 of the Employment Act 1982, no statutory immunities are available to a person who induces or attempts to induce another to incorporate into a contract a term requiring work to be done by union or non-union members only, or requiring a party to recognise one or more trade unions, or to negotiate or consult with any trade union official. Nor is protection available to employees of one employer, A, who breach or threaten to breach or interfere with their contracts of employment, resulting in tortious interference with the supply of goods or services to B, because B uses or is likely to use union or non-union labour or refuses to recognise one or more trade unions, or to negotiate or consult with any trade union official. Protection is similarly withdrawn from the organisers of such action. It does, however, remain open to employees to put pressure on their own employer to achieve these ends.

C. Ballots before industrial action

493. Even if a trade union has satisfied both section 13 of the Trade Union and Labour Relations Act 1974 (para. 485, above) and not lost the immunity by virtue of section 17 of the Employment Act 1980 (para. 490, above) the union and any individuals involved will lose their immunity from civil action in respect of certain torts if the balloting provisions of Part II of the Trade Union Act 1984 are not fulfilled. The remedy is placed not in the hands of a member of the union as such, but in those of any person who suffers harm, or threatened harm as a result of acts which constitute the specific common law torts, such as an employer, supplier or customer or a worker prevented from working. (The member's remedies lie either for a breach of the union's rule book or under the statutory provisions relating to exclusion in closed shop situations, above, paras. 393 and 424). So, while Part II of the 1974 Act is based on the idea of increasing membership participation, it places a tactical weapon in the hands of employers and others harmed by industrial action. The reason given for this by the government was that if members could trigger ballots this could be 'used by militants to force the hand of more responsible leaders and to put at risk the functioning of established collective bargaining procedures. If the initiative for the holding of ballots lay with employers these risks would be reduced'.[1] The introduction of statutory ballots before industrial action has important consequences for bargaining processes.[2] Ballots tend to lengthen the bargaining process; delay tends to give time for 'cooling-off' in which both sides can assess the situation, but, on the other hand, it may increase membership commitment, especially if seen to be externally imposed. Ballots increase formality, and reduce the flexibility of negotiations because firm proposals are necessary, so reducing the possibilities of compromise by implicit undertakings. It may also make it more difficult to end a strike because it will be argued that a strike authorised by ballot should only be ended by ballot. Research findings indicate[3] that ballots as such do not usually reduce the likelihood of industrial conflict; during a recession members are more likely to vote against strikes, while in times of prosperity ballots reinforce the stand of union executives with no reduction in the level of conflict. In practice, the ballot provisions in their first year of operation (since September 1984) have had more influence on union procedures than any of the Conservative Government's other measures. The provisions have proved attractive to employers who seek to delay action, and in a considerable number of cases unions have complied with the Act, although sometimes only after the employer has obtained an injunction. Most ballots have resulted in majority support for industrial action; indeed, it can be argued that the Act has strengthened democratic procedures within the unions and in many cases increased the pressure on employers where a successful ballot has been held.

1. *Democracy in Trade Unions*, Cmnd. 8778, London 1983, para. 67.
2. See generally R. Undy and R. Martin, *Ballots and Trade Union Democracy*, London 1984.
3. *Op. cit.*, p. 167.

494. The ballot provisions apply only to 'official' industrial action by a union. Difficult questions may arise as to when there is an 'act done by a trade union' which attracts the balloting requirements, and this turns on the question of the union's vicarious liability. It is not yet clear whether this will be resolved by reference to the criteria in section 15 of the Employment Act 1982 or by common law principles (see above, para. 421). If the union is responsible then the immunity is lost where the union 'authorises' or 'endorses'[1] a strike or other industrial action without the requisite ballot. Failure to comply with the provisions does not mean that *all* the immunities are lost; those which are lost are for the torts of inducing breach of or interference with contracts of employment and indirectly inducing breach of or interference with the performance of commercial contracts by the unlawful means of inducing breach of or interference with contracts of employment. Perhaps surprisingly liability for intimidation by the threat of industrial action is not affected, although any threats may be empty ones if the union cannot carry them out without a ballot.

1. This is determined by EA 1982, s. 15 (above, para. 421).

495. The conditions which must be met for the ballot to afford immunity are complex. Where the strike or other industrial action has not yet begun, the union's authorisation and the action itself must be within four weeks of the date when the ballot is held. Where the action has already begun the union's endorsement of it must be within that four-week period. The ballot has to be secret, the union having the option between a postal or workplace ballot. Entitlement to vote must be accorded equally to all members whom it is reasonable to believe at the time of the ballot will be called on to break or interfere etc. with their contracts of employment, and to no others. This poses a dilemma for unions who are contemplating action at different times by different groups of members. It needs only *one* relevant member to have been denied a vote, or one irrelevant member to have been given one for the whole ballot to be invalidated, with consequent loss of immunity. Every voter must be allowed to vote without 'interference' or 'constraint' from the union and any of its members, officials or employees. Employer interference does not invalidate the ballot, otherwise it would have been possible for the employer to expose the union and others to civil action simply by preventing workers from voting. Interference by another union than that conducting the ballot does not invalidate it. The majority of those voting must have answered the appropriate question in the affirmative. This question (however framed) is whether the member is prepared to take part (or continue to take part) in a strike – or industrial action short of a strike – involving him or her in a breach of his or her contract of employment. Curiously the members have to be asked whether they are willing to break their contracts even if the kind of action does not involve an actual breach of contract. Government funds are available to cover the costs of postal ballots, but the policy of the Trades Union Congress has been that unions should not apply for such funds. Two major affiliated unions, the EETPU and AUEW, however, have done so, and the TUC policy is currently under review.

§6. PICKETING

496. Picketing has been a traditional feature of industrial action in Britain. Striking workers gather at the gates of the workplace in order to persuade non-strikers or substitute workers not to undermine the strike by continuing to work. Picketing may also take the form of secondary action, with employees in the primary dispute picketing other places of work in an attempt to gain support from other workers, or other workers picketing their own places of work in support of the primary strikers. Large scale picketing was a favoured tactic of the National Union of Mineworkers (NUM) and was widely used in the protracted miners' strike of 1984–1985. Picketing is one area of industrial conflict in which the criminal law plays a central role. Indeed, in the 1984–1985 miners' strike, the criminal law was far more extensively used than the civil law regulating industrial action. A range of criminal laws are applicable to picketing, especially where violence takes place or is apprehended. These include: (a) conduct likely or intended to cause a breach of the peace; (b) obstructing the police; (c) criminal damage; (d) obstructing the highway; (e) unlawful assembly; (f) riot and affray. One criminal offence which relates specifically to picketing is contained in section 7 of the Conspiracy and Protection of Property Act 1875, which outlaws actions such as 'watching or besetting' a person's house or place of business, with a view to compelling that person to do or abstain from doing any 'act which such other person has a legal right to do or abstain from doing'. Despite its anachronistic flavour, this offence was brought back into use during the miners' strike when almost 650 such charges were laid, particularly in cases of picketing of working miners' homes.[1] During the same strike, the police made use of traffic control powers and general preventitive powers to stop pickets massing at working pits, often by turning back pickets hundreds of miles from their intended destinations. In a White Paper issued in May 1985,[2] the Government proposed to strengthen and expand the applicable criminal laws. Thus it was proposed that the offence of 'watching and besetting' be made an arrestable offence and the penalties increased to a maximum of 6 months' imprisonment or a fine of up to £2,000. The lynchpin of the proposals was to replace the common law offence of unlawful assembly by a statutory offence of violent disorder, which covers the use or threat by 3 or more persons of unlawful violence to persons or property. Legislation is expected in 1986.

    1. (1985) 14 *Industrial Law Journal* 145 at 151.
    2. Cmnd. 9510.

497. Picketing may also lead to the commission of similar torts as those described in paras. 479–483, above (the 'economic torts'), as well as the tort of nuisance. In addition, it has been held in one case that it is a tort unreasonably to harass others in the exercise of their right to use the highway for the purposes of going to work.[1]

    1. *Thomas* v. *NUM* [1985] 2 All ER 1, Ch. D.

498. The freedom to picket peacefully is delimited by section 15 of the Trade Union and Labour Relations Act 1974, which was amended and substantially circumscribed by section 16 of the Employment Act 1980. Section 15 states that 'it shall be lawful for a person in contemplation or furtherance of a trade dispute to attend (a) at or near his own place of work or (b) if he is an official of a trade union, at or near the place of work of the member of the union whom he is accompanying and whom he represents for the purpose only of peacefully obtaining information or persuading any person to work or to abstain from work'. This section differs from secion 13 of the Trade Union and Labour Relations Act 1974 in that it is not limited to specific torts, but applies to all criminal and civil liability, provided the statutory conditions are observed. However, the extent of the immunity afforded for criminal liability has been limited by highly restrictive judicial interpretation, which held that the section protects only the 'attendance' at or near the workplace, and not the detention of persons or invitations to them to stop and listen to the pickets' arguments.[1] Above all, pickets generally have to follow police instructions.

1. *Broome* v. *DPP* [1974] ICR 84, HL.

499. The scope of the immunity afforded by section 15 was substantially narrowed by the requirement introduced by the Employment Act 1980 that picketing should take place at or near the person's own place of work. Where section 15 does not apply, neither does the usual immunity afforded by section 13 of the Trade Union and Labour Relations Act 1974.[1] Immunity is thus withdrawn not only from employees who picket premises of other employers but also from those who picket other premises of their own employer in a multi-plant group. There are only three exceptions: (i) a trade union official may accompany a member to the latter's place of work; (ii) an employee who has been dismissed in connection with the industrial action may attend at his or her former place of work; (iii) where a person does not normally work at any one place or the location of the place (*e.g.* an oil rig) makes it impracticable to picket that place, he or she may picket any premises from which he or she works or from which his or her work is administered.

1. EA 1980, s. 16(1).

500. There is a complex inter-relationship between the picketing provisions and those relating to secondary action. Employees picketing their own work-place may well find that they have interfered with a commercial contract between two parties, neither of whom is a party to the primary dispute. (For example, a road haulier delivering goods to the employer in dispute from a supplier may be in breach of contract with the supplier if his drivers turn back at the picket line.) Section 17(5) of the Employment Act 1980 contains an express provision protecting such employees from what would otherwise be unlawful secondary action. However, the protection only applies to workers employed by a party to the dispute. Thus, workers who are not employed by a party to the dispute may lose their immunity to action in tort if in the course of picketing their own place of work in support of other workers they procure the breach of a contract between two parties neither of whom is the primary employer.

§7. Labour Injunctions

501. The most important intervention of the law in collective labour disputes is through the power of the High Court to issue injunctions before, during or after the trial of an action. The most common form of injunction in such disputes is interlocutory, that is pending trial of the action. This may be negative, for example restraining the union and organisers from acts of interference with trade by unlawful means, or mandatory, requiring the union executive to withdraw instructions which are alleged to constitute some tort. Frequently an action is started for the sole purpose of enabling the employer or a third party to obtain interlocutory relief to stop a boycott or industrial action. The commission of a large number of torts may be alleged, and the court will not have the opportunity at this stage of assessing the evidence fully. In the ordinary non-industrial case, so long as the person seeking the injunction can show that there is a serious issue to be tried, the court will then determine where the 'balance of convenience' lies. This nearly always favours the plaintiff whose tangible business interests are being threatened rather than the defendants (the union and its officials) whose industrial objectives are intangible. Once the interlocutory injunction is granted, the plaintiff usually (but not always) has little interest in bringing the matter to trial and so the substantive issue – whether torts were in fact committed – is never decided. The view that this is unfair in trade disputes resulted in the provisions of section 17 of the Trade Union and Labour Relations Act 1974. Section 17(1) requires reasonable steps to be taken to give notice of the application and an opportunity to be heard to a party likely to claim a 'trade dispute' offence, but this has not allayed trade union criticisms that excessive speed is usual in granting such injunctions, giving the union defendants little time to prepare their evidence and denying them the opportunity to cross-examine those on whose allegations the application is based. Section 17(2) requires the court to have regard to the likelihood of the defendant establishing the 'trade dispute' defence, but despite this the courts have insisted on retaining their residual discretion to grant the injunctions where this factor is outweighed by the 'disastrous' consequences of the industrial action to the employer or the public.[1] Prior to 1982, when trade unions were immune from liability in tort, an important factor in the 'balance of convenience' was that the employer was unlikely to be able to recoup damages from the individual defendant at trial. In theory, the fact that, since 1982, unions may be held liable to pay damages and costs, should lead the court to find that the matter may come to trial and the plaintiff may be able to enforce any judgment for damages.[2] However, in practice, this consideration has done little to curb the judiciary's willingness to grant interlocutory injunctions.

1. *NWL Ltd.* v. *Woods* [1979] 3 All ER 614; *Express Newspapers Ltd.* v. *McShane* [1980] 1 All ER, 65; *Duport Steels Ltd.* v. *Sirs* [1980] 1 All ER, 529, HL.
2. *Dimbleby & Sons Ltd.* v. *NUJ* [1984] ICR 386, HL.

502. Although many employers are reluctant to use judicial remedies, preferring to resolve matters through the bargaining process, injunctions have been sought in a significant number of cases, particularly since 1982. According to one research study, at least 34 injunctions were sought between 1980 and 1984 and nearly all of these were granted. Most of these were based on the picketing and secondary action provisions. It is notable that between 1982 and 1984 several of these were ignored by the union defendants,[1] but successful contempt of court proceedings against the National Graphical Association in the Stockport Messenger dispute (1983), and the National Union of Mine-workers (1984–1985) followed by sequestration of assets, and, in the latter case, the appointment of a receiver, has been followed by a greater degree of compliance with injunctions (see above, paras. 422 and 423). It is significant as well that more actions are now being brought to trial to obtain awards of damages after the dispute has ended. This is not usually the case where the plaintiff is a large employer anxious to maintain a continuing relationship with a union, but rather where the employer or a third party supplier can rely on non-union labour or labour supplied by members of another union.[2]

1. S. Evans, 'The use of injunctions in industrial disputes' (1985) *British Journal of Industrial Relations* 133; and Ch. 5 in *Industrial Relations and the Law in the 1980s: Issues and Future Trends* (eds. P. Fosh and C. R. Littler), London 1985.
2. Prominant examples are the *Stockport Messenger* dispute (1983) and the action against the South Wales miners (1984): see above, paras. 422 and 423. In the first major dispute under the 1984 Trade Union Act, Austin-Rover obtained injunctions against 6 unions; one of these, the Transport & General Workers' Union, was fined £20,000 for contempt of court for refusing to comply; Austin-Rover also proceeded with a claim for damages against the unions concerned: *The Times*, 27 November 1984.

§8. Other State Intervention

503. Under the Emergency Powers Act 1920 (as amended in 1964) the Government can make a proclamation and then govern with special powers if essential supplies are threatened for the community.[1] Parliamentary approval must be forthwith and regularly obtained. The powers are extensive, but they fall short of 'industrial conscription'. Nor may the Government use their powers to make it an offence to take part in a strike or peacefully persuade other persons to do so. The powers have been used on twelve occasions, most recently in 1973–1974, and since 1964, due to a little-noticed amendment, the Government has been able to use troops, without consultation with Parliament, for work of 'national importance'. This power has been used on several occasions, for example to remove refuse during a 'dustmen's strike' in Glasgow, thereby offsetting the impact of the strike. During the period of the Industrial Relations Act 1971 there were provisions for 'cooling-off' periods, along the lines of United States legislation, and for compulsory ballots of union members in 'emergencies'. These powers were used in only one dispute (in the railways) and failed abysmally.[2] Although there were occasions on which they could have been used after this, they were never again invoked before the Act was repealed. *Ad hoc* measures have been used on a few occasions for example to deal with a strike by prison officers.

1. See generally G. S. Morris, *Strikes in Essential Services*, London 1986.

2. B. Weekes *et al.*, *Industrial Relations and the Limits of Law*, Oxford 1975, p. 213.

504. Apart from some special provisions restricting the right to strike of the police, armed forces, postal and telecommunications workers, and merchant seamen, workers in the public sector have not been singled out for special attention. Although there is still a provision dating back to 1875, which makes it an offence to break a contract of service with cause to believe that it will result in serious bodily injury or serious property damage, this has never been invoked. Special sanctions against gas, water and electricity workers (also never successfully invoked) were repealed in 1971. Civil servants are not subject to special restraints, but disciplinary sanctions may be imposed on them for individual action.

505. The most important form of governmental intervention in 'trade disputes' is in fact through the Advisory, Conciliation and Arbitration Service using methods of conciliation, inquiry and arbitration with the consent of both parties. Occasionally the Government may set up a special Court of Inquiry, under the Industrial Courts Act 1919, s. 4, to inform Parliament and the public about the causes of a dispute, but this too is a form of 'public conciliation'. The functions and work of ACAS are described above, para. 70 and the common meaning of terms such as conciliation and arbitration are discussed in para. 48.

506. Finally, a significant example of state intervention is the withholding of social security benefits from those affected by industrial action. There are two relevant sources of social security benefit:
(1) Unemployment benefit: This benefit, paid out of a fund to which employees and employers make compulsory contributions, is normally available for a limited period of time to those who are involuntarily unemployed. Unemployment benefit is not payable to striking workers, on the principle that they are voluntarily unemployed. However, the disqualification is not limited to those who participate in the industrial action itself but extends to those workers who are laid off as a result of the stoppage. In such cases, workers are disqualified from receiving unemployment benefit, unless they can prove (i) that they were not participating in the trade dispute, and (ii) that they were not directly interested in the trade dispute causing the stoppage.[1] A recent House of Lords decision has held that a person is 'directly interested' in a dispute if, despite the fact that he or she is not participating in the industrial action, the outcome of the dispute will be applied to him or her by virtue of a collective agreement or established custom and practice in the workplace.[2]

1. Social Security Act 1975, s. 19(1), as amended by s. 111(1) of EPA 1975.
2. *Presho* v. *Department of Health and Social Security* [1984] ICR 463, HL.

507. (2) Supplementary benefit: This is a non-contributory benefit, usually payable if a family's income falls below a given minimum and the head of the household is unemployed. The family of a striking worker may be entitled to supplementary benefit. However, by section 6 of the Social Security (No. 2) Act 1980, a striking worker is deemed to be in receipt of £16 per week strike pay whether or not the relevant trade union actually pays strike pay. The amount of supplementary benefit payable to the family is reduced accordingly. Single people without dependent families are entitled to no state benefits at all, save in very restricted situations of 'urgent needs'. Where no strike pay is in fact paid by the trade union, these provisions could lead to great hardship, increasing the pressure on strikers to return to work. This was clearly manifested during the 1984–1985 miners' strike, since the National Union of Mineworkers did not pay strike pay.

Appendices

APPENDIX 1 – SELECTED BIBLIOGRAPHY

§1. Bibliographical

B. A. Hepple, J. M. Neeson, and P. O'Higgins (eds.) *A Bibliography of the Literature on British and Irish Labour Law*, London, 1975; and B. A. Hepple, J. Hepple, P. O'Higgins and P. Stirling *Labour Law in Great Britain and Ireland to 1978* (companion volume), London, 1981 (a comprehensive working bibliography from the earliest times, kept up to date in regard to periodical literature, once a year, in the *Industrial Law Journal*, London).

§2. Reference Works

R. J. Harvey (ed.) *Industrial Relations and Employment Law*, London 1971 with supplements (2 vols.) (texts of selected legislation and commentary).

B. A. Hepple & P. O'Higgins (eds.) *Encyclopedia of Labour Relations Law*, London, 1972, with six supplements each year (3 vols.) (comprehensive texts and digests of all relevant case law, legislation, rules and orders, awards, reports and inquiries, precedents and EEC and international law with commentaries).

V. Craig, R. Hay, D. Littlejohn, B. Napier and I. Truscott 'Employment' in *Stair's Encyclopedia of the Laws of Scotland* (forthcoming 1986).

§3. Specialist Law Reports

Industrial Cases Reports, London, 1975–
Industrial Court Reports, London, 1972–1974
Industrial Relations Law Reports, London, 1972–
Industrial Tribunal Reports, London, 1966–1978

§4. Periodicals

British Journal of Industrial Relations, London, 1963–
Equal Opportunities Review, London, 1985–
European Industrial Relations Review, London, 1974–
Incomes Data Service Ltd., *Incomes Data Reports, Incomes Data Brief* and *Incomes Data Studies*, and *International Report*, London, 1971–
Industrial Law Journal, London, 1972–
Industrial Relations Journal, London, 1972–
Industrial Relations Review and Report, London 1972– (including *Industrial Relations Legal Information Bulletin*)

Appendix 1

§5. Official Reports etc. Published by Her Majesty's Stationery Office (HMSO)

Advisory, Conciliation and Arbitration Service, Annual Reports (1975–)
Central Arbitration Committee, Annual Reports (1975–)
Certification Officer, Annual Reports (1976–)
Commission for Racial Equality, Annual Reports (1977–)
Department of Employment, *Guides* on labour legislation (*e.g.* Contracts of Employment, Dismissal etc.)
Equal Opportunities Commission, Annual Reports (1976–)
Report of the Royal Commission on Trade Unions and Employers' Associations 1965–1968. Chairman: The Rt. Hon. Lord Donovan, Cmnd. 3623, and 11 research papers published by the Commission.
Report of the Committee on Safety and Health at Work. Chairman: Lord Robens, 1972, Cmnd. 5034.
Report of the Committee of Inquiry on Industrial Democracy. Chairman: Lord Bullock, Cmnd. 6706

§6. General Books

G. S. Bain (ed.), *Industrial Relations in Britain*, Oxford, 1983.
H. A. Clegg, *The Changing System of Industrial Relations*, Oxford, 1979.
P. L. Davies and M. R. Freedland, *Labour Law: Text and Materials*, 2nd ed., London, 1984.
P. Fosh and C. R. Littler (eds.), *Industrial Relations and the Law in the 1980s: Issues and Future Trends*, London, 1985. ·
B. A. Hepple and Paul O'Higgins, *Employment Law*, 4th ed. by B. A. Hepple, London, 1981.
O. Kahn-Freund, *Labour and the Law*, 3rd ed. by P. L. Davies and M. R. Freedland, London, 1983 (also available in German and Italian translations).
—, *Labour Relations: Heritage and Adjustment*, London, 1979.
—, *Selected Writings*, London, 1978.
Roy Lewis and Bob Simpson, *Striking a Balance? Employment Law after the 1980 Act*, Oxford, 1981.
R. W. Rideout, *Principles of Labour Law*, 4th ed., London, 1983.
I. T. Smith and J. C. Wood, *Industrial Law*, 2nd ed., London, 1983.
Lord Wedderburn, *The Worker and the Law*, 3rd ed. (forthcoming 1986).
Lord Wedderburn, Roy Lewis and Jon Clark (eds.), *Labour Law and Industrial Relations: Building on Kahn-Freund*, Oxford, 1983.

§7. Specialist Books

S. D. Anderman, *The Law of Unfair Dismissal*, 2nd ed., London, 1985.
W. Brown (ed.), *The Changing Contours of British Industrial Relations*, Oxford, 1981.
W. B. Creighton, *Working Women and the Law*, London, 1979.

W. W. Daniel and Neil Millward, *Workplace Industrial Relations in Britain*, The DE/PSI/SSRC Survey, London, 1983.

L. Dickens, M. Jones, B. Weekes and M. Hart, *A study of unfair dismissal and the industrial tribunal system*, Oxford, 1985.

S. Dunn and J. Gennard, *The Closed Shop in British Industry*, London, 1984.

K. D. Ewing, *Trade Unions, the Labour Party and the Law*, Edinburgh, 1982.

M. R. Freedland, *The Contract of Employment*, London, 1976.

M. J. Goodman, *Industrial Tribunals – Practice and Procedure*, 3rd ed., London, 1985.

C. Grunfeld, *The Law of Redundancy*, 2nd ed., London, 1980.

Bob Hepple, *Race, Jobs and the Law in Britain*, 2nd ed., Harmondsworth, 1970.

—, *Equal Pay and the Industrial Tribunals*, London, 1984.

—, A. Jacobs, T. Ramm, B. Veneziani, E. Vogel-Polsky, *The Making of Labour Law in Europe: a comparative study of 9 countries to 1945* (forthcoming 1986).

P. Kahn, N. Lewis, R. Livock and P. Wiles, *Picketing: Industrial Disputes Tactics and the Law*, London, 1983.

R. Kidner, *Trade Union Law*, 2nd ed., London, 1983.

G. S. Morris, *Strikes in Essential Services* (forthcoming 1986).

B. Perrins, *Trade Union Law*, London, 1985.

Appendix 2

[An asterisk* signifies that the legislation is still in force in whole or in part]

1813	Repeal of Statute of Artificers: removal of remnants of Elizabethan wage-fixing system.
1823	Master and Servant Act: extended power of magistrates to punish deserting servants (modified 1867, repealed 1875).
1824	Combination Laws Repeal Act (Francis Place and the reformers): limited recognition of freedom of association.
1825	Peel's Combination Act. Only combinations concerned with wages, prices, hours free from criminality; penalised undefined crimes of violence, threats, intimidation, molestation and obstruction, so precluding freedom to strike. Modified by Molestation of Workmen Act 1859.
1831	Truck Act (reforming some abuses of 'tommy' shop and deductions from wages) amended in 1887, 1896, 1940.
1833	Factory Act. Creation of factory inspectors to enforce child labour statutes, *viz.* Health and Morals of Apprentices Act 1802, Factory Acts 1819, 1825, 1831.
1834	The 'Tolpuddle' martyrs (*R* v. *Loveless* [1834] 6 C & P 596: transportation for union initiation ceremony contrary to Unlawful Oaths Act 1797).
1834	New Poor Law. Aimed at driving unemployed on to 'free' labour market.
1844	Factory Act (inclusion of women; fencing of machinery).
1847	Ten Hours Act (limited hours of young persons and women).
1845–1861	Factory Acts extended to factories allied to textiles.
1864–1867	Factory Acts extended to non-textile factories (consolidating measures in 1878, 1901, 1937 and 1961*).
1871	Trade Union Act (adopting Minority report of Erle Royal Commission on Trade Unions) reversed effect of *Hornby* v. *Close* (1867) 2 QB 153. Trade union objects not unlawful by reason only that in restraint of trade (s. 3); members not liable for criminal conspiracy by reason thereof (s. 2); but union agreements not directly enforceable (s. 4).
1871	Criminal Law Amendment Act: repealed 1825 and 1859 Acts but penalised most forms of picketing by defining 'molestation', 'obstruction', 'threats' etc. and creating new offences.
*1875	*Conspiracy and Protection of Property Act* (adopting Report of Cockburn Royal Commission on Labour Laws). (1) Repealed Master and Servant Acts (criminal liability for breach of contract by servants). (2) Codified crimes relating to molestation and picketing (s. 7). (3) Imposed criminal liability for strikes in certain essential services (s. 4 repealed in 1971); and for strikes in breach of contract where life endangered (s. 5 still in force).

(4) Reversed effect of *R* v. *Bunn* (1872) 12 Cox 316, in which London gasworkers convicted of conspiracy by 'an unjustifiable annoyance and interference with the masters in the conduct of their business . . .' (s. 3).

1896   Conciliation Act. To encourage conciliation and voluntary arbitration (following Report of Devonshire Royal Commission on Labour).

1906   Trade Disputes Act (adopting Minority Report of Dunedin Royal Commission on Trade Unions).

(1) Immunity to 'any person' acting 'in contemplation or furtherance of a trade dispute' (defined for the first time) (i.f.c.t.d.) in respect of new civil tort of conspiracy (s. 1).

(2) Immunity to 'any person' 'i.c.f.t.d.' in respect of peaceful picketing (s. 2).

(3) Immunity to 'any person' 'i.c.f.t.d.' inducing breach of contract of employment (s. 3 first limb); or interfering with business (s. 3 second limb 'for avoidance of doubt').

(4) Immunity to trade unions in tort (s. 4).

1909   Trade Boards Act. Minimum wage legislation for 'sweated' trades, later replaced by *Wages Councils Acts* currently of 1979.*

*1913   *Trade Union Act.* To enable unions to finance political objects with safeguard for individuals to contract-out of political fund. Overcomes *Osborne* case [1910] AC 87. (Definition of political objects and balloting requirements substantially altered, 1984.)

1916–1919   Committee on relations between employers and employed (Chairman: J. H. Whitley M.P.) leading to voluntary establishment of Joint Industrial Councils in many industries.

1919   Industrial Courts Act. Machinery for voluntary arbitration by Industrial Court, renamed Industrial Arbitration Board in 1971 and Central Arbitration Committee 1974, and machinery for Courts of Inquiry (s. 4, still in force).*

1927   Trade Disputes and Trade Unions Act. To make 'general strikes' like that in 1926 illegal. (Repealed in 1946.)

1940   Conditions of Employment and National Arbitration Order No. 1305. (Compulsory arbitration superimposed on collective bargaining. Industrial action prohibited.)

1951   Industrial Disputes Order No. 1376 replacing 1940 order. (Penal sanctions against strikes removed.)

1959   Order of 1951 repealed. Terms and Conditions of Employment Act 1959, s. 8 retained procedure for extending collective agreements on *ad hoc* basis to employers in otherwise well-organised industries who fail to observe 'recognised' terms. (Replaced by Employment Protection Act, Sched. 11, repealed 1980.)

1963   Contracts of Employment Act (consolidating Act in 1972): minimum statutory periods of notice; written statements of employment terms.

Appendix 2

1965	Trade Disputes Act to reverse effect of *Rookes* v. *Barnard* [1964] AC 1129 (new tort of intimidation) in trade disputes.
1965	Redundancy Payments Act (compensation for dismissal by reason of redundancy).
1965–1968	Donovan Royal Commission on Trade Unions and Employers' Associations. Diagnoses 'problems' of unofficial and unconstitutional strikes, wages drift, abuse of union power and restrictive practices as being caused by shift in power from relatively formal industry-wide level to relatively informal shop floor. Proposes reform of rules to encourage plant and company bargaining, to reduce fragmentation of bargaining and widen subject-matter of bargaining, largely by voluntary means.
1971	Industrial Relations Act (based on Conservative Party policy as in *A Giant's Strength*, 1958, and *Fair Deal at Work*, 1968).

(1) Protection of 'public interest' and the individual against abuse of union power; emergency provisions (taken from US Taft-Hartley Act); other restrictions on freedom to strike (unfair industrial practices); union responsibility for acts of officials; restrictions on closed shop; right to be 'non-unionist'; regulation of union rules and member's rights.

(2) Extension of individual protection; unfair dismissal; extension of minimum periods of notice.

(3) Reform of collective bargaining by legal means; presumption that collective agreements legally enforceable as contracts; rights to union recognition; disclosure of information (not brought into force); notification of procedure agreements.

The main institutions set up to achieve these purposes were the National Industrial Relations Court (NIRC), Commission on Industrial Relations (CIR) and Registrar of Trade Unions and Employers' Associations (all abolished in 1974).

*1974	*Health and Safety at Work Act* (first comprehensive legislation on safety and welfare, gradually to replace all earlier measures in specific industries).
*1974	*Trade Union and Labour Relations Act*

(1) Repealed 1971 Act.

(2) Abolished registration as device for controlling unions except for certificate of status (s. 8) and tax immunity.

(3) Restored and updated immunity from liability for certain torts committed by persons in contemplation or furtherance of a trade dispute (s. 13).

(4) Restored and modified trade union immunity from tort actions (s. 14) (repealed 1982).

(5) Restored immunity for peaceful picketing i.c.f.t.d. (s. 15) (narrowed in 1980).

(6) Restored presumption that collective agreements not legally binding (s. 18).

(7) Re-defined 'trade dispute' (s. 29) (narrowed in 1982).

(8) Re-enacted, with minor improvements, unfair dismissals legislation (Sched. 1).

*1975   *Employment Protection Act*

(1) Establishes ACAS on statutory basis (ss. 1–6).

(2) Establishes CAC to replace Industrial Arbitration Board (s. 10).

(3) Extends jurisdictions of industrial tribunals and establishes Employment Appeal Tribunal (EAT) (ss. 87–88, 109).

(4) Establishes Certification Officer to take over functions of Chief Registrar of Friendly Societies re unions (s. 7).

(5) Re-introduces unilateral compulsory arbitration for recognition of trade unions (ss. 11–16); and extension of recognised or general level of terms and conditions (sched. 11) (repealed 1980).

(6) Provides for disclosure of information for bargaining (ss. 17–21).

(7) Creates new individual employment rights, *e.g.* guarantee payments (ss. 22–23); maternity pay (ss. 36–39), right to return to work after confinement (ss. 48–52) and protection from dismissal for pregnancy (ss. 35–47); right to participate in activities of independent union (ss. 53–56), time off for union duties (ss. 57–58) and public duties (s. 59) and to look for new employment if redundant (ss. 63–69); itemised pay statements (ss. 81–84); removal of certain trade disputes disqualifications from unemployment benefit (s. 111).

(8) Improves unfair dismissal provisions (written statement of reasons for dismissal (s. 70), orders for reinstatement (s. 71), basic and compensatory awards (ss. 72–77); interim relief for dismissal for union activity (ss. 78–80).

(9) Procedural limits on employer's power to make collective dismissals for redundancy (Part IV).

*1975   *Sex Discrimination Act* (prohibits sex discrimination in employment) supplementing *Equal Pay Act* 1970 (in force from 31 December 1975).

1976   Trade Union and Labour Relations (Amendment) Act. Removed House of Lords amendments to 1974 Act by

(1) Broadening protection against tort liability (s. 13).

(2) Removing safeguards for members (s. 5) and provisions for rules of unions (s. 6).

(3) Making dismissal fair in nearly all closed shop situations, and requiring Press Freedom Charter.

(Substantially amended in 1980 and 1982.)

*1976   *Race Relations Act* (prohibits racial discrimination in employment) replacing legislation of 1968.

*1977   *Criminal Law Act* (abolishes common law crime of conspiracy, but creates new statutory offences of relevance to industrial action).

Appendix 2

*1977 *Patents Act* (creates new rights for employees in respect of their inventions).

*1978 *Employment Protection (Consolidation) Act 1978* (consolidates, without alteration, most of the existing law relating to individual employment rights). It now includes: right to written particulars of employment (ss. 1–6) and to itemised pay statements (ss. 8–10); right to guarantee payments (ss. 12–18); right to remuneration on suspension from work on medical grounds (ss. 19–22); rights protecting employees from action short of dismissal for membership or non-membership of a trade union (ss. 23–26A); right to time off work for trade union and public duties, job seeking and ante-natal care (ss. 27–32); rights in connection with pregnancy and confinement, maternity pay and return to work (ss. 33–48); rights to minimum periods of notice and written statements of reasons for dismissal (ss. 49–53); right not to be unfairly dismissed (ss. 54–80); rights to redundancy payment (ss. 81–120); rights on employer's insolvency (ss. 121–127); provisions on industrial tribunals, conciliation officers and EAT (ss. 128–136).

*1979 *Wages Councils Act* (consolidates earlier legislation on wages councils which lay down minimum wages for workers in industries where collective bargaining is inadequate) (to be amended 1986).

*1980 *Companies Act* (fiduciary duty placed on directors to have regard to interests of company's employees. The duty is owed to and enforceable by the company, with no right of enforcement given to employees).

*1980 *Social Security (No. 2) Act* (supplementary benefit to families of striking workers reduced by £15 per week, on the assumption that £15 of strike pay is available from the worker's trade union, whether or not this is in fact the case; amount increased upwards from time to time).

*1980 *Employment Act.*

(1) Provision for State funds in respect of secret ballots and for workplace ballots (ss. 1–2).

(2) Power of Secretary of State to issue Codes of Practice (s. 3).

(3) Right not to be unreasonably excluded or expelled from a trade union in a closed shop situation (ss. 4–5).

(4) Modification of certain rights in EPCA 1978, namely unfair dismissal, maternity rights (ss. 6, 8, 9), guarantee payments (s.14) and action short of dismissal (s. 15).

(5) Amendment of picketing provisions in TULRA 1974 to limit immunity to picketing at place of work (s. 16).

(6) Removes immunity from civil action for unlawful secondary action (s. 17).

(7) Repeals recognition procedure (ss. 11–16 EPA 1975), extension of terms and conditions of employment (s. 98 and Sched. 11, EPA 1975), and Road Haulages Act 1938 (fixing of statutory remuneration).

*1981   *Transfer of Undertakings (Protection of Employment) Regulations* (UK government's implementation of obligations under EEC Directive 77/187 relating to safeguarding employees' rights on the transfer of undertakings, businesses and parts of business).

*1982   *Industrial Training Act* (replaces earlier Acts of 1964, 1973 and 1981 modifying functions of industrial training boards which have power to impose a levy on employers to meet the board's expenses and to pay grants to employers who provide approved training).

*1982   *Social Security and Housing Benefits Act* (provides for payment of statutory sick pay by employers)

*1982   *Employment Act*
    (1) Narrows closed shop exceptions to unfair dismissal legislation (EPCA 1978, ss. 58, 58A); substantially increases compensation for closed shop unfair dismissals, allows trade union to be joined as a defendant in such cases (ss. 3, 4, 5, 7).
    (2) Prohibits union membership or recognition requirements in contracts of supply (ss. 12–13) and removes immunity in tort for inducing incorporation of such requirements (s. 14).
    (3) Removes trade union's immunity from tort actions (s. 14 TULRA 1974 repealed). Limits amount of damages which may be awarded against unions in tort actions (ss. 15–16) and protects political funds and provident benefits from legal process (s. 17).
    (4) Narrows meaning of 'trade dispute' (s. 29 TULRA 1974).

*1983   *Equal Pay (Amendment) Regulations 1983* (amended Equal Pay Act 1970 to introduce equal pay for work of equal value for men and women in compliance with decision of ECJ in *Commission of European Communities* v. *UK* [1982] ICR 578).

*1984   *Trade Union Act*
    (1) Requires secret ballots for election to certain leadership positions in trade unions (Part I).
    (2) Requires secret ballot confirming industrial action in order to retain immunity under s. 13 TULRA 1974 (Part II).
    (3) Requires periodic ballots for maintenance of political fund; modifies definition of political objects; and regulates check-off arrangements for collection of political contributions.

1986   *Wages Bill* proposes (1) repeal of the Truck Acts and related legislation so as to remove restrictions on payment of wages and to regulate deductions for all workers; (2) removal of workers under 21 years of age from scope of wages councils; (3) wages councils to be limited to setting one basic hourly rate, an overtime rate and a limit on amount charged for accommodation; (4) simplified procedure for amending scope of wages councils or abolishing them; (5) abolition of rebate for employers with 10 or more employees who pay statutory redundancy payment.

1986   *Sex Discrimination Bill* proposes (1) coverage of employers of 5 or less employees and (2) provision to make discriminatory provisions in collective agreements void, both in compliance with decision of ECJ in *Commission of European Communities* v *UK* [1984] ICR 192. In addition (3) removal of restrictions on night work by women.

[The 1986 Bills may be altered before enactment.]

Table of Cases

The numbers given refer to paragraphs.

Table of Cases

273

Table of Statutes

The numbers given refer to paragraphs.

Table of Statutes

Table of Statutory Instruments and Orders in Council

The numbers given refer to paragraphs.

Index

The numbers given are paragraph numbers.

Index

282

Index

Index

Index

Index

Index